Descartes's Dualism

Descartes's Dualism

MARLEEN ROZEMOND

HARVARD UNIVERSITY PRESS
Cambridge, Massachusetts, and London, England 1998

Printed in the United States of America

Library of Congress Cataloging-in-Publication Data

Rozemond, Marleen.
Descartes's dualism / Marleen Rozemond.
p. cm.
Includes bibliographical references and index.
ISBN 0-674-19840-9
1. Descartes, René, 1596–1650—Contributions in dualist doctrine of mind and body. 2. Mind and body—History—17th century. I. Title.
B1878.M55R68 1998
128′.2–dc21 97-42399

For Sam

Acknowledgments

I am indebted to a number of people for their support. Many contributed comments on the book or parts of it. Among them were Marilyn M. Adams, Robert M. Adams, John Carriero, Vere Chappell, John Etchemendy, Dan Garber, Paul Hoffman, Steve Nadler, Alan Nelson, Derk Pereboom, John Perry, Houston Smit. Jeremy Hyman read all of the book in stages and contributed his great knowledge of the history of philosophy and the secondary literature. Hannah Ginsborgh helped not just with her comments, but also with her enthusiastic reactions to my work. The book's existence owes much to those who were my teachers, especially Marilyn Adams, Alan Nelson, Rogers Albritton. I am greatly indebted to Tyler Burge for many years of encouragement and friendship. Bob Adams was a terrific thesis advisor. Not only did I learn from him intellectually, but his steady confidence in me and his enthusiasm about my work continue to be a great source of support. After I graduated, I continued to learn—from Dan Garber's feedback about parts of the book, from Eckart Förster and Peter Galison's advice about how to present my views, and especially from John Etchemendy. John has also been an invaluable friend and senior colleague in these early years of my career.

I doubt that I would have written a book without a fellowship from the Stanford Humanities Center. In addition to time for research, the Center provided an ideal environment for productive work, a splendid office where I spent scores of hours, and excellent company in the other fellows. Its director, Wanda Corn, associate director, Charlie Junkerman, and staff created a marvelously supportive atmosphere where I flourished in many ways. I finished the book in a perfect study endowed with nine windows, and we owe our inimitable real estate agent, Steve Bellumori, for helping us find that house.

An earlier version of Chapter 1 appeared previously as "Descartes's Case for Dualism," *The Journal of the History of Philosophy,* 33. pp. 29–63, 1995. Chapter 2 is a revised version of "The Role of the Intellect in Descartes's Case for the Incorporeity of the Mind," in *Essays on the Philosophy and Science of René Descartes,* Stephen Voss, ed., Oxford: Oxford University Press, 1994. I thank Oxford University Press and *The Journal of the History of Philosophy* for permission to reprint.

Last but not least, I thank my husband, Philip Clark. Philip considerably refined his ability to put up with my obsessiveness and got very good at laughing at my fits of exasperation. Had he been less good-natured, writing this book would have been much harder.

Contents

Preface

Few views are as central to Western philosophy as Descartes's dualism. Its historical prominence is undeniable, and while contemporary philosophers generally reject dualism, they continue to pay attention to it. Introductions to philosophy and courses in the philosophy of mind commonly include discussion of Descartes, and his principal argument for dualism still attracts considerable attention from the philosophical community at large. Descartes's dualism is widely regarded as a major influence on the formulation of our modern mind-body problem, and indeed he has sometimes been held responsible for creating the mind-body problem.

Consequently, understanding of Descartes's dualism is obviously of great significance. Nevertheless, one may well ask: Given the large volume of literature on Descartes's thought, why write a book about this subject? It is true that much has been written on Descartes. There are many articles on his conception of the mind and his argument for dualism. A large number of books have been written; some cover a range of issues in his writings, many focus on the *Meditations,* others address one specific aspect or other of his thought. But there is a remarkable absence of books that attempt to give a systematic interpretation of his dualism and his defense of the position. This is what I set out to do.

One reason why Descartes continues to attract so much attention is because much of what he says speaks to the contemporary mind.

Clearly, arguments and views proffered long ago continue to engage us, in spite of differences in intellectual, cultural, political, and social environment. Nevertheless, it is important for understanding Descartes to acknowledge that, like that of any thinker, his thought was embedded in the intellectual climate of his time. So consideration of historical context is very instructive about his views and arguments. We all know, for instance, that which beliefs we take for granted and which we labor hard to defend depend significantly on the views of our contemporaries and predecessors. The focus of this book is historical: I will examine Descartes's dualism in relation to his seventeenth-century philosophical context, a perspective that has been sorely neglected. This perspective gives rise to questions that have received insufficient attention and often places Descartes's views in a very different light. This approach is often distinguished from a philosophical one, but to some extent at least the distinction is misleading. In-depth examination of the thought of a thinker from the past requires much philosophical activity. And while the history of philosophy is of abiding interest because of the intrinsic significance of historical matters, we can also benefit from it philosophically. We can learn from the different answers offered in the past to questions we still pose, sometimes because these answers appeal to us, but sometimes because the difference with our perspective is thought-provoking. And at other times what we find instructive is that the questions that were raised are not the same.

In relation to Descartes's historical background we need to ask ourselves: To what extent was his dualism new? How did he defend it in light of differences and similarities with his predecessors? These questions are fundamental to the book. I do consider other predecessors and contemporaries of Descartes's along the way, but I will examine these questions primarily in relation to Aristotelian scholasticism, which constitutes the most important aspect of Descartes's historical context. His education, especially on the issues relevant to this book, was based on the teaching of the Schools.[1] One of his main goals was to propose a system of thought that would supplant Aristotelianism, and so the question where Descartes and the scholastics agreed and disagreed is of great significance. Much of his argumentation is directed against them, and understanding his target improves our grasp of his arguments. In addition, similarities in their views help explain other important features of his thought. Many scholars now acknowledge an interest in exploring the scholastic background of Descartes's thought, but relatively little in-depth work has been done as yet.

Contemporary discussions usually focus on Descartes's view that the mind is an incorporeal entity, but this is not the only aspect of his dualism that is significant. Equally important is his view about the *nature* of both body and mind. The way in which we approach the mind-body problem depends to a large degree on our view of what belongs to the mental and on our conception of the physical world. This was true for Descartes, and it is true for us now. But the way in which we divide things up today finds its first major expression in Descartes. His writings contain roughly the list of mental states about which we ask whether they can be understood as corporeal, or how they can be so understood. Furthermore, although the scientific conception of the physical has changed significantly, ours, like Descartes's, is quite remote from the apparent nature of our conscious lives. Many contemporary philosophers are optimistic, but others continue to find it difficult to understand the mental as corporeal.

From a historical point of view Descartes's position that the mind is incorporeal was not at all new: the idea that the mind or soul is an incorporeal entity that is separable from the body is, of course, at least as old as Plato. More directly relevant for understanding Descartes is the fact that the Aristotelian scholastics also accepted it. Unlike today, in the seventeenth century materialism was not dominant, and a commitment to personal immortality provided a strong motive for belief in the incorporeity of the mind. But Descartes did initiate a significant departure from Aristotelian scholasticism in regard to the question what belongs to mind, soul, and body, and when I speak of his dualism, I mean to include his view on these issues. A fundamental difference lies in his conception of the physical world, according to which bodies only have mechanistic qualities, and not sensible qualities: he accepted the distinction between what we now call primary and secondary qualities. Furthermore, he regarded the mind as the principle of thought and for him it constitutes the entire soul. But the scholastics regarded the mind as the principle of intellectual activity, and for them the mind is merely a "part" of the soul, as Descartes put it. The soul was also the principle of nutrition, growth, locomotion, and it was the form of the body.

In this book I pursue this perspective on Descartes's dualism in depth. His continuity with the past in regard to the incorporeity of the mind (or soul) and his shifting of the conception of the mind have sometimes been noted. But this perspective has had no noticeable impact on the study of his thought by historians of philosophy. There is much to be gained from pursuing it. In doing so I learned much about the scholastics, about Descartes's own views, and about the relationship between them. Sometimes his views or arguments will look different in light of this relationship; at other times it will become more intelligible just why he held the views scholars have detected in his writings.

Descartes's commitment to mechanistic science is crucial for his dualism and for his relationship to Aristotelianism, since it motivates his reconfiguration of the notions of body, mind, and soul: he wanted to develop a conception of body such that everything in the physical world could be explained mechanistically. His conception of the mind accommodates those aspects of human beings that he thought could not be so explained. While philosophers have generally focused their attention on his conception of the mind rather than his conception of body, Descartes himself had far more to say about the physical world than about the mind. Taking this fact into account, I will emphasize his concern to defend a mechanistic conception of body in relation to his dualism. In sum, the approach I take is based on Descartes's aim to provide a metaphysics that accommodates mechanistic science and supplants Aristotelian scholasticism.

The book divides into three parts. In chapters 1 and 2 I address the question of what Descartes's dualism is and how he defends the view that mind and body are two different substances. Chapter 1 examines various metaphysical ideas fundamental to his dualism (the notion of substance, real distinction, essence) and contains a detailed analysis of Descartes's main argument for dualism. This argument is quite subtle, and I offer an interpretation that differs markedly from ones common in the literature. In chapter 2 I discuss central differences and similarities with the scholastics and how they affect his defense of the incorporeity of the mind.

Descartes's main argument for dualism concludes that mind and body are two different substances, but it does not yet settle just what belongs to the realm of the mental, what to the realm of the physical, and so it is not sufficient for establishing a mechanistic conception of body. Chapters 3 and 4 are concerned with this issue. In chapter 3 I discuss how Descartes eliminates sensible qualities from the physical world and propose a very different account from ones common in the literature. Chapter 4 is devoted to the rejection of the specifically Aristotelian scholastic entities real qualities and substantial forms—entities that have been widely misunderstood by his interpreters.

Descartes's dualism generates a number of questions and objections. The question how, on his view, mind and body are united is particularly important for understanding his dualism, and it is the subject of the final two chapters. His writings raise expectations for two different answers to this question. First, some of his statements suggest that he accepted the Aristotelian, hylomorphic conception of soul-body union, that is, the view that the soul is the form of the body. In chapter 5 I discuss the relationship between Descartes's dualism and scholastic conceptions of the soul and its union with the body: this relationship is quite complex in interesting ways. Secondly, on various occasions Descartes offers a defense of the union of mind and body on the basis of the nature of sensation, which I examine in chapter 6. In recent years both these ideas have inspired interpreters to argue that his dualism is not as sharp as is usually thought, despite his description of mind and body as substances of entirely different kinds. I disagree with this trend and must confess to more pessimism about Descartes's conception of the union than this trend allows.

Let me close with a few remarks about the scholastics I discuss. Descartes's rejection of Aristotelian scholasticism often concerned views that were fundamental to this entire system of thought, and to the extent that this is true, differences among the scholastics are not important. But this is not the entire story. Major departures in late scholasticism from both Aristotle himself and also from Aquinas will be quite important. Various scholastics make appearances in this book. I focus on a few whose thought Descartes seemed to know, but I generally do not rely on the views of just one of these scholastics. References to all of them, although not numerous, can be found in Descartes's writings. The first scholastic is Thomas Aquinas, whose thought was important in the teaching of the Jesuits who educated Descartes. The others are nearly all Descartes's immediate predecessors or contemporaries. A particularly prominent one is Francisco

Suárez, who was a very influential thinker early in the seventeenth century. Eustachius of St. Paul wrote a succinct textbook of philosophy, which Descartes praised as the best of its kind and at one point considered publishing, furnished with comments, in conjunction with a work of his own. Finally, I have used the commentaries by the Jesuits of Coimbra, which were widely used in Jesuit teaching.[2] I have confined myself to a few scholastics, but no doubt examination of others, as well as of non-scholastic contemporaries and predecessors of Descartes's, would result in further insights into his thought.

The study of scholastic philosophers in relation to Descartes, as well as other early modern philosophers, is enormously helpful, and it reveals new and illuminating perspectives on their thought. Much work needs to be done in this area. I hope that, among other things, this book will serve as an illustration of the fruitfulness of this approach.

Abbreviations

Translations provided in the text and notes are my own, although I have consulted and benefited from published translations. For Descartes's writings I provide references to the standard edition as well as to the translations in the volumes by Cottingham, Stoothoff, and Murdoch. Some texts of Descartes's are not available in translated form, however. Several of the scholastic texts I use have not been translated into English at all.

Alquié I–III — Fernand Alquié, ed., *Œuvres philosophiques de Descartes,* 3 vols.

AT — The standard edition of Descartes's writings, *Œuvres de Descartes,* Charles Adam and Paul Tannery, eds. I provide references to this edition by volume and page number, except for the *Principles* and the *Passions,* to which I refer by part and article.
Coimbra Commentators, *De anima separata,* cited by disputation and article.
Coimbra commemtaria in tres libros de anima Aristotelis, cited as Coimbra Commentators, *De anima,* by book, chapter, question, article, and page number.
Commentarii in octo libros physicorum Aristotelis, referred to as Coimbra Commentators, *Physics,* cited by book, chapter, question, article, and page number.

CSM — *The Philosophical Writings of Descartes,* John Cottingham, Robert Stoothoff, and Dugald Murdoch, transl., 3 vols. I provide references to this edition for translations of Descartes's writings, again by volume and page number. This edition provides the AT page numbers in the margins.

DA	Francisco Suárez, *De anima, Opera omnia,* vol. 3, referred to by book, chapter, section.
DM	Francisco Suárez, *Disputationes metaphysicae, Opera omnia,* vols. 25–26, referred to by disputation, section, and article.
Essay	John Locke, *An Essay Concerning Human Understanding,* cited by book, chapter, section. Ockham, references to which specify parts of the works in question, as well as volume and page numbers in *Opera Philosophica* (OPH) and *Opera Theologica* (OTH).
SCG	Thomas Aquinas, *Summa contra gentiles,* referred to by volume and chapter.
SP	Eustachius of St. Paul, *Summa philosophica quadripartita,* 4 vols., referred to by part and page number.
ST	Thomas Aquinas, *Summa theologiae.* I have used the standard practice of referring to part, question, article, and where appropriate, the number of an objection or a reply.

Descartes's Dualism

CHAPTER ONE

The Real Distinction Argument

One of Descartes's most lasting contributions to philosophy is his well-known argument for dualism. This argument continues to attract attention, not just from historians of philosophy, but from the philosophical community at large, at least in the English-speaking world. It continues to interest even many a convinced materialist.[1] In this chapter I will provide a detailed analysis of this argument. I will propose that Descartes's argument is radically different from ones that have been attributed to him and that various serious objections that have been advanced in the literature simply do not apply to it.

Most interpreters believe that the claim that mind can exist unextended or the claim that it can exist without body is central to this argument, and many equate Cartesian dualism with these claims. On one very common interpretation the basic idea of the argument is this. Descartes begins by contending that it is conceivable that mind exist without body, and then he argues for dualism by deriving that it is possible for mind to exist without body. It is certainly true that Descartes was concerned with the possibility of mind existing without body, but I will argue that this idea is not central to his argument. His dualism does not consist in this possibility, nor is it fundamental to the argument. Instead, crucial to the argument is Descartes's conception of substance, including important claims about the relationship between the nature or essence of a substance and the properties it can have.

Indeed, I believe that these claims embody what still grips us about this argument.

In Descartes's own terms, the conclusion of the argument is that mind and body are really distinct, and I will speak of the Real Distinction Argument.[2] Its most prominent statement is to be found in the *Meditations,* where it has two focal points, one in the Second and the other in the Sixth Meditation. As a result of the skeptical arguments of the First Meditation, in the Second Meditation Descartes doubts that there are any bodies. Nevertheless, he is certain that he exists and thinks. Next he uses these observations to argue that he has a clear and distinct perception of the mind as a thinking, unextended thing. In the Sixth Meditation he employs this perception to show that the mind is an incorporeal substance, really distinct from the body.

Perhaps the most important questions about this defense of dualism are the following. What exactly does Descartes think he accomplishes in his discussion of the mind in the Second Meditation? And how does he think he can get from the results of the Second Meditation to the real distinction of mind and body in the Sixth Meditation? The argument is often criticized on the ground that the claims about the mind that Descartes is entitled to in the Second Meditation are insufficient to lead to dualism. I will propose that we can answer these questions and objections by considering them in relation to Descartes's conception of substance.

In addition to offering an account of the Real Distinction Argument, this chapter serves to introduce this conception of substance, which will continue to be important throughout the book. For Descartes each substance has a principal attribute, a property which constitutes its nature or essence, and other properties of the substance are its modes. The modes of a substance presuppose this attribute: they cannot exist, nor be clearly and distinctly understood without it. In section 1.1 I will examine Descartes's conception of substance in depth, and sections 1.2–1.5 explain how it is used in the Real Distinction Argument. In section 1.6 I address the relationship of the argument to the idea that mind and body can exist without one another. I briefly discuss some serious problems for prominent interpretations that focus on that idea and argue that these problems do not affect the argument as I see it.

The present chapter does not complete my treatment of the Real

Distinction Argument. Some important issues will be addressed in chapter 2, where I discuss the argument in the broader context of Descartes's relationship with Aristotelian scholasticism and his interest in developing a mechanistic conception of body.

1.1 Substance, Essence, and the Real Distinction

Before analyzing the argument we need to develop a firm grip on its intended conclusion and the metaphysical notions central to it, in particular, the notions of real distinction, substance, and essence. Let me begin with the conclusion. In the Sixth Meditation we find this formulation of the final stage of the argument:

> Since I know that anything that I clearly and distinctly understand can be brought about by God just as I understand it, it is sufficient that I can clearly and distinctly understand one thing without another in order for me to be certain that one is different from the other, since they can be placed apart [*seorsim poni*] at least by God. And it does not matter by what power that happens, in order for them to be regarded as different. Consequently, from the very fact that I know that I exist, and that at the same time I notice nothing else at all to pertain to my nature or essence, except that I am a thinking thing, I conclude correctly that my essence consists in this one thing, that I am a thinking thing. And although perhaps (or rather, as I will soon say, certainly) I have a body, which is very closely joined to me, nevertheless because I have on one hand a clear and distinct idea of myself, insofar as I am only a thinking, not an extended thing, and on the other hand a distinct idea of body insofar as it is only an extended thing, not thinking, it is certain that I am really distinct from my body, and can exist without it. (AT VII 78/ CSM II 54)

Now Descartes is clearly interested in establishing the modal claim that mind and body are separable, that is, that each can exist without the other. He is particularly interested in the idea that he, or his mind, can exist without the body because this idea provides hope for an after-life, as he explains in the Synopsis to the *Meditations* (AT VII 13/ CSM II 10). And indeed, in this passage in the Sixth Meditation he does conclude that mind can exist without body. But on this occasion he does not discuss the issue of the after-life. In fact, a different concern is much more prominent, namely, the purpose of establishing that mind and body are different kinds of substances, each with different kinds of modes. Descartes's interest in this idea becomes evident very quickly, because immediately after the passage just quoted he discusses the question which modes belong to which substance:

> Moreover, I find in me faculties for certain special modes of thinking, namely the faculties of imagining and sensing. I can clearly and distinctly understand myself as a whole without them; but not vice versa them without me, that is, without an intelligent substance in which they inhere: for they include some intellection in their formal concept, and hence I perceive that they are distinguished from me as modes from a thing. I also recognize certain other faculties, such as the capacity to change place, to have various shapes and the like, which can no more be understood without some substance in which they inhere than the preceding ones, and which therefore can also not exist without it: but it is manifest that if these [faculties] exist, they must inhere in a corporeal or extended, not an intelligent substance, because their clear and distinct concept certainly contains some extension, but no intellection. (AT VII 78–79/ CSM II 54–55)

So right after the conclusion of the Real Distinction Argument Descartes argues that sensation and imagination belong to him, that is, to his mind; the 'faculties' for changing location, taking on various shapes, and the like belong to a corporeal substance. The idea that mind and body are different kinds of substances with different kinds of modes is very important to him because it allows him to assign to body only those modes that can be dealt with by mechanistic explanations.[3] The mind is the incorporeal subject of states that cannot be so understood. In this way he aims to provide metaphysical support for his view that mechanistic explanations can account for all phenomena in the physical world.[4] There are important connections between this purpose and the aim of providing support for the immortality of the soul, some of which will emerge in chapter 2. But the concern with mechanism relates only to the idea that mind and body are substances with different types of properties, and not to their ability to exist apart. This concern and its implications for the question just what could be assigned to the incorporeal mind will be particularly important in this book.

The conclusion of the Real Distinction Argument is most properly understood to consist in the claim that mind and body are different substances—*diversae substantiae* (AT VII 13, 78, 226, 423/ CSM II 9, 54, 159, 285–286). In the *Principles of Philosophy,* which contains the most extensive and most formal exposition of his metaphysics, Descartes characterizes the notion of real distinction in accordance with the interpretation I propose. He writes there: "a real distinction obtains properly only between two or more substances" (*Principles* I.60). Now the notion of real distinction was not new with Descartes and had its roots in the scholastic theory of distinctions. And in fact, the characterization from the *Principles* is very close to the one used by such scholastics as Suárez and Eustachius, who defined real distinction as distinction of one thing from another: *una ab alia re*. It is crucial in this context that the term thing—*res*—is for them a technical term: modes are not *res* in this sense, as is particularly clear in Suárez.[5] In this sense of the term for Descartes only substances are *res*, modes are not, and he too sometimes uses the term *res* in a sense that excludes modes.[6]

On the common understanding of the real distinction of mind and body, it simply consists in their separability, contrary to the view I am proposing.[7] This interpretation derives support from Descartes's definition of real distinction in the appendix to the Second Replies entitled "Reasons that Prove the Existence of God and the Distinction of the Soul from the Body Expounded in Geometrical Fashion" (henceforward Geometrical Exposition). He writes there that "two substances are said to be really distinct when each of them can exist without the other" (AT VII 162/ CSM II 114). But we must be careful, for elsewhere in the Second Replies Descartes considers separability as a *sign* of real distinction. The objectors had argued that he had failed to show that body cannot think. In response he writes:

> I don't really see what you can deny here. That in order to recognize that they are really distinct it is sufficient that we clearly understand one thing without another? Provide then some more certain sign of real distinction; for I am confident that none can be given. For what will you say? That those things are really distinct of which each can exist without the other? But again I ask, how do you know that one thing can exist without another? For in order for something to be a sign of real distinction, it must be known. (AT VII 132/ CSM II 95)

One might think that Descartes here rejects the idea that separability is a sign of real distinction. But in fact his point is that by itself separability is not enough: one also needs to know, with certainty, that separability obtains. Consequently, he contends, this sign is not an alternative to his way of proving the real distinction; rather, it leads to his own requirement that we clearly and distinctly understand one thing without another. In addition, the way in which Descartes here considers separability as a candidate for being a sign of real distinction is hard to reconcile with the idea that for him it is constitutive of real distinction: that idea is conspicuously absent. If he thought that real distinction simply consists in separability, one would surely expect him to say so in this context. So this discussion strongly suggests that separability does not constitute real distinction. In section 1.6 we shall see that there is an important distinction between establishing that mind and body are two different substances and establishing that they are separable. The reason is that, philosophically speaking, establishing that mind can exist without body, or can exist without being extended, is not sufficient to show that the mind is actually a substance that is not extended. But clearly Descartes wants that result: the conclusion he aims for is that mind and body are different subjects of inherence, each of which actually has an entirely different set of properties.[8]

It is worth noting that Descartes's position so understood is also the one taken by Suárez, whose theory of distinctions shows remarkable similarities to Descartes's. Suárez characterizes real distinction as the distinction of one thing *(res)* from another, and he devotes considerable attention to the question how one can detect such a distinction. He discusses various signs of real distinction, and separability is one of them. He holds that separability is sufficient but not necessary to conclude that the entities in question are really distinct, and so for him separability is not constitutive of real distinction.[9] He also thinks that separability is sufficient for something being a *res,* and that it distinguishes *res* from modes. Interestingly enough, like Descartes, Suárez thought that, in relation to the distinction between modes and *res,* it does not matter by what power separation can occur. Any mutual separability is sufficient for real distinction, and modes cannot be separated from their subjects, even by God. On the other hand, a crucial difference between the two philosophers is that anything that is a *res* for Suárez is a substance for Descartes. Suárez admits accidents that are *res,* Descartes does not, as we shall see in chapter 4.

It is now time to turn to the notion of substance. In the *Principles* Descartes defines substance as a thing "that so exists that it needs nothing else in order to exist."[10] It is tempting to read this definition as saying that being a substance simply consists in having the ability to exist apart from anything else, and indeed, Descartes's notion of substance is often understood in precisely this way. On this interpretation the real distinction of mind and body, the idea that they are different substances would, after all, reduce to their separability.[11] But the definition in the *Principles* makes clear that there is more to his notion of substance. For it presents the idea that a substance needs nothing else in order to exist, not as fundamental, but *as a result* of its actual mode of existence: a substance "*so exists* that it needs nothing else in order to exist." What could this mean?

Descartes's basic ontology contains substances and modes. A mode exists in or through something else, that is, a substance, whereas a substance exists through itself. He quite frequently characterizes substances as things existing through themselves—*res per se subsistentes* (AT III 502/ CSM III 207; AT VII 222, 226/ CSM II 157, 159; AT VIII-2 348/ CSM I 297).[12] In his definition of substance in the Geometrical Exposition this way of distinguishing modes and substances is presented from a different angle. There Descartes does not describe substance as a *res per se subsistens,* but as that through which properties exist. He writes: "Each thing in which inheres [*inest*] immediately, as in a subject, or through which exists something that we perceive, that is, some property, or quality, or attribute, of which a real idea is in us, is called substance" (AT VII 161/ CSM II 114; see also AT VII 222/ CSM II 156). Again, this characterization follows the Aristotelian scholastics, who commonly distinguished substances and qualities in this way. For instance, Eustachius of St. Paul wrote that a substance is a "being that subsists or exists *per se.*" And he explains that "to subsist or exist *per se* is nothing other than not to exist in something else as in a subject of inherence, in which a substance differs from an accident, which cannot exist *per se* but only in something else in which it inheres."[13]

Intuitively, the idea is that a substance, unlike a mode, is a thing in its own right. A substance has its own existence, unlike a mode.[14] Descartes expresses precisely this idea in one of his discussions of the scholastic notion of a real quality—a quality that is supposed to be a *res*. He often criticizes this notion, arguing that it is the result of regarding a quality as a substance—which he thinks is incoherent. Sometimes when he makes this point he says that we think of such a quality as a substance because we ascribe to it the capacity to exist separately (AT VII 434/ CSM II 293 and AT V 223/ CSM III 358). But in a letter to Elizabeth he characterizes real qualities as qualities "that we have imagined to be real, that is, *as having an existence distinct from that of body,* and consequently as substances, although we called them qualities" (AT III 667/ CSM III 219, emphasis mine).

The connection with separability is now as follows: A substance can exist without anything else *because* it has existence in its own right, *per se*. Modes are different because they exist by virtue of inherence in something else. Consequently, a mode cannot exist without such a subject of inherence. In non-Cartesian terms the idea is very simple. The world contains things and properties. The primary entities are things, which exist in their own right, whereas properties don't; they exist by belonging to things. The basic idea of the distinction between these two categories does not consist in modal claims about separability, but it does have modal consequences. To take an arbitrary example, a piece of wax is a thing, which exists in its own right. Its shape and size are properties of it, which exist by belonging to the piece of wax. As a result, if one were to destroy the piece of wax, the shape and size would disappear. But the piece of wax itself is not a property of something else such that its existence depends on that entity in this way. This is not to say that it has no dependence relations other than this ontological one. It does, in particular, causal ones. But causal relations are irrelevant to the notions of mode and substance.[15] So what Descartes wants to establish, regarding mind and body, is that each is a thing in its own right, and they are different kinds of things.

There is another feature of Descartes's theory of substance that is crucial for our purposes, and that is his conception of the essence of a substance, which consists in its principal attribute. The notion of principal attribute has received relatively little attention in the literature, but it is absolutely central to Descartes's conception of substance as well as to the Real Distinction Argument. The notion of such an attribute is presented most clearly at *Principles* I.53:

> there is one principal property for each substance, which constitutes its nature and essence and to which all the other ones are referred. Namely, extension in length, width and depth constitutes the nature of corporeal substance; thought constitutes the nature of thinking substance. For everything else that can be attributed to body presupposes extension, and is only some mode of an extended thing; and similarly anything we find in the mind, is only one of the different modes of thinking. So for

> instance, figure can only be understood in an extended thing, motion in extended space; and imagination, sensation or the will only in a thinking thing. But on the other hand, extension can be understood without shape or motion, and thought without imagination or sensation and so on—as is obvious to anyone who attends to the matter.

In his discussion of the essences of substances one might expect Descartes to insist that a substance cannot exist without its principal attribute. Now he does believe this to be the case, but this is not distinctive of the attribute that constitutes the essence of a substance: for other attributes also necessarily belong to a substance (if it exists), such as duration, number, and existence (*Principles* I.56, 62). Indeed, Descartes does not even mention that idea in this passage, and instead he insists on something very different, namely, the idea that all the other (intrinsic) properties of a substance are 'referred to' this attribute. They are modes, ways of being of the principal attribute, and, as he often says, *presuppose* it.[16] The principal attribute determines what properties a substance has. Descartes does not use the term principal attribute in the *Meditations,* but the picture of *Principles* I.53 is already present there. Thus we saw that he writes in the Sixth Meditation that sensation and imagination are modes of him, that is, the mind, because "I can clearly and distinctly understand myself as a whole without them; but not *vice versa* them without me, that is, without an intelligent substance in which they inhere." And he claims that motion, shape, and size are modes of body because their clear and distinct conception contains extension (AT VII 78–79/ CSM II 54–55).

This notion of essence is very different from our usual conception of essences as consisting in necessary properties. But the intuition behind Descartes's view is not difficult to grasp. A principal attribute is like the atomic structure of, say, gold, which determines the properties of gold, such as its color, weight, solubility in aqua regia. His view is a particular version of the idea that a substance has a nature that determines and explains what properties that substance has. Questions about the essence of body and, especially, mind play an important role in the Real Distinction Argument. It is usually assumed that for this argument the separability of thought or extension from one's mind is what matters. But as we shall see, the relationship between modes and attributes is far more important.

There is another feature of the notion of principal attribute that deserves attention. In regard of this feature it is useful to compare

Descartes's conception of substance to two other ones, namely, a view one might call the Bare Subject View and the Aristotelian scholastic conception of corporeal substance. On the Bare Subject View a substance just is a subject of inherence of properties. Properties inhere in the subject, but are not constituents of a substance. The subject constitutes the entire substance.[17] According to the Aristotelian scholastics, on the other hand, a corporeal substance is a composite of prime matter and substantial form. Prime matter is a bare subject in the sense that it, too, is in itself featureless and the bare subject for substantial form. But an important difference with the Bare Subject View is that prime matter is just one constituent of the substance besides substantial form.[18]

Descartes clearly rejects the Bare Subject view and agrees with the Aristotelians in thinking that the substance itself is more than just a bare subject: he thinks it contains the principal attribute. Thus on several occasions he makes clear that in order to think of something as a complete thing, that is, a substance, one must include the principal attribute. In the Fourth Replies he writes that surfaces and lines can be understood as complete things, that is, substances, only if one adds, besides length and width, depth (AT VII 228/ CSM II 160). The point is that one needs to include the principal attribute of extension in order to get completeness, substancehood. In a letter to Gibieuf he says that in order to have a complete idea of shape—which is the same as understanding shape as a complete thing (AT VII 221/ CSM II 156)—one needs to include extension and substance, not just substance.

In fact, Descartes seems to hold a view that is exactly the opposite of the Bare Subject View. For much of what he says suggests that the principal attribute constitutes the entire substance and that there is no bare subject of inherence at all. On this view there is nothing to the substance over and above the principal attribute, as he indeed suggests in the *Principles:*

> Thought and extension can be regarded as constituting the natures of intelligent and corporeal substance; *and then they must be conceived not otherwise than as thinking substance itself and extended substance itself, that is, as mind and body.* In this way they are understood most clearly and distinctly. And indeed, we understand extended or thinking substance more easily than substance alone, when the fact that it thinks or is extended is omitted. For there is some difficulty in abstracting the notion

> of substance from the notions of thought and extension, because these are different from it only by reason. (*Principles* I.63, emphasis mine)

Descartes here presents a principal attribute and its substance as the same thing considered in different ways.[19] Furthermore, in the *Comments on a Certain Broadsheet* he uses 'thought' and 'mind' interchangeably, and he writes: "I have not said that those attributes [thought and extension] are in [incorporeal substance and corporeal substance] as in subjects different from them" (AT VIII-2 348/ CSM I 297).

The identification of substance and attribute is also suggested by Descartes's rejection of the scholastic notion of prime matter. In *The World* he dismisses this notion as unintelligible: "it has been so deprived of all its forms and qualities that nothing remains that can be clearly understood." Matter must be conceived as extended, he contends, and the scholastics make a mistake in distinguishing it from its extension (AT XI 33, 35/ CSM I 91, 92). Since Descartes eliminates prime matter from the hylomorphic conception of corporeal substance, the result in Aristotelian terms is that a substance just consists in a substantial form. In Descartes's own terms the result is that the substance just consists in a principal attribute. I think that this is indeed his view. But his commitment to this view is not entirely without problems. Most importantly, he writes that we do not know substances immediately but through their attributes, which require that a substance be present (AT VII 176, 222/ CSM II 124, 156; *Principles* I.52). A full discussion of this issue would, however, lead us too far afield.[20]

Finally, whereas the notions of substantial form and principal attribute are different in many ways, the latter inherited some important features from the former, in particular, from a version of this notion found, for instance, in Aquinas and Suárez. Thus substantial forms constitute the natures of substances; for Descartes the principal attribute plays this role. The substantial form of a hylomorphic substance is the principle or source of the properties, faculties, and activities of a substance, and it determines what kinds a substance can have, or, at least, those proper to a certain kind of substance. For Descartes its principal attribute determines what kinds of modes belong to a substance.[21] Aquinas and others held that the substantial form is what gives the substance its being, its actuality. It makes something a substance.[22] For Descartes the principal attribute makes something a substance, a being in its own right, as opposed to a mode, which has being through something else.

Now that we have a good sense of Descartes's conception of substance, we can turn to the Real Distinction Argument itself. I will use its presentation in the *Meditations* as a guideline and analyze the argument as ruling out, one by one, various ways in which mind and body could be the same substance. First, the discussion of the mind in the Second Meditation leads to the conclusion that thought is not a mode of body but a principal attribute. Second, the argument relies on the claim that extension constitutes the nature of body and is its principal attribute. Consequently, mind and body are not identical by virtue of thought being a mode of extension or *vice versa*. But this is not yet sufficient to establish the real distinction because so far the argument leaves open the possibility that mind and body constitute one substance with two principal attributes. This third possibility is ruled out, since for Descartes a substance has only one principal attribute. I will discuss these three stages of the argument in this order.

1.2 Against Thought Being a Mode of Extension

Let me begin with the question of what Descartes means to accomplish in the Second Meditation. Interpreters have answered this question in different ways. On one view, his point is that he clearly and distinctly perceives that the mind is not extended. In that case dualism would follow quite simply from the validation of clear and distinct perceptions. But Descartes himself makes clear that the Second Meditation should not be understood in this way. In a letter to Clerselier he writes:

> I said in one place that, while the soul doubts the existence of all material things, it only knows itself precisely taken—*praecise tantum*—as an immaterial substance; and seven or eight lines below, in order to show that by these words *praecise tantum,* I do not understand an entire exclusion or negation, but only an abstraction from material things, I said that nevertheless one was not assured that there is nothing in the soul that is corporeal, although one does not know anything corporeal in it. (AT IX 215/ CSM II 276)

The Second Meditation itself is in fact explicit about this point. Descartes argues there that in spite of the skeptical arguments of the First

Meditation he is certain that he exists and that he is a thinking thing. Throughout this discussion the crucial skeptical doubts are about bodies. Next he considers the question whether he might be a body, but he concludes that he cannot settle that issue yet:

> What else am I? I will use my imagination. I am not that complex of limbs, which is called the human body; I am also not some thin air infused in these limbs, nor a wind, fire, vapor, breath, nor anything that I imagine. For I have supposed that those things are nothing. The position remains: I am nevertheless something. Perhaps it happens to be the case, however, that these very things which I suppose to be nothing, because they are unknown to me, do not in reality differ from that I that I know? I don't know, I don't dispute about this yet: I can only judge about those things that are known to me. (AT VII 27/ CSM II 18)

So here Descartes points out that he has not established that he (clearly and distinctly) perceives that the mind is not corporeal. Whereas he does not mention extension explicitly in this passage, it is covered by what he says. For earlier he had announced: "By body I understand all that which is apt to be limited by some shape, confined in a place, and which can fill a space in such a way that it excludes any other body from it" (AT VII 26/ CSM II 17). This last characteristic, filling space in a way that excludes other bodies or other things, Descartes identifies with extension, and he sometimes specifies the essence of body in terms of it. For instance, in writing to Hyperaspistes he denies of the mind "real extension, that is, that by which it occupies a place and excludes something else from it" (AT III 434/ CSM III 197).[23]

Descartes does think the Second Meditation establishes something about his nature or essence. He uses a variety of descriptions that are not clearly consistent. For instance, he claims that extension can be denied of the mind (AT III 475–476/ CSM III 202 and AT VII 121, 227/ CSM II 86, 159). We saw above that he writes to Clerselier about the Second Meditation "I do not understand an entire exclusion or negation, but only an abstraction from material things," but in a letter to Mesland he claims we need an exclusion rather than a negation (AT IV 120/ CSM III 236).[24] In the Fifth Replies he simply says that we don't have to regard the mind as an extended thing and that the concept of it developed in the Second Meditation does not contain corporeal characteristics (AT VII 355/ CSM II 245). In the Sixth Meditation he writes: "I noticed nothing else to pertain to my nature or essence except that I am a thinking thing" [*nihil plane aliud ad naturam sive essentiam meam pertinere animadvertam, praeter hoc solum quod sim res cogitans*] (AT VII 78/ CSM II 54; see also AT VII 8, 219/ CSM II 7, 154). Now this phrase clearly raises a problem because it is ambiguous.[25] It could mean either (1) that he did not notice that anything else belongs to his nature or essence, or (2) that he noticed that nothing else belongs to his nature or essence. Descartes's argument might rely on ambiguities of this kind in a way that is fatal to it.[26] The first of these claims is weaker and easier to establish than the second one. But the question is often raised whether it would be sufficient for establishing dualism. The second claim, on the other hand, is obviously harder to defend. Thus a common objection to the argument is that the Second Meditation fails to show that the mind is not essentially extended. Philosophers have questioned the idea that this claim, and dualism, can be established *a priori* by means of a thought experiment of the kind found in the Second Meditation.[27]

These problems are very serious if one assumes that the question whether the mind is essentially extended comes down to the question whether it is necessarily extended. But we have seen that this approach does not capture Descartes's conception of essence, and so let us interpret the thought experiment of the Second Meditation in light of this conception. The contribution of this Meditation is a clear and distinct perception of the mind that shows that thought is a principal attribute. Once we take this perspective, I will argue, we will be able to see that the argument does not fall victim to ambiguities of the sort noted above.

To see how Descartes establishes that thought is a principal attribute we must begin with his claim that he has a clear and distinct conception of the mind as a complete thing (AT VII 120–121, 221–227/ CSM II 85–86, 156–159). As has been pointed out by Margaret Wilson and others, this notion is very important for the Real Distinction Argument.[28] A complete thing, for Descartes, is "a substance endowed with those forms or attributes which are sufficient for recognizing it as a substance" (AT VII 222/ CSM II 156). He writes: "The mind can be perceived distinctly and completely, or sufficiently for it to be regarded as a complete thing, without any of those forms or attributes from which we recognize that body is a substance, as I think I have sufficiently shown in the Second Meditation" (AT VII 223/ CSM II 157). Now in the Second Meditation Descartes considers the mind only as a *thinking* thing. So the import of the idea that mind can be conceived as complete without any corporeal attributes is that thought is perceived to be sufficient for the mind to be a substance.

This is what the Second Meditation is supposed to establish, and in terms of Descartes's theory of substance, it means that thought is a principal attribute and not a mode.[29] And it should be pointed out that the idea that thought is sufficient to constitute a complete thing must not be understood merely modally. One might think the idea is that thought and extension *can* each constitute a complete thing, but that they don't necessarily do so. Instead, however, the idea is that they are the sorts of items that constitute complete things and always do so. In other words, Descartes thinks that thought and extension are always principal attributes. The thought experiment contributes to this result by showing that thought is not a mode of body. In other instances the point is that thought does not presuppose *extension,* which is what Descartes regarded as sufficient to argue that thought is a principal attribute. For he held that extension is the principal attribute of body, and he is concerned with the question whether mind is the same substance as body. I will return to this point later.[30]

But how does the thought experiment of the Second Meditation show that thought is not a mode of body or of extension? In the *Comments on a Certain Broadsheet* Descartes provides an explanation:

> it belongs to the nature of a mode that although we can easily understand a substance without it, we cannot, however, *vice versa* clearly understand a mode unless we conceive at the same time a substance of which it is a mode; as I explained at *Principles* I, 61, and as all philosophers agree. It is manifest from his fifth rule, however, that our author [Regius] had not attended to this rule: for there he admits that we can doubt about the existence of body, when we do not at the same time doubt the existence of the mind. Hence it follows that the mind can be understood by us without the body, and that therefore it is not a mode of it. (AT VIII-2 350/ CSM I 298)

So the mind is not a mode of body because we can doubt the existence of body while not doubting, indeed, while being certain of the existence of mind, and because a mode cannot be clearly understood without conceiving of the kind of substance to which it belongs. In this text Descartes identifies the claim that the mind is not a mode of body with the idea that thought is a principal attribute. A little later he makes basically the same claim entirely in terms of attributes: "From this fact that one [attribute] can be understood in this way [that is, distinctly] without the other [attribute], it is known that it is not a mode of the latter, but a thing or an attribute of a thing which can subsist without it." The point is really that the Second Meditation is supposed to show that *thought* is not a mode of body. So the Second Meditation shows that thought is not a mode of body, because a mode depends not only ontologically but also epistemically on its attribute. A mode cannot be conceived clearly and distinctly without the substance of which it is the mode or without the attribute of that substance.

The picture becomes yet clearer in the letter to Gibieuf of January 19, 1642:

> when I consider a shape without thinking of the substance or the extension of which it is a shape, I make an abstraction of the mind which I can easily recognize afterwards, by examining whether I did not draw that idea that I have of figure alone from some other, richer idea that I also have in me, to which it is so joined that, although one can think of one without paying attention to the other, one cannot deny it of the other when one thinks of both. For I see clearly that the idea of figure is so joined to the idea of extension and of substance, given that it is not possible for me to conceive a shape while denying that it has extension, nor to conceive of extension while denying that it is the extension of a substance. But the idea of an extended and shaped substance is complete because I can conceive it all by itself, and deny of it everything else of which I have ideas. Now it is, it seems to me, quite clear that the idea I have of a substance that thinks is complete in this way, and that I have no other idea that precedes it in my mind, and that is so joined to it that I cannot conceive them well while denying one of the other; for if there were such an idea in me I would necessarily know it. (AT III 475–476/ CSM III 202)

So Descartes allows that we can think of a mode without thinking of its attribute by means of an abstraction of the mind—that is to say, by not thinking of the attribute at all (see also AT III 421/ CSM III 188). But when we consider both the mode and its attribute together, we will see that the mode depends on that attribute. Consequently, in order to establish whether some property F is a mode of another property G, one would have to consider them both together and then see whether one can deny G of F. Or, more properly, the question is whether one could conceive of something as a thing that has F while denying G of it.[31]

And of course, what is at issue is the question whether we can have *clear and distinct* conceptions of the right kind. Descartes does not always specify the requirement of clarity and distinctness, and in the *Meditations* the notion of a clear and distinct idea or conception does not emerge until after the discussion of the mind in the Second Meditation. Like Descartes, I will often omit it. The notion of clear and distinct perception enters into the argument only to make the point that a reliable cognition is at issue, a perception of the kind we know to be true. If skeptical worries are ignored, the philosophical structure of the argument does not include explicit reference to the notion of clear and distinct perception. The same goes for God, whose role in the argument, in my view, consists in validating clear and distinct perceptions. This view of the role of God is certainly not uncontroversial, but Descartes himself describes it this way in the Fourth Replies (AT VII 226/ CSM II 159).[32]

Let us now return to the strategy described in the letter to Gibieuf. In the Second Meditation it is carried out as follows. Descartes doubts that there are bodies, yet he is certain that he exists. He establishes that he is a thinking thing. Then he turns to the question whether he might be a body, and he concludes that he cannot settle that issue yet. But after he has made that point he explains that there is something that is certain already: "It is very certain that the notion of this [I] so precisely taken does not depend on those things which I do not yet know to exist; it does not depend therefore on any of those things that I feign in the imagination" (AT VII 27–28/ CSM II 18–19). In light of his theory of substance, and in particular the letter to Gibieuf, this passage has the following significance for the Real Distinction Argument. Before the above quote Descartes establishes that he is a thinking thing: he focuses his attention just on thought while not considering corporeal characteristics—that is, in abstraction from such characteristics. Then, in effect, he considers thought and extension (as well as other corporeal characteristics) together: he wonders whether he is a body in addition to being a thinking thing. At first he claims he is not a body, since he assumes there are none. But then he considers the possibility that he is, after all, a body, and he says he does not know, that he cannot settle the question now. But what he does think he can claim is that his *notion* of himself does not depend on the objects of the imagination, that is, bodies or extended things.[33] This is as one should expect in light of the letter to Gibieuf. For according to that letter, if thought were in fact a mode of extension, Descartes would recognize at this point that his idea of himself, a thinking thing, depends on the idea of extension, or of extended substance. Given that he knows he is a thinking thing, he would now see that he also is a body. But he doesn't. So he concludes that this notion of himself does not depend on bodies.[34]

We are now in a position to see that the Real Distinction Argument does not rely on a problematic equivocation in the phrase "I know nothing else to belong to my nature or essence except that I am a thinking thing." And we can see that the weaker version of this claim is sufficient. Indeed, in the Synopsis to the *Meditations* Descartes explicitly makes that weaker claim: "I clearly had no cognition of [*cognoscere*] anything that I knew [*scirem*] to pertain to my essence, except that I was a thinking thing" (AT VII 8/ CSM II 7), and he himself was clearly confident that it is enough (see also AT VII 219, 355/ CSM II 155, 245). Descartes wants to establish that thought is not a mode of extension. And he believes that a mode depends epistemically on its attribute in such a way that one would see the connection between a mode and its attribute *when considering them together*—as opposed to merely not paying attention to corporeal characteristics, as happens in abstraction, as he writes to Gibieuf. So the crucial result for the Real Distinction Argument is that considering thought and extension together does not force us to ascribe extension to the thinking thing. And the weak claim that we do not clearly and distinctly perceive extension to belong to the essence of the mind (as opposed to the stronger claim that we perceive that extension does not belong to its essence) is sufficient if this claim is established while considering whether extension does belong to the essence of the mind.[35] Also one could say that extension can be omitted from the concept of a thinking thing. This claim is insufficient if it is made while abstracting from extension, but it is sufficient if the omission of extension is found possible while considering the question whether extension should be included. Alternatively, we could say that we can deny extension of the mind, or that we can form a conception of the mind that excludes extension from it in the sense that we can exclude it coherently. Similarly, Descartes would say also that sensation can be denied of the mind: it is merely a mode of it. But it does not follow that the mind does not have the faculty of sensing or does not actually sense.[36]

So in terms of Descartes's theory of substance, it follows from the thought experiment of the Second Meditation that thought is not a mode of extension and of body. And as will become even clearer in the sequel, Descartes does not rely on the so-called 'Argument from Doubt', which runs as follows: "I can doubt that body exists, I cannot doubt that I exist, therefore I am not identical with body." Here the conclusion is supposed to follow simply by an application of Leibniz' Law. Sometimes this argument is attributed to Descartes, but its shortcomings are obvious, and others have also pointed out that matters are more complicated.[37] But the importance of the doubt is that it allows us to discover that mind, or rather thought, is not a mode of body.[38]

1.3 Thought a Principal Attribute

The idea that thought is not a mode of extension is not by itself enough to establish that it is a principal attribute. Thought could be a mode of some other attribute. It could also be identical with extension, although Descartes does not pay much attention to this possibility. He regarded it as fairly obviously wrong, but let me address it briefly. In the Sixth Replies he does seem to say that he used to identify thought and extension: "although the mind had the idea of thought no less than of extension, since it did not understand anything unless it also imagined something at the same time, it took them for one and the same [*utrumque pro uno et eodem sumebat*], and referred all the notions which it had of intellectual things to the body" (AT VII 441/ CSM II 297). Elsewhere he addresses the question whether thought might be identical with motion. At one point he allows that one might think so, but only if one made the mistake of relying on one's imagination (AT VII 425/ CSM II 287). And a little before he writes that identifying thought and motion is out of the question if one understands what motion is, and that the only error one might make is ascribing both thought and motion to the same thing (AT VII 422–423/ CSM II 285). The passage quoted above combines both ideas applied to extension instead of motion: the problem there is really that one might refer thought and extension to the same thing. And so Descartes is not so much concerned with an identification of thought with a corporeal property as with the ascription of thought and corporeal properties to the same substance.

Furthermore, it is important to note that for him the method for distinguishing thought from motion or extension consists in using one's pure intellect, rather than the senses or the imagination. This is one instance in which the withdrawal from sense is important. But I think Descartes did not mean to be *arguing* that thought is not extension, and that the point struck him as obvious. Surely he was right about this. If thought is corporeal, it isn't by virtue of being identical with *extension.* And indeed, it is worth contemplating that many cases of nonidentity strike us as obvious without making us feel the need for an argument. To take an extreme example, consider the nonidentity of the number 7 and a piece of wax. In the sequel I will assume that the idea that thought is a principal attribute includes its nonidentity with extension. I will return to the relationship of thought to motion in chapter 2.2.

The possibility that thought presupposes some other property is sometimes raised as an objection to Descartes's argument, and it calls for more discussion. The first thing to note is that this possibility does not necessarily threaten the attempt to show that the mind is an incorporeal substance. For if thought were a mode of some other property that is, however, a principal attribute distinct from extension, then the intended conclusion could still be established. So this objection would pose a problem for the argument only if either (a) thought were a mode of some other *corporeal* property, or (b) thought were a mode of some property that is presupposed by *both* thought and extension. These are the possibilities Descartes needs to rule out.

So what could he say? The following considerations address (a). In the Second Meditation Descartes does not merely try to establish that *extension* can be denied of the mind. He uses the assumption that bodies don't exist and lists various corporeal characteristics. So all corporeal properties are supposed to be ruled out on the basis of the thought experiment. Consequently, in the *Meditations* Descartes does not assume that thought's not being a mode of extension is sufficient for its being a principal attribute.

Often he does make this assumption, however, and the reason is that extension is the crucial property. On his view it is the principal attribute of body. If one grants him this view, he has an additional reply to (a). For then all the other properties of body presuppose extension. And in that scenario, if thought presupposes some corporeal property other than extension, it would turn out in the end that thought also presupposes extension.[39] Thus if one grants Descartes that extension is the principal attribute of body, then showing that thought does not presuppose extension is enough to show that thought is either (i) a principal attribute or (ii) a mode of some principal attribute that is different from extension and that is neither presupposed by extension, nor presupposes it. I have pointed out that (ii) is not a problem. So I will disregard it.

Let us now turn to (b), the possibility that there is some other property that is presupposed by both thought and extension. Now Descartes generally neglects this possibility. He seems to assume that he just needs to show that thought is not a mode of body. Nevertheless, he would have something to say to (b). A passage in the Third Replies suggests that (b) can be ruled out by considering thought and extension together, for it suggests that if one considers modes that presuppose the same attribute together, one will see that they have this attribute in common. So when we consider the various modes of mind together we see they have thought in common, and similarly for the modes of body. And Descartes claims that we see no connection between thought and extension (AT VII 176/ CSM II 124; see also the Sixth Replies, AT VII 423–424/ CSM II 285–286).[40]

This reply may well leave a critic unsatisfied. After all, Descartes's approach can only establish that thought does not presuppose extension by virtue of some *a priori* dependence. This is enough, on his view, to show that it is not a mode of extension. But one might question the idea that the mode-attribute relation is always detectable *a priori*. Alternatively, one might grant that it is, but doubt that a strategy like the one pursued in the Second Meditation and described in the letter to Gibieuf is enough to determine whether there is an *a priori* connection of the relevant kind between two properties.

This is a very serious problem for the argument. Descartes needs to rule out the possibility that thought might be a way of being extended despite there being no *a priori* connection between thought and extension, or none that is so easily detected. But it is not an objection to my interpretation because, given Descartes's use of the thought experiment of the Second Meditation, this kind of problem is bound to arise in one form or another on any interpretation. One may have different views about the full import of this thought experiment. But it certainly relies on the idea that the absence of an *a priori* connection between thought and extension or other corporeal properties is enough to establish that thought itself is not, or need not be, a property of body, and that it is independent of matter in some crucial sense. Consequently, the question how much one can establish in this *a priori* fashion about the nature of thought is essential for the success of Descartes's argument for dualism, regardless of one's interpretation. On the present objection, even in the absence of an *a priori* connection between thought and corporeity, it might well be that thought is not at all possible without body and that it is necessarily a corporeal process. This problem arises in particular when one accepts the view that there are necessary truths that are not *a priori*.[41]

My interpretation is distinguished from others, however, in that it presents Descartes as giving a justification for his reliance on *a priori* considerations in his mode-attribute conception of substance. It is a justification, furthermore, that is compatible with there being *a posteriori* necessary truths about other matters: Descartes's conception of substance merely commits him to the specific claim that the relationship between mode and attribute is detectable *a priori*. So the mere existence of necessary *a posteriori* truths does not entail that the thought experiment cannot provide him with what he needs. Rather, in order to question his *a priori* approach we specifically need to address his view about the relationship between modes and attributes. This view is plausible for various examples of modes found in his writings, such as motion, shape, sensation, imagination; but it is a very strong view about the relationship between the essence of a substance and its modes.

1.4 The Nature of Body

How close are we to the conclusion that mind and body are different substances? Thought being a principal attribute is not enough to establish that my mind is not actually extended. If my mind is a thinking, complete thing by virtue of the attribute of thought, it follows that my mind could exist as just a thinking thing that is not extended. But that conclusion is compatible with the idea that it is actually extended. Descartes relies on two further premises; the claim that extension is the principal attribute of body, and the claim that a substance has exactly one principal attribute.

The claim that extension is the principal attribute of body rules out the possibility that mind and body are identical by virtue of extension being a mode of thought. It is easy to overlook the importance of this premise, and generally, discussions of the argument focus on the mind without paying attention to body. But Descartes's conception of body is crucial. I will confine myself here to making clear how this conception is important to the Real Distinction Argument and leave further discussion of body for chapters 3 and 4.

The claim that extension is the principal attribute of body is essential in two ways. (1) *Extension,* rather than some other property, is the principal attribute of body. Descartes thought that existing views of body confused what belongs to body and what belongs to the soul. He singled out Aristotelian scholasticism for mixing 'ideas of body and soul,' in particular, in their notions of real qualities and substantial forms, as he explains in a letter of July 1641. Once we clean up the notions of body and soul, and we think of body as what is extended and of the soul as what thinks, he contends, we can easily see they are different for the following reason: "When things are separated only by a mental abstraction, one necessarily notices their conjunction and union when one considers them together. But one could not notice any between the body and soul, provided that one conceives them as one should, the one as that which fills space, the other as that which thinks" (letter of July 1641, possibly to de Launay, AT III 420–421/ CSM III 188).

(2) The extension claim is also crucial to the argument that body has a *principal attribute* different from thought. That is to say, it is important that body is a substance by virtue of some property different from thought and does not have to think in order to be a substance.[42] Descartes takes the idea that body has a principal attribute different from thought to be pretty obvious, and it will surely strike most people as not in need of defense. One can easily conceive of a corporeal, nonthinking complete thing, such as a stone, and we easily grant that there are such things. But this point is important, because the argument relies on the idea that extension is a *principal attribute* to show that the mind is not extended. And it is worth noting that this claim was denied, for instance, by Leibniz, who thought that all substances are perceiving substances. In Cartesian terms, Leibniz did not regard extension, but only perception as a principal attribute, that is, as a property that constitutes the nature of a substance. Although Descartes thought it was an advantage of his conception of body that he regarded its essence as consisting in extension, the argument could have gone through, in principle, on a conception of body as having a

different principal attribute. The present point is that in order to get the conclusion that the mind is not a body Descartes needs the claim that some property different and independent from thought is the principal attribute of body.

The role of claims about body in the Real Distinction Argument is generally neglected, and this is no doubt due to the fact that the possibility of corporeal, nonthinking substances seems so obvious. But claims about the nature of body are indispensable to the argument and central statements of it should make this clear. Thus in the Sixth Meditation Descartes relies on clear and distinct conceptions of both mind and body—not just of the mind.

1.5 The Attribute Premise

At this stage of the argument we are supposed to be convinced that both thought and extension are principal attributes. Consequently, two ways in which the mind might be a body are ruled out: thought cannot be a mode of extension, and extension cannot be a mode of thought. What is left is the possibility that the mind has two principal attributes, thought and extension. But this possibility is eliminated by what I will call the Attribute Premise, according to which a substance has exactly one principal attribute.

We have, in fact, already encountered this premise in Descartes's account of substance. For we saw that at *Principles* I.53 he writes that each substance has one principal attribute that constitutes its nature or essence. The premise is generally not at all explicit when he argues for the real distinction of mind and body, but he does appeal to it in the *Comments on a Certain Broadsheet.* Regius had written: "since those attributes [extension and thought] are not opposites but diverse, there is no obstacle to the mind being some attribute belonging to the same subject as extension, although one is not comprehended in the concept of the other" (AT VIII-2 343/ CSM I 294–295). Descartes responds that this is possible for modes, but:

> About other attributes that constitute the natures of things it cannot be said that those that are different and of which neither is contained in the concept of the other belong to the same subject. For it is the same as saying that one and the same subject has two different natures, which implies a contradiction, at least when the question concerns a simple and

non-composite subject, as is the case here. (AT VIII-2 349–350/ CSM I 298)[43]

Less obviously, the premise is just below the surface in his discussion of the argument in the Fourth Replies, where Descartes writes: "No one who perceived two substances through two different concepts has ever failed to judge that they are really distinct" (AT VII 226/ CSM II 159). On a simple-minded reading of this sentence he would be suggesting something like this: whenever we have two concepts, and we wonder whether they correspond to one or two substances, we must think there are two. But he cannot mean to say that. The concepts in question are those of the mind as a thinking complete thing, and the body as an extended complete thing, where neither concept contains what belongs to the other substance. Thus the idea is that mind and body are perceived through thought and extension respectively. I think that what is behind this comment is Descartes's view that two principal attributes yield two substances. The comment suggests that he regarded this view as pretty obvious, or that he simply assumed it—which might explain why he does not make the Attribute Premise more explicit when he states or discusses the Real Distinction Argument.

Now in the passage from the *Comments on a Certain Broadsheet* Descartes draws a distinction between simple and composite subjects; the human being is a complex subject, a composite of mind and body, which contains more than one attribute. This suggests that we need to make a modification in the statement of the Attribute Premise, for it seems to suggest that he allows for complex *substances,* which have more than one principal attribute. If so, the Attribute Premise would apply to simple substances only. We must be cautious, however, for Descartes does not use the term 'substance' here, and in fact I am convinced that he did not regard the human being as a substance. But that question has to wait until chapters 5 and 6. Fortunately, the question does not need to be settled here, because insofar as its role in the Real Distinction Argument is concerned, the Attribute Premise is perfectly compatible with the possibility of complex substances. The premise entails that when there are two principal attributes, there are two substances. But this is, in principle, consistent with two substances, such as mind and body, in turn composing a third substance.

To put the point slightly differently: the Attribute Premise entails that if there are substances that both think and are extended they are always composites of two different substances, a thinking one and an extended one. In the sequel I will leave this complication out. My discussion will concern simple substances, regardless of whether or not Descartes allows for complex ones.[44]

Scholars have overlooked the role of the Attribute Premise, no doubt due to the fact that Descartes does not make it explicit in his discussions of the Real Distinction Argument. Indeed, he himself may not always have appreciated its importance.[45] Nevertheless, the reasons for thinking that the argument does rely on it are very strong indeed. Descartes did clearly commit himself to the Attribute Premise, as at *Principles* I.53, and in the *Comments* he does explicitly ascribe a role to the premise in his defense of dualism. Furthermore, there is the philosophical consideration that the argument requires *something* to do the work the premise does. Without it the argument establishes the possibility of a thinking, nonextended substance. But it simply does not rule out for any particular thinking substance—such as my mind or Descartes's or human minds in general—that it is in fact extended and corporeal (without being composites of a thinking and an extended substance).

This finally leaves us with the following question: Why did Descartes hold the Attribute Premise?[46] The premise makes a strong claim, and the question whether one should accept or reject it is not easy to answer. Descartes himself never really defends it. For him the premise may well have been fundamental, and in that case one should not expect a defense, but one might well wish for an explanation of its appeal. The closest he comes is in the passage from the *Comments:* he says that a substance cannot have two natures, because this would imply a contradiction. But that remark does not teach us much. The question why he might have held this premise is an interesting one, however, and I wish to pursue it briefly, although doing so is necessarily speculative.

One possible explanation is this. We saw in section 1.1 that Descartes identified substance and principal attribute. A substance contains nothing over and above the principal attribute: there are no additional constituents. This view provides a very simple hypothesis about why he adhered to the Attribute Premise: for it would seem to follow that where there are two such attributes there must be two substances. By contrast, on the view that there is a bare subject—which either is an additional constituent or entirely constitutes the substance—two attributes could be accommodated within one (simple) substance because one could say they both inhere in this one subject. Indeed, when Descartes makes explicit in the *Comments on a Certain Broadsheet* that a (simple) substance can only have one principal attribute, his identification of substance and attribute is quite present. For instance, as I pointed out in section 1.1, he speaks interchangeably about substances and attributes and claims that attributes are not in substances as in something different from them.

But when he writes that a substance cannot have two natures, I suspect that he expresses a rather different idea. Here the sense in which a principal attribute constitutes the nature of a substance is important. Being its nature means in part determining what kinds of properties, modes, a substance has: a particular kind of substance cannot have just any kind of property. In this regard a Cartesian principal attribute is like a scholastic substantial form, but also like the atomic structure of gold, which determines the properties of gold, and how gold behaves.[47] The properties of a substance are unified by this attribute, which accords with the idea, common in the history of philosophy, that a substance is a unity in a strong sense: the principal attribute generates a qualitative unity. But this picture presupposes that a substance only has one such attribute. I think that this is the idea Descartes refers to when he claims that a substance cannot have more than one nature.

For a proper understanding of the role of the Attribute Premise, it is useful to consider that one may reject its contribution to the argument in various ways. Thus one may not accept the idea that a substance has one single nature and reject the premise. Locke's position seems to exemplify this attitude. He accepted the view that there is a great disparity between the mental and the physical, but he held that God could have added thought to matter.[48] Alternatively, one may reject the view that thought and extension constitute two such natures and argue that in fact they both pertain to one single nature. For Descartes, principal attributes are distinguished by their relations of conceptual independence. The modes that pertain to one such attribute depend on it conceptually: we must conceive of shape as inhering in something extended. Thought and extension turn out to be two different principal attributes because, as he explains in the *Comments on a Certain*

Broadsheet, "neither is contained in the concept of the other." Each can be clearly and distinctly conceived without the other, and so each is "a thing or the attribute of a thing that can subsist without the other" (AT VIII-2 350/ CSM I 299). But one could argue that thought and extension are not two such natures on the ground that Descartes is wrong in thinking that natures can be identified by the kind of conceptual independence he regarded as essential. And one could contend that, in fact, thought and extension do have some sort of crucial dependence, so that thought must inhere in an extended thing, and they are united in one nature.

Or one could contend that *human* thought and extension have such dependence because, in fact, the way we humans think presupposes a body; indeed, the scholastics held this last view. As we shall see in chapter 2, they held that human intellectual states do not inhere in a body, and they regarded this idea as a basis for concluding that the mind or soul is incorporeal and can exist without the body. But as we shall see, in particular, in chapter 5, they thought that human intellectual states require the cooperation of the imagination, which does take place in a corporeal organ.[49] For them this dependence establishes a connection between the human intellect and the body that was crucial for their view that the human being is a single substance with a single nature, despite the incorporeity and separability of the soul.

1.6 Separability

The previous section concludes my account of the structure of the Real Distinction Argument for now, although some issues will be addressed in the next chapter. At this point I wish to return to the issue of the separability of mind and body. I have argued that the real distinction of mind and body consists not in their separability, but in their being different substances. Nevertheless, as we saw earlier, the question of their separability was on Descartes's mind, and he cared in particular about the possibility of the mind existing without the body. So we may well ask: What is the relationship between the separability of mind and body and their being different substances, and what is the connection of separability with the Real Distinction Argument?

One connection between real distinction and separability, as we have seen, is that the first entails the second. For Descartes a substance is a thing that exists in its own right, and for this reason it can exist without anything else. So it follows from the idea that mind and body are really distinct, that is, are different substances, that they can exist without one another. Nevertheless, it does not follow from these considerations that Descartes infers the separability of mind and body from their being different substances and really distinct. According to many interpreters the inference goes in the opposite direction, and indeed, I argued that he regarded separability as a sign of real distinction. I believe, however, that this approach misrepresents the precise significance of separability for the Real Distinction Argument and overestimates its importance.

One place where Descartes clearly does infer the real distinction of mind and body from their separability is the Geometrical Exposition. He argues there that mind can be without body and *vice versa,* at least by God's power. Then he concludes: "Substances that can be without one another are really distinct (by definition 10). But mind and body are substances (by definitions 5, 6, and 7), that can be without one another (as has already been proved). Therefore mind and body are really distinct" (AT VII 170/ CSM II 120, see also AT VII 227/ CSM II 160). But the Geometrical Exposition is unusual in this regard. Thus, whereas the separability of mind and body is in evidence in the Sixth Meditation and in the *Principles,* in neither of these texts does Descartes seem to derive real distinction from it. At *Principles* I.60 Descartes concludes that mind and body are really distinct before he addresses their separability. The text of the crucial passage in the Sixth Meditation is quite complicated and difficult to interpret. Descartes first makes general claims about how to establish a real distinction. He seems to be saying that it is established via separability, when he writes "Since I know that anything that I clearly and distinctly understand can be brought about by God just as I understand it, it is sufficient that I can clearly and distinctly understand one thing without another in order for me to be certain that one is different from the other, since they can be placed apart [*seorsim poni*] at least by God." When he moves to the discussion of mind and body in particular, however, their separability does not figure as a premise, although it does show up. Descartes concludes the argument by saying "it is certain that I am really distinct from my body, and can exist without it." But this sentence is more easily read as presenting the direction of inference as being from real distinction to separability!

Furthermore, on various occasions Descartes presents the real distinction as derived simply from the claim that he has clear and distinct conceptions of mind and body as different substances. The Sixth Meditation can be read that way, but most strikingly, in the Synopsis Descartes presents the final stage of the argument as follows: "it must be concluded that all those things which are clearly and distinctly conceived as different substances, as are mind and body, are substances really distinct from one another" (AT VII 13/ CSM II 9). Now statements of the argument in which he infers that mind and body are different substances simply from the fact that he had different conceptions of them, or, as here, from the observation that he clearly and distinctly conceives them to be different, might be elliptical. There might be an implicit step to the effect that mind and body are separable. But there are two philosophical points to be made here. First, in fact that step is not needed: on my reconstruction the argument arrives at the real distinction without any appeal to separability. Second, interpretations that do see the argument as deriving the real distinction from the separability of mind and body, or from the separability of extension from mind, tend to run into serious trouble with respect to this inference. I will consider two examples.

Margaret Wilson reconstructs the argument as follows. If A can exist apart from B, and *vice versa,* A is really distinct from B, and B from A. Furthermore, the argument relies on premises that establish the following: If I clearly and distinctly perceive that A can exist apart from B and *vice versa,* then they can so exist, because God can bring it about, and thus they are really distinct. The question is now: What does it take to perceive that A can exist without B? Wilson says: "I can clearly and distinctly perceive the possibility that A and B exist apart, if: there are attributes ϕ and ψ such that I clearly and distinctly understand that ϕ belongs to the nature of A, and that ψ belongs to the nature of B (and $\phi \neq \psi$), and I clearly and distinctly understand that something can be a complete thing if it has ϕ even if it lacks ψ (or has ψ and lacks ϕ)."[50] Thought and extension then fulfill the conditions on ϕ and ψ for myself (that is, my mind) and body, and it follows that I (my mind) and body are really distinct.

On this interpretation the argument relies on the perceptions that thought belongs to me and that thought is sufficient to constitute a complete thing. Consequently, it establishes that my completeness, my existence as a substance, does not require extension, and that I *can* exist without being extended. But on this interpretation nothing in the argument rules out that *actually* I am extended and a body. This would not be a problem if Descartes was merely concerned to establish that I can exist without body, or, to put it differently, that I can exist in an entirely incorporeal form. Now Wilson thinks that this is all Descartes wants to establish; she thinks that real distinction is nothing over and above separability and that for Descartes mind and body are different things just in the sense that they can exist apart.[51] Her view leaves open the possibility that mind and body are like a statue and the bronze it is made of. Each can exist without the other, and they are distinct in that sense, but in their current form of existence they coincide to share properties. I have argued, however, that there is more to Descartes's notion of real distinction. Mind and body are different substances for him, in the sense that each is a thing in its own right, entirely different in nature from the other, and each is the subject of inherence for entirely different types of properties.

Adding the Attribute Premise to Wilson's reconstruction would result in the conclusion that I am a different substance from body in this stronger sense. But doing so would make the appeal to separability superfluous. For, as Wilson sees it, Descartes bases the claim that he clearly and distinctly perceives the separability of his mind and body on the claim that he perceives that thought belongs to his mind, and extension to body, and that each of these is complete with just the attribute in question.[52] She is right on this point. But, given the clear and distinct perceptions of mind and body as complete with just thought and extension, respectively, the real distinction can be established without an appeal to separability of mind and body—by adding the Attribute Premise (and the validation of clear and distinct perceptions via God). For Descartes these clear and distinct perceptions allow us to conclude both that thought and extension are principal attributes and that mind and body are separable. But the first of these two claims is more fundamental philosophically: mind and body can exist without one another because thought and extension are different principal attributes. More importantly for the argument, this first claim is what we need to establish the real distinction, since in combination with the Attribute Premise it allows the inference to mind and body actually being nonextended and nonthinking, respectively. The conclusion that they are different substances follows immediately.

Descartes himself did, however, seem to think that one can infer from the separability of mind and body that they are different substances, and he did not seem to see any problem with this inference. But these problems are not serious for him since his conception of substance allows the argument for the real distinction to go through without running afoul of them.

The other interpretation I wish to consider is the following. Versions of it are widespread in the literature, and unlike Wilson's interpretation, it purports to offer a way of establishing that the mind is actually not extended. In the Second Meditation Descartes argues that it is conceivable that he (his mind) exists and thinks without being extended. Furthermore, he believes that whatever is conceivable is possible. Let us call this the Conceivability Premise. It follows that it is possible for him to exist and think without being extended. The argument needs a further premise to show that he is *actually* not extended and thus not a body. This job can be done by what I will call the Essentialist Premise: What is extended is necessarily extended, where this claim must be understood *de re*. The conceivability and possibility of Descartes existing without being extended should also be understood as *de re* claims about a particular (Descartes, his mind). Let us call this the Essentialist Argument.[53]

This argument is stated in terms of the ability of the mind to exist without being extended, rather than in terms of separability of mind from body. But their separability is at stake in the following sense. The question at issue is whether a person's mind is identical with her body, or, for that matter, any body. If the mind can exist without being extended, it can exist without a body with which it might be identical. (Or at least, it can exist without a body in the relevant sense: it might need a body for reasons of causal dependence.)

There are two serious problems with this interpretation. From a historical point of view, the trouble is that the Essentialist Premise is introduced just on the basis of the philosophical need for it, and not at all on the basis of textual evidence. It seems very plausible that Descartes believed the premise to be true, but he never states it, and there certainly is no textual evidence that he relied on it in the Real Distinction Argument.[54] Secondly, the argument suffers from a very serious philosophical defect. For Descartes might find it conceivable that he exists without being extended and from this infer, by way of the Conceivability Premise, that it is possible for him not to be extended. But we often find it conceivable that an entity lack a certain property that it does in actuality have. So it might be that Descartes finds it conceivable that he not be extended, while he is actually extended. But then, by the Essentialist Premise, he would be necessarily extended. So, given this premise, the conceivability of a particular entity existing unextended is insufficient to establish its possibility. Thus, whereas the argument needs both the Essentialist Premise and the Conceivability Premise, they are in fact in tension.[55]

The problem at hand is not that *thinking* might require extension. As I pointed out in section 1.3, on *any* interpretation the question arises whether one can establish that thought is independent of extension (or other corporeal properties) by way of the thought experiment of the Second Meditation. But the trouble that specifically affects the Essentialist Argument is that, even if thought is independent of corporeity, the particular individual Descartes might be extended (or his mind might be extended) in addition to and independently from his being a thinker. And then, by the Essentialist Premise, he would be necessarily extended.

So let's compare this argument with the Real Distinction Argument as I interpret it. The latter argument does not rely on the two clashing premises and so their conflict poses no problem for it. The Conceivability Premise is supposed to capture how one can use the result of the thought experiment of the Second Meditation. It is a very strong claim about *a priori* access to what is possible, as it contends that *anything* that is conceivable is possible. (There are other relevant notions of conceivability that would not be appropriate in an interpretation of the Real Distinction Argument, which is meant to be *a priori*.) But the Real Distinction Argument only requires the narrower claim that the connection between modes and attributes is an *a priori* matter—which allows one to conclude, on the basis of the thought experiment, that thought is not a mode of extension. And this claim is compatible with the Essentialist Premise, which, moreover, is simply not used in the argument as I see it.

But perhaps an even more important difference between the two arguments is this. The Essentialist Argument uses the thought experiment to establish that a particular entity is conceivable without extension. It is natural to interpret Descartes's argument this way, as he claims that he can conceive of *himself* as a thinking, unextended thing. But the Real Distinction Argument does not rely on the full force of that claim, since it merely cares about the idea that the *attribute of thought* is conceivable without extension—which it uses to establish its status as a principal attribute. This feature of the argument derives from Descartes's conception of essence. As I argued in section 1.1, this conception turns on the relationship of presupposition between attributes and modes rather than on the question whether a property necessarily belongs to a substance. So it is not surprising that the Real Distinction Argument, which involves claims about the essence of the mind, relies on questions about the relations between attributes and modes, rather than on the question whether a particular entity is necessarily extended. This is another reason why the philosophical difficulties that affect the Essentialist Argument do not arise for the Real Distinction Argument. For the source of those difficulties includes *de re* modal claims about a particular entity, claims that are based on the conceivability of that entity without extension.

This point is connected to the following important difference between the two arguments. Sidney Shoemaker has claimed that the Essentialist Argument may be thought to work because it is assumed that if dualism is true for *some* thinking subject, then it is true for *every* thinking subject.[56] What he has in mind, I take it, is this. One might find coherent the notion of a thinking substance that is not extended and infer that it is possible for there to be such an entity. But supposing that these claims are correct, it still does not follow about any *particular* thinking thing, such as Descartes or his mind, that it is unextended. On my interpretation, however, the argument tries to establish directly that dualism is true for *any* thinking subject: it purports to establish that it is impossible for *any* thinking thing to be an extended thing.

So, unlike Wilson's reconstruction, the Real Distinction Argument aims to establish that the mind is actually not extended. And unlike the Essentialist Argument, it does not rely on incompatible premises to do so. In sum, the reconstruction I propose avoids serious philosophical problems that arise from focusing on separability of mind from body or from extension. These are considerable advantages. At the same time it reveals, I believe, the ideas that are fundamental to the argument.[57] But this is not to say that the argument succeeds in establishing dualism, and it has not been my aim to argue that it does. As on any interpretation, the argument faces the question of the significance of the *a priori* independence of thought and corporeity exploited by the Second Meditation. Problems peculiar to my interpretation arise from its reliance on the Attribute Premise, which Descartes does not justify and does little to motivate. The premise is puzzling, but I find it interesting and thought-provoking. It needs defending, but this is surely a better problem to have than reliance on conflicting premises. Furthermore, the philosophical interest of looking at Descartes's argument does not necessarily lie in its succeeding to establish dualism. After all, we can often learn from historical figures because they articulate views different from ours in ways that stimulate our thought. Indeed, contemporary philosophers often examine Descartes's argument in order to determine the force of dualistic intuitions that they wish to render harmless. And whatever the philosophical strengths and weaknesses of this argument, I hope I have established that it is the one offered by Descartes.

Conclusion

The argument can now be schematized as follows:

(1) I can doubt that I am extended but I cannot doubt (that is, I am certain) that I think.
(2) For any (intrinsic) properties ϕ and ψ, if it is possible to doubt that something is ψ while not doubting (that is, while being certain) that it is ϕ, then ϕ is not a mode of ψ.
(3) Thought is not a mode of extension. (1, 2)
(4) Extension is the principal attribute of body, that is, corporeal substance.
(5) If thought is not a mode of extension, it is a principal attribute distinct from extension.
(6) Thought is a principal attribute distinct from extension. (3, 5)
(7) Every substance has exactly one principal attribute.
(8) The substance that is the subject of my thoughts (=my mind) is not extended. (4, 6, 7)
(9) My mind is a different substance from body. (4, 8, Leibniz' Law)
(10) If A and B are different substances, they are really distinct.
(11) My mind is really distinct from body. (9, 10)

So understood, Descartes's argument escapes various philosophical problems, which I have discussed throughout this chapter. And this interpretation explains his confidence in the argument in terms of views he clearly held, and which he himself adduces in relation to it.

Descartes's conception of substance explains why he thought the kind of *a priori* reasoning displayed in the thought experiment of the Second Meditation could establish dualism: it is supposed to show that thought is a principal attribute. This virtue of my interpretation of the argument helps meet the following objection. Descartes's theory of substance is not in evidence in the Second Meditation, and so one might be puzzled by the idea of understanding that Meditation in terms of this theory. But I have argued that the contribution of that Meditation *can* be understood in the context of this theory, and that doing so explains Descartes's confidence in the Real Distinction Argument. And he does express his conception of the relationship between modes and principal attributes in the Sixth Meditation, immediately after the conclusion of the Real Distinction Argument, when he discusses the question what modes belong to what substance.

I do not wish to claim that in writing the *Meditations* Descartes had his conception of substance in mind in precisely the terms in which he expounded it in the *Principles*. I don't know whether he did. Descartes did report working on the *Principles* fairly soon after finishing the *Meditations*. He completed the *Meditations* early in 1640 and wrote to Mersenne that he was working on part I of the *Principles* as early as December 31, 1640 (see AT III 35–36, 61, 63, 276/ CSM III 146, 167).[58] But for the purpose of understanding the argument in the *Meditations* it is sufficient that the ideas fundamental to this conception of substance were already operative in Descartes's mind—whether or not he had formulated them to himself as he did in the *Principles*.

I have argued that the Real Distinction Argument is considerably different from the picture of this argument that is common, in particular, in the literature in English, which has often examined the argument in great detail. Given the continued interest in this argument, one may well ask what relevance it could still have to contemporary concerns on my interpretation. It is not a question I can pursue adequately here, but let me summarize the basic idea of the argument. It relies fundamentally on Descartes's view that the categories of the mental and the physical are radically different: they constitute two entirely different types of properties. This idea connects his argument to contemporary concerns, since late twentieth-century doubts about materialism often focus precisely on the sense that there is such a radical difference between the mental and the physical. It is hard to see, skeptics worry, how the mental could reduce to the physical, in the sense that everything is, ultimately, corporeal. Nevertheless, this much may seem compatible with mind and body being one and the same *thing*. Thus the question arises how we should individuate things: How should we decide whether mind and body are the same thing or two different ones? This is the question on which the argument focuses. Descartes believes that mind and body must be different because one thing cannot have two sets of properties that are different and unrelated in the way mental and corporeal properties are. His mode-attribute conception of substance embodies a strong conception of an individual substance as unified by means of a nature that determines and explains what types of properties it can have. And he holds that extension and thought are two such natures.[59] So the Real Distinction Argument exploits the perceived radical gap between mental and physical properties by combining it with a view of the nature of individual entities.

Finally, I have emphasized the importance of Descartes's conception of body for the Real Distinction Argument. Whereas this fact is often overlooked, the question of what we find hard to regard as corporeal is determined to a high degree by our view of the nature of the corporeal. In chapters to come the importance, for his dualism, of Descartes's conception of body as mechanistic will become more evident. Our twentieth-century conception of body is quite different from his, but it is continuous with his insofar as it is quite remote from the mental as we experience it or as we conceive of it. As for Descartes, for at least some of us there is a gap that means that we continue to be troubled by the mind-body problem.

CHAPTER TWO

Scholasticism, Mechanism, and the Incorporeity of the Mind

In the previous chapter I offered a detailed analysis of Descartes's main argument for dualism, the Real Distinction Argument. I now wish to step back and consider his dualism in a broader context. Understanding of both the view itself and Descartes's defense of it benefit considerably from consideration of his preoccupation with mechanistic science and his relationship to Aristotelian scholasticism.

On the common understanding of Descartes's dualism, the view stands out by virtue of the claim that the mind (or soul) is an incorporeal entity. This is what is striking from a twentieth-century perspective. But when we consider the similarities and dissimilarities between Descartes's views of mind and body and those common among the scholastics, a very different perspective emerges. First, the view that the human soul is an incorporeal entity and can exist without the body was by no means new or unusual at the time, and it was common fare among the Aristotelian scholastics. This fact should not be surprising given their commitment to the immortality of the soul, but it is never discussed in relation to Descartes's dualism. This is not to say that the scholastics had entirely the same view of the soul's ontological status as Descartes. As we shall see in chapter 5, there is an important difference insofar as for them the soul is an incomplete substance and for Descartes it is a complete one. But the most significant departure from scholastic doctrine concerns the questions what activities should be ascribed to the human soul and mind, and what qualities can be found in the physical world. This departure constitutes a radical change concerning the boundaries between the corporeal and the incorporeal.

The discussion in this chapter will center around Descartes's treatment of the intellect and its role in his defense of dualism. On the usual interpretation of his view, intellectual activity is just one among different kinds of modes of the incorporeal mind. After all, Descartes regards the mind as the subject of thought, and he describes it as "a thing that doubts, understands, affirms, denies, is willing, is unwilling, imagines also and senses" (AT VII 28/ CSM 11 19). But in fact, in regard to his dualism, he treated intellectual activity quite differently from most other mental states. He held that most mental states, for instance sensation and imagination, involve the body as well, but he believed that purely intellectual activity does not. Furthermore, Descartes regarded the intellect as the essence of the mind, and the Real Distinction Argument relies on claims about intellection, but not about sensation, imagination, and other types of thoughts. Once we recognize these features of his view, we can see that there are important points of continuity between Descartes and the scholastics regarding the intellect. They, too, regarded it as pertaining to the mind and as entirely incorporeal. On the other hand, for the scholastics the mind was not the whole soul, whereas for Descartes mind and soul were the same. Interestingly, he differs from the scholastics in excluding various activities from the soul, while at the same time he expands the notion of the mind to include activities besides the intellect, in particular, sensation and imagination. These differences are intimately connected to his preoccupations with mechanistic science.

Section 2.1 relates Descartes's conception of the intellect to his views of the scope of mechanistic science, the question of the immortality of the soul, and his Aristotelian scholastic background. In section 2.2 I will turn to the Real Distinction Argument and defend the view that it relies on claims about intellection and not about sensation and imagination. We will see that the fact that the argument relies only on the intellect is important for its strength, given views of the various types of mental activity held by Descartes and the scholastics. In section 2.3 I will explain the precise significance of Descartes's conception of the intellect for the Real Distinction Argument.

2.1 The Intellect, Science, and Immortality

Descartes contrasts the intellect with sensation and imagination with respect to their relationship to the body on various occasions. For example, in the Sixth Meditation Descartes writes that imagination differs from intellection in that "when the mind understands, it turns in some way towards itself and inspects one of the ideas which are in itself; but when it imagines, it turns towards the body and intuits something in the body which conforms to an idea understood by the mind or perceived by the senses" (AT VII 73/ CSM II 51). In the Fifth Replies he claims: "I have also often distinctly shown that the mind can operate independently of the brain; for certainly the brain can be of no use to pure intellection, but only to imagination or sensation" (AT VII 358/ CSM II 248).[1] From a twentieth-century perspective, these descriptions of the intellect are quite striking, as is brought out quite clearly by Margaret Wilson. She notes that Descartes's conception of the intellect shows that his dualism differs rather dramatically from "Cartesian dualism" as it is usually understood in contemporary discussions.[2] The main point of the latter view is, in her words, that "mental events *are not identical* with events in the body (brain, or whatever)." This "Cartesian" view is compatible with the idea that "*every* type of mental occurrence, from twinges of pain to metaphysical reflection—has a *corresponding* or *correlated* type of physical occurrence." But for Descartes, she points out, acts of intellection are not even *paralleled* by any physical acts.[3]

Wilson considers the question why Descartes held this view of the intellect. She contends that this form of dualism not only distinguishes him from twentieth-century dualists, but means he was also an odd man out in the seventeenth century. For instance, Hobbes, Leibniz, and Spinoza all accepted forms of either materialism or parallelism. Furthermore, she suggests that the Real Distinction Argument does not support this form of dualism. In light of these observations it is remarkable and rather puzzling that Descartes holds this version of dualism. Wilson does not think that a concern with personal immortality fully explains it because Leibniz and Spinoza were more concerned with this issue. Instead, she suggests, Descartes was *motivated* by his "universalist pretensions" in physics and the observation he had no account of the human intellect. A *reason* for his view that intellection is completely immaterial may be that he was committed to mechanistic explanations in physics—explanations that he thought could not account for human intellectual activity.[4] I wish to offer a very different perspective, however, which emerges when we consider Descartes's view of the intellect not in relation to other early modern philosophers, but in relation to the Aristotelian scholastics.

We must begin by noting that his point in the passages in question is not that there are no physical events that *parallel* intellection—the idea emphasized by Wilson. Rather he is concerned to claim that, unlike sensation and imagination, intellection is *independent* from the body. Intellection is an operation of the mind alone in which the body does not take part. This is literally what he says in the second of the passages quoted above, from the Replies to Gassendi.[5] I will call this conception of intellection the Independence Thesis. This claim is different from the claim of nonparallelism because one could hold that intellectual acts are in and of themselves independent of body even though they are paralleled by states of body.

But now it becomes possible to see that Descartes's view was not unusual in his time, for the Independence Thesis was widely accepted among the Aristotelian scholastics, including Aquinas, Eustachius, Suárez, and the Coimbra Commentators. They also believed that intellection is an activity of the soul alone and that it differs in this respect from sensation and imagination. For them the soul alone is the subject of intellection, but the body or the body-soul composite is the subject of sensation and imagination.[6] The scholastics often addressed this question when wondering what powers the soul retains when separated from the body. Thus Aquinas writes: "Certain powers are related to the soul alone as their subject, such as the intellect and the will. And such powers necessarily remain in the soul when the body is destroyed. But other powers inhere in the composite [*conjuncto*] as their subject, such as all the powers of the sensitive and nutritive parts" (ST I.77.8).[7] So Descartes was not an odd man out with respect to his Aristotelian scholastic predecessors and contemporaries in holding the Independence Thesis. Consequently, his adherence to this thesis is not as urgently in need of an explanation as it would be if he were very unusual in this regard. And given that the view was common among the scholastics, it is unlikely that Descartes's scientific preoccupations actually moved him to adopt it. On the contrary, it probably seemed quite natural to him to think that the human capacity for intellection can only be exercised by an incorporeal entity (which may, however, be joined to a body).

But there is more. Descartes's perspective on the relationship between science and his conception of the intellect is remarkably different from what one would expect from a twentieth-century point of view. This becomes clear in his well-known treatment of the difference between human beings and animals in part V of the *Discourse* (AT VI 55–59/ CSM I 139–141).[8] Descartes there argues that animals cannot be distinguished from machines, but that humans can, by means of two criteria. The first consists in our linguistic abilities: no machine could "use words, or other signs in composing them, as we do in order to express our thoughts to others." We can imagine a machine that has some sort of capacity for speech and can utter words when prompted in various ways. But we cannot imagine of a machine that "it arranges them in different ways, in order to respond to the meaning of everything that is said in its presence, as even the most stupid of men can do." Second, a machine might be able to do various things as well as we can or better, but there would always be some activities beyond its reach. This shows that machines "do not act from knowledge, but in virtue of the disposition of their organs" (AT VI 56–57/ CSM I 140). These criteria also distinguish humans from animals, and this fact, he concludes, shows "not merely that animals have less reason than human beings, but that they do not have reason at all." Whereas he does not explicitly say so on this occasion, the implication is that animals have no souls.[9]

For us it is striking that the scope of Descartes's mechanistic explanation is *limited* in the sense that it cannot account for our capacity for language and for the wide variety of our abilities. But Descartes himself clearly sees his own position as significant because of his *optimism* about the scope of mechanistic explanation. In the *Discourse* he is much concerned to point out the great power of mechanism. He emphasizes that it *does* cover all animal behavior, as well as whatever human beings do that they have in common with animals. And indeed, this aspect of his position is what would be surprising for his contemporaries, as is illustrated by Arnauld's skeptical reaction to Descartes's claim that all animal behavior can be explained mechanistically:

> As far as the souls of the brute animals are concerned, M. Descartes elsewhere suggests clearly enough that they have none. All they have is a body with a certain configuration, made up of various organs in such a way that all the operations which we observe can be produced in it and by means of it. But I think that in order for this conviction to find faith in the minds of men, it must be proved by very valid reasons. For . . . it seems incredible at first sight that it can happen without the help of any soul that the light reflected from the body of a wolf into the eyes of a sheep move the very thin optical nerves, and that upon that motion reaching the brain, animal spirits are diffused through the nerves in such a way as is necessary to make the sheep flee. (AT VII 205/ CSM II 144)

In short, Descartes was out of step at the time because he extended the scope of mechanistic explanation as far as he did, rather than because he did not extend it to intellectual operations.

In addition, the discussion of animals in the *Discourse* brings out a striking aspect of Descartes's view of the relationship between science and religion. Wilson contrasts the issue of immortality with Descartes's preoccupations with mechanistic science, and she suggests that the latter have more to do than the former with his adherence to the view that intellection is entirely immaterial. Others have connected the two issues in a way that results in a limit on the explanatory powers of science: religious reasons moved Descartes to regard the intellect as not susceptible to scientific explanation and as incorporeal.[10] But, in fact, Descartes's thinking is interestingly different from what either of these approaches suggest. It is true that for him the incorporeity of the intellect does support the immortality of the human soul, and he does think the intellect cannot be explained mechanistically. Furthermore, these issues are indeed connected for him because if one could explain intellectual activity mechanistically it would no longer support the immortality of the soul. But, again, in relation to this issue, Descartes himself emphasizes his *optimism* about the scope of mechanistic science. In the *Discourse* he insists that this optimism counts in favor of the immortality of the human soul. This view is remarkable, since usually the increasing scope of modern science is regarded as a threat to religious beliefs. Indeed, Descartes's contemporaries often worried that his optimism about mechanistic science might lead to the view that everything about human beings can also be explained mechanistically, thus making the human soul superfluous.[11]

So why does he think that his optimism about science supports the soul's immortality?

In his conclusion of the discussion of animals Descartes raises the issue of the human soul and observes that it is very important to see that the souls of animals are radically different from our souls. For if one clearly sees this difference "one has a much better understanding of the reasons that prove that our soul is of a nature entirely independent of the body, and that, consequently, it is not subject to dying with it. Furthermore, since one does not see any other causes that destroy it, one is naturally brought to judge that it is immortal" (AT VI 59–60/ CSM II 141). What he has in mind, of course, is that animals don't have souls, but are machines. For Descartes the idea that mechanistic explanation covers all animal behavior, in combination with the view that mechanistic explanation does not cover certain human abilities, shows that our soul is radically different from the soul of an animal. This difference counts in favor of the immortality of our soul, Descartes alleges, because it allows us to see better that our soul is completely independent of the body.

There are two reasons why he takes this stance. First, if animals and humans had the same kind of soul there would be a problem for the immortality of the human soul, since animals were not supposed to have immortal souls. The problem is then how to distinguish between animal souls and human souls. This was a live issue at the time, and in the *Discourse* Descartes is in fact responding to arguments by Montaigne and Charron to the effect that there is no radical difference between animals and humans.[12] Descartes argues that the only ground for thinking that animals have souls would be that their behavior shows that they have reason. But, he contends, animal behavior does not show that they have reason, and it can be explained mechanistically. So he concludes that there is no basis for ascribing souls to animals, and in fact he believes that animals do not have souls at all. Consequently, we need not doubt the immortality of our souls on the ground that animals have souls like ours.[13]

The second reason is as follows. Descartes meant to supplant a traditional conception of the human soul common among the Aristotelian scholastics. According to this conception the soul is the substantial form of the human being and the principle of a variety of functions, which include nutrition, growth, locomotion, sensation, imagination, and intellection. Plants, animals, and human beings all have souls. The human soul is the principle of all the functions mentioned above and shares them all, except for intellection, with the souls of animals.[14] The functions humans and animals have in common take place in a body and are performed by the ensouled body, or body-soul composite. But as we saw, intellection is an operation of the soul alone; this activity distinguishes our souls from those of animals. In scholastic thought, this difference was crucial to the question of the immortality of the human soul. For the idea that in intellection the soul operates independently of the body—the Independence Thesis—was used to argue that the soul is not merely the form of the body, but an incorporeal, spiritual entity, which can exist without the body. Aquinas relied on this argument, and other scholastics followed his example, including Descartes's immediate predecessors, Eustachius, Suárez, and the Jesuits of Coimbra. They all held that the human soul is an incorporeal substance, albeit an incomplete one. In Aquinas' words:

> The intellectual principle which is called the mind or intellect has an operation through itself [*per se*] in which the body does not participate. Nothing, however, can operate through itself unless it subsists through itself; for activity only belongs to a being in act, and hence something operates in the same way in which it is. For this reason we do not say that heat heats, but that something hot heats. Consequently, the human soul, which is called intellect or mind, is something incorporeal and subsisting. (ST I.75.2)[15]

As one might expect, the idea that the soul is a substance that can exist without the body was important for the view that the decay of the body did not necessitate the death of the soul, and it was used to defend its immortality.[16]

Consequently, for these Aristotelian scholastics the human soul is an unusual entity. On one hand, it is the form of the body. As such its proper mode of existence is in union with the body, and it needs the body to exercise its functions. On the other hand, the soul is an incorporeal entity that can exist without the body. These two aspects of the human soul are in tension with each other, as Aquinas saw very clearly.[17] Other Aristotelians thought, in fact, that they are incompatible. In particular, Averroes had concluded from the idea that intellection is not an operation of the body but of the intellect alone that its subject cannot be the form of the body, and, consequently, that it is not an operation of the soul. He inferred that intellection is the operation of a separate entity.[18]

We can now see the second reason why Descartes thought his view of the scope of mechanistic science strengthens the case for the independence of the human soul from the body. On the view he presents in the *Discourse* all operations the Aristotelians ascribed to the soul, other than intellectual ones, can be accounted for mechanistically and do not require a soul. Descartes restricts the soul to the mind, whereas for the Aristotelians there was much more to the soul.[19] That means that, in effect, he restricted the human soul precisely to those activities that were thought to show that the soul is independent from the body. On the other hand, the functions that Descartes relegated to the realm of mechanistic explanation are ones that, on the Aristotelian view, imply the soul's dependence on the body. The soul is their principle, and it needs to be united to a body to exercise them.[20] As we shall see in detail in chapter 5, Descartes eliminated precisely those features of the human soul in virtue of which the scholastics called it a substantial form, and it becomes simply a spiritual substance. Furthermore, by confining the soul to the mind, he eliminated from the soul those functions that, on the scholastic view, human and animal souls had in common. In this way the human soul becomes radically different from the souls of animals.

Descartes insists in particular that the *essence* of the soul consists in thought alone. For him this confinement of the essence of the soul was very important for proving its incorporeity. Thus he emphasizes on a number of occasions the fact that thought constitutes the *entire (tota)* essence or nature of the soul, and this phrase is intended to exclude other traditional functions of the soul. He does so, for instance, in the Second Meditation, when he is trying to determine what he is. He first considers but quickly dismisses what he regards as belonging to the nature of body. Then he writes:

> But what about those things that I attributed to the soul? Nutrition or walking? Since I do not now have a body, these things are also nothing other than fictions. Sensation? This also does not happen without a body, and I have seemed to see many things in dreams about which I later noticed that I had not sensed them. Thought? This I do find: there is thought: this alone cannot be taken away from me. I am, I exist—that is certain. But for how long? For as long as I think. For it could be that if I ceased to have any thought, I would entirely *(totus)* cease to exist. At this

> point I admit nothing unless it is necessarily true; I am then, strictly speaking *(praecise tantum)*, a thinking thing, that is, a mind, spirit, intellect or reason, words whose meaning was previously unknown to me. (AT VII 27/ CSM II 18)[21]

So he considers the traditional functions of the soul: nutrition, locomotion, sensation, and thought. He rejects all of them except thought as belonging to his essence: without thought he would cease to exist entirely.

Descartes's transformation of the notion of the soul is quite explicit in the Fifth Objections and Replies. Gassendi reacted with bafflement to Descartes's claim in the Second Meditation that he is just a thinking thing:

> You conclude: "I am therefore strictly speaking a thinking thing, that is a mind, spirit, intellect, reason". Here I acknowledge that I am confused. For I thought that I was speaking to a human soul, or that internal principle by which a man lives, senses, moves in space, understands; but I am only speaking to a mind, which has not only lost its body, but also its soul. (AT VII 263/ CSM II 183)

Descartes responds by explaining that the term 'soul' had been used in an inappropriate way:

> the first men did not perhaps distinguish between, on one hand, that principle in us by which we are nourished, grow, and perform without any thought all the other functions we have in common with the brutes, and on the other hand, that principle by which we think. They applied to both the single term 'soul'. Then, noticing that thought is different from nutrition, they called that which thinks 'mind', and believed that it is the principal part of the soul. I, however, noticing that the principle by which we are nourished is entirely different from the principle by which we think, have said that the term 'soul' is ambiguous when it is used for both. And in order to understand it as the first act or principal form of man, it must only be understood as the principle by which we think. To this I have as much as possible applied the term 'mind', in order to avoid ambiguity. For I do not regard the mind as a part of the soul, but as the whole soul, which thinks. (AT VII 356/ CSM II 246)

So Descartes was quite conscious of his transformation of the conception of the soul. Incidentally, the expression "part of the soul" should not be taken literally here. The point of the claim that the mind is not *part* of the soul is clearly that he regards the soul only as the principle of thought, contrary to others, in particular the scholastics.

What have we learned from this discussion of Descartes's conception of the intellect and the mind? In the first place, his view that intellectual activity was entirely incorporeal was not at all unusual, because it was common among the Aristotelian scholastics, and so it may have seemed natural for Descartes to accept this view. For us it may be striking that he thought intellectual activity cannot be accounted for mechanistically. But from an early seventeenth-century perspective his view was remarkable because he extended the scope of mechanistic explanation quite far.[22] Furthermore, the discussion in the *Discourse* shows that Descartes had a very interesting view of the relationship between the scope of mechanistic science and religious beliefs. As one might expect, he regards the impossibility of accounting for intellectual activity mechanistically as support for the immortality of the rational soul. But on his view, his optimism about the scope of mechanistic explanation, which *only* leaves out thought, constituted a significant contribution to support for its immortality.

2.2 The Real Distinction Argument and the Intellect

Descartes also saw his own conception of the essence of the soul as important for his most prominent argument for dualism, the Real Distinction Argument. Thus in a letter of July 1641, probably to de Launay, he attributes the difficulty many people have in recognizing the distinction between mind and body to their confusing what belongs to mind and what belongs to body. He optimistically suggests, referring to ideas fundamental to the Real Distinction Argument, that once one sees that the essence of the soul consists in thought and the essence of the body in extension, it is pretty obvious that they are different:

> By examining physics carefully, one can reduce all those things in it which fall under the knowledge of the intellect to very few kinds, of which we have very clear and distinct notions. After considering them I do not think one can fail to recognize whether, when we conceive one thing without another, this happens only by an abstraction of our mind or because the things are truly different. For when things are separated only by an abstraction of the mind, their conjunction and union would necessarily be noticed when they are considered together. But none could be noticed between the body and soul, provided that they are conceived

> as they should, the one as that which fills space, the other as that which thinks. (AT III 420–421/ CSM III 188)

I now wish to return to the Real Distinction Argument. As I have pointed out, Aquinas and other scholastics argued that the soul is independent of the body on the basis of the nature of intellectual activity, and in doing so they relied on the Independence Thesis. I will argue that in both respects Descartes follows their example in the Real Distinction Argument, in particular in its occurrence in the *Meditations,* where we find its most elaborate presentation. I will defend this interpretation in two stages. In the present section I will argue that the argument relies only on claims about intellection, and not about sensation and imagination. Section 2.3 will address the role of the Independence Thesis in the argument. My defense of the view that the argument only relies on claims about intellectual activity will also occur in two stages: (1) In the Real Distinction Argument Descartes is concerned with substance dualism: he wants to show that the soul is an incorporeal substance, and he argues for this conclusion by relying on the nature of its activity. (2) The activity he relies on is intellection. I will begin by discussing (1) while assuming (2) for expository purposes.

(1) One might think that the Real Distinction Argument is supposed to support the immateriality of intellection.[23] But the argument does not aim to establish the incorporeity of the activity of intellection; instead it aims to establish that the *mind* is an incorporeal *substance.* Recognition of this point is crucial for understanding the argument, as is especially clear in the Sixth Replies. The objectors had claimed that Descartes had failed to show that thought is not motion (AT VII 413/ CSM II 278–279). His reply is revealing about what he takes his task to be:

> When someone notices that he is thinking, and he understands what motion is, it is impossible that he believes that he is mistaken and is "not thinking but merely moving". Since the idea or notion that he has of thought is quite different from his idea of corporeal motion, he necessarily understands the one as different from the other. But because of his habit of attributing many different properties to one and the same subject without seeing any connection between them, it can happen that he doubts, or even affirms, that he is one and the same being who thinks and who moves. (AT VII 422–423/ CSM II 285)

So Descartes claims that it is quite impossible for anyone to confuse thought and motion, and he does not seem to worry about this kind of confusion. He then points out what mistake a person might indeed make: someone might think that thought and motion *belong to the same subject.*

On the other hand, later in the Sixth Replies Descartes acknowledges that some people did regard thought as motion. He writes that he is very certain that thought is not corporeal motion, but that he is not sure he can convince those who "turn their attention not to objects of the pure intellect but only to objects of the imagination" (AT VII 425/ CSM II 287). As we saw in chapter 1.3, he offers the same diagnosis for the error of identifying thought with extension later in the Sixth Replies (AT VII 441/ CSM II 297). But this diagnosis suggests that what is needed is not an argument, but a change in epistemic perspective, namely, the withdrawal from sense, which consists in a turning away from reliance on the sensory powers, including the imagination. Once one relies on the pure intellect, he believes, it is obvious that thought is not motion. So Descartes does not think that he needs to give an *argument* for the view that thought is not motion any more than he sees a need to argue that thought is not extension. Since the form of materialism that was current in his time consisted in the view that thought is motion, it is clear that he did not think he needed to argue that thought is incorporeal.

One would expect materialists contemporary with Descartes to balk at this point. But I must confess that it strikes me that Descartes has the upper hand on this issue. Thought might perhaps consist in some corporeal process, but it seems quite implausible that it would simply consist in matter in motion, although this is perhaps less obviously implausible than the identity of thought with extension.

Be that as it may, Descartes does clearly see a need to argue that the *thing* that thinks is really distinct from the *thing* that moves. And so the purpose of the Real Distinction Argument is not to show that intellection is an incorporeal activity, but that the mind is an incorporeal thing.[24] Consequently, the Independence Thesis, which concerns the nature of intellectual activity, should not be expected to be the conclusion of the Real Distinction Argument. Instead this thesis comes at the beginning of the argument: it is used to support the conclusion. It is worth noting that this is as one should expect: Given his views about the way we know substances, it is right that Descartes should base the conclusion that mind and body are different substances on the nature of intellection rather than the other way around. For he thinks we do not know substances directly, but via their properties (AT VII 222/ CSM II 156 and *Principles* I.52). Furthermore, on the usual interpretation, Descartes derives the incorporeity of the mind from the nature of thought broadly conceived. Once it is seen that the argument involves only claims about intellection, the incorporeity of the mind should be expected to be derived from the nature of intellection.[25]

It is important to pause over the fact that Descartes does not think he needs to argue against the idea that thought is a corporeal activity. For this is quite surprising, especially from our contemporary point of view.[26] But this fact is much less surprising if we regard Descartes as more focused on supplanting Aristotelian scholasticism than on defeating materialism of the type that regards thought as a corporeal process like motion (as opposed to the type that regards thought as belonging to the same entity as motion). In the Third and Fifth Objections Descartes was faced with objections from the perspective of this type of materialism, and the reader of his replies cannot fail to be struck by the impression that he simply did not take them very seriously. On the other hand, in a letter to Mersenne he admitted that supplanting Aristotelianism was his purpose in the *Meditations*.[27] Similarly, the *Principles* were meant to replace scholastic textbooks. In fact his correspondence contains many discussions of his relationship to scholasticism. Furthermore, we saw that he did regard the restriction of the soul to intellection as important for establishing its incorporeity, and this restriction was directed against Aristotelianism rather than against the view that thought is a corporeal process. In arguing for dualism Descartes certainly means to offer a view that is directly opposed to any kind of materialism. But my point is that he thought he only had to *argue* against the view that thought belongs to the same substance as motion (and other corporeal properties). And the form of his argument is influenced by the fact that he took Aristotelian scholasticism more seriously than the view that thought is a corporeal process like motion. So since the scholastics generally agreed that intellection is incorporeal, he probably did not feel as great a need to argue against its identity with corporeal processes as we might expect.

(2) It is now time to defend the claim that the Real Distinction Argument relies on intellection, and not on sensation and imagination.

Let us return to Descartes's introduction of his conception of the soul, or mind, at the beginning of the Second Meditation. We saw that he there considers the traditional functions of the soul, nutrition, locomotion, sensation, and thought, and that he retains only thought as belonging to his essence. The first thing to notice about this passage is that, as in the *Discourse,* we find Descartes again focusing on the restriction of the soul to the mind. This feature of the passage brings out the importance of this move for the Real Distinction Argument. For the passage serves to develop the clear and distinct conception of the mind used in that argument, and we can see now that, to a significant extent, developing that conception consists in restricting the soul in this way. But in the second place, we must consider the question what Descartes has in mind when he speaks about thought on this occasion. Elsewhere he gives quite a broad characterization of thought, but at this point in the Second Meditation thought only includes intellection. This is already indicated by the fact that he here retains thought but rejects sensation. In addition, he proceeds to use the claim that thought alone belongs to him to conclude that he is a mind, intelligence, intellect, or reason *(mens, sive animus, sive intellectus, sive ratio)*. All of these terms were used to refer to the intellectual part of the soul, or rather, the soul insofar as it is the principle of intellectual activity. It is not until two paragraphs later that he includes other activities among thoughts, when he describes the mind as a thing that "doubts, understands, affirms, denies, is willing, is unwilling, imagines also and senses" (AT VII 27/ CSM II 18).[28]

This broader characterization of thought is usually presumed to be the basis for the Real Distinction Argument. But the text of the Sixth Meditation makes clear that this is not so, since immediately after the conclusion of the argument in that Meditation Descartes writes:

> Moreover, I find in me faculties for certain special modes of thinking, namely the faculties of imagining and sensing. I can clearly and distinctly understand myself as a whole without them; but not *vice versa* them without me, that is, without an intelligent substance in which they are. For they include some intellection in their formal concept: hence I perceive that they are distinguished from me as modes from a thing. (AT VII 78/ CSM II 54)

So Descartes argues that imagination and sensation belong to him *after* the Real Distinction Argument. More importantly, he makes clear here that sensation and imagination do not belong to the essence of the mind; he says that he can clearly and distinctly understand himself without them, and the Real Distinction Argument relies on claims about the essence of the mind. He writes in the course of the argument: "because I notice nothing else at all to pertain to my nature or essence, except that I am a thinking thing, I conclude correctly that my essence consists in this alone, that I am a thinking thing" (AT VII 78/ CSM II 54). So claims about sensation and imagination are not included in the Real Distinction Argument. Furthermore, Descartes says that imagination and sensation are modes of the mind because they include *intellection.* Consequently, the Real Distinction Argument relies on a conception of the mind as a thing that engages in intellection.

Descartes's position in the history of philosophy and science should in fact make it quite unsurprising that the Real Distinction Argument relies only on intellection and not on imagination and sensation. Modern considerations against the corporeity of the mind often rely on qualia such as those occurring in sensations of secondary qualities—sensible qualities, in Descartes's terms. Centuries of successful science have relied on the idea that such qualities as they appear to us do not characterize the physical world. Thus the phenomenological nature of our sensations of colors, flavors, and the like is sometimes taken as a reason to doubt that these sensations and the subjects that have them are part of the physical world. But for Descartes it would not have been a good strategy to rely on this argument, since he simply could not look back on a tradition of exile of sensible qualities from the physical world. On the contrary, he was one of the founders of this view, whereas on the Aristotelian view, which he sought to replace, bodies do have such qualities. Part of Descartes's rejection of Aristotelianism consisted in eliminating sensible qualities from the physical world to make it safe for his mechanistic conception of science.

Furthermore, there was an important difference between Descartes and the scholastics in regard to sensation and imagination. I will focus on sensation, but similar comments apply to imagination. As we saw, the Aristotelians regarded sensation as inhering in the body or body-soul composite. The representations, which they called 'species', that give these acts of the soul content are part of the physical world, and the existence of the subject of inherence of sensation requires that the soul is united to the body. So for the scholastics sensation indicated the dependence of the soul on the body—and not its independence, as the Real Distinction Argument requires. Consequently, sensation would have made a poor foundation for the Real Distinction Argument.

Descartes did agree with the scholastics that sensation and imagination are dependent on body, but he had a very different view of the nature of this dependence, which I will discuss at length in chapter 6. For now, it is important to focus on the following issue. For the scholastics sensation occurs entirely in the body or body-soul composite, and there simply is no stage of sensation that inheres in just the incorporeal mind.[29] Descartes, on the other hand, relocated the species we have in sensation and imagination, which he called 'ideas', in the incorporeal mind. He regarded sensations as consisting in several stages:

> To the first grade pertains only that through which the corporeal organ is immediately affected [*afficitur*] by external objects; and this can be nothing other than the motion of the particles of that organ and the change in figure and position resulting from that motion. The second [grade] contains everything that results immediately in the mind from the fact that it is united to the corporeal organ so affected, and such are the perceptions of pain, pleasure, thirst, hunger, colors, sound, flavor, smell, heat, cold, and the like, which result from the union and, as it were, intermixture of mind and body, as explained in the Sixth Meditation. The third grade comprises all those judgements about external objects which we have been used to making since our earliest childhood on the occasion of the motions of the corporeal organ. (AT VII 436–437/ CSM II 294–295)

A crucial difference with the scholastics is that for Descartes the second stage of sensation is a mode of the mind. This difference constitutes a significant departure from their notion of the mind. Whereas for them the mind is only the subject of intellectual activity (and volition), Descartes adds (a stage of) sensation, and similarly for imagination.

Given this difference between Descartes and his scholastic predecessors and contemporaries, he very much needed to argue for his view that sensation and imagination (or a part or aspect of these operations) are modes of the mind. On the other hand, the scholastics thought that intellectual activity does not take place in a corporeal organ, and they used this idea to argue for the incorporeity of the soul. Consequently, from the point of view of Descartes's historical context, reliance on considerations about the intellect was clearly a much better strategy than reliance on considerations about sensation for defending the incorporeity of the soul.

In fact his own comments suggest that he thought that sensation and imagination would constitute an obstacle for recognizing the real distinction. For instance, he writes in the Fourth Replies: "I do not deny, however, that the close union of the mind with the body, which we experience constantly through the senses, is the reason why we do not notice the real distinction of mind from body without attentive meditation" (AT VII 228–229/ CSM II 160). Furthermore, on various occasions he claims that sensation shows the union of mind and body rather than their distinction. In the Sixth Meditation he contends that through inner sensation we know that we are not united to our body merely as a pilot to his ship. If we were, then damage to and needs of our bodies would be perceived by us intellectually. But in fact we perceive such states by means of such sensations as hunger, pain, thirst, which, he claims, "are nothing other than certain confused modes of thinking that arise from the union and, as it were, intermingling of the mind with the body" (AT VII 81/ CSM II 56).[30] Earlier in the same Meditation he had argued, although tentatively, for the union of the mind with body on the basis of the nature of imagination (AT VII 73/ CSM II 51).

It would perhaps go too far to conclude that Descartes thought it entirely impossible to establish the real distinction on the basis of considerations about sensation and imagination. In the Third Replies he seems to rely on intellection and volition as well as sensation and imagination, but there he uses a rather different argument from the one he usually deploys (AT VII 176/ CSM II 124). In particular, in the *Meditations* Descartes first gives the Real Distinction Argument, then he claims that sensation and imagination belong to the mind. In the Third Replies he claims that intellection, volition, sensation, and imagination belong to the same substance because they all "fall under the common concept [*ratio*] of thought, perception or consciousness" (AT VII 176/ CSM II 124). Then he contends that these types of thought have nothing in common with corporeal modes and uses this observation to support the real distinction of mind and body. But in the *Meditations* Descartes clearly relies only on intellection, and at the very least he thought that sensation and imagination cause problems for the recognition of the real distinction of mind and body. This attitude clearly distinguishes him from twentieth-century philosophers who are concerned about the mind-body problem, because they tend to regard sensations as the type of mental state that poses the most problems for materialism.

But at this point an important question arises. In chapter 1, I defended the view that the Real Distinction Argument relies on principal attributes. So on that view, it would seem, the argument relies on the attribute of thought, which underlies the various kinds of modes of the mind, rather than on intellection, which is just one of these modes. So now it seems as if what I argued in chapter 1 is inconsistent with the thesis of the present chapter.

On my view, however, intellection, or as Descartes sometimes says, pure intellection, is not just a mode of the mind on a par with other kinds of thought: rather, intellection constitutes the attribute of thought, the essence of the mind. This point is just under the surface when he says in the Sixth Meditation that sensation and imagination are modes of him, that is, his mind, because they include intellection in their formal concept. And there is the following striking passage earlier in this same Meditation. After comparing imagination and pure intellection at some length, Descartes writes: "Moreover I consider that insofar as it differs from the power of intellection this power of imagining that is in me is not required for my essence, that is the essence of my mind. For even if it were absent from me, I would no doubt remain that same I that I am now. Hence it seems to follow that it depends on something different from me" (AT VII 73/ CSM II 51). The thing other than the mind that the imagination depends on, he argues, is probably the body. He relies here on the idea that the essence of the mind is the intellect.

Descartes's view that the essence of the mind is the intellect is also implied by his use of the term 'pure intellection'. He also speaks of the 'pure mind' to refer to this operation; he regards intellection as a pure manifestation of the attribute of thought, which is the essence of the mind.[31] On the other hand, sensation and imagination involve an intellectual component but contain something else as well, which comes in some way from the union with the body, and they are impure forms of thought or intellection. Thus Descartes writes to Regius in January 1642, that "we perceive the sensations of pain and all others not to be pure thoughts of the mind distinct from the body, but confused perceptions of it really united to the body" (AT III 493/ CSM III 206).

And on January 19, 1642, he writes to Gibieuf that sensation and imagination "are sorts of thoughts without which one can conceive the soul entirely pure—*toute pure*" (AT III 479/ CSM III 203, emphasis mine). Since intellection is a pure manifestation of the attribute of thought, reliance on it to demonstrate the real distinction between mind and body amounts to relying on the attribute of thought. Sensation and imagination are less suitable for recognizing the real distinction, given that they are impure manifestations of this attribute due to a corporeal element. So the view that the Real Distinction Argument relies on consideration of the principal attribute of thought is entirely compatible with the view that it relies on consideration of intellection.

But now one may well wonder what it means when Descartes writes that "sensation and imagination include some intellection in their formal concept." And in what sense are they impure forms of intellection or thought? These questions invite discussion of just what his conception of intellection was. I will not attempt a full treatment of this issue, but the following observations are crucial for present purposes. We have already seen that the Independence Thesis distinguishes pure intellection from imagination and sensation. Clearly essential to this difference is the idea that pure intellection is an operation that does not involve images; it is purely abstract. Thus at the beginning of the Sixth Meditation he contrasts imagination with intellection, saying "when I imagine a triangle, for example, I do not only understand that it is a shape comprehended by three lines, but also at the same time I intuit those three lines with the eye of the mind [*acie mentis*] as if they are present." Later in the Sixth Meditation and elsewhere Descartes makes clear that the presence of contents like pain, color, and the like distinguishes both imagination and sensation from the intellect (AT VII 72, 74, 81/ CSM II 51, 56).[32]

So pure intellection does not include images of mechanistic or sensible qualities, or internal sensations like pain. Descartes particularly insists on the nonimagistic nature of the pure intellect. We see examples of its activity in thinking about the mind or God, and nonimagistic mathematical reasoning. We can also think about these items by means of images, but that would be different. Where God and the mind are concerned, it would be a mistake to use faculties other than the pure intellect, a mistake that would result in confused ideas. Mental images can only give us knowledge of physical objects, not of incorporeal entities, because "imagining is nothing other than to contemplate a figure or image of a corporeal thing" (AT VII 28/ CSM II 19).[33] Descartes thinks that the intellect has much wider scope than the other cognitive faculties. In the case of God and the mind this is so because they are entirely the wrong type of entity to be contemplated by anything but the pure intellect. But in addition, in the case of body and mathematical truths, the intellect reaches further than the other faculties. In the Second Meditation he argues that the wax is known by the pure mind rather than the imagination because "I comprehend that [the wax] is capable of innumerable changes [in shape], and I cannot run through innumerable ones in my imagination" (AT VII 31/ CSM II 21). In the Sixth Meditation he argues that we can imagine simple geometrical figures like triangles, but not polygons like myriagons and chiliagons. This difference he uses for a tentative argument for the existence of body on the supposition that the imagistic content of the imagination is due to the role of the body. He clearly thinks that this difference derives from the fact that an intellectual grasp does not involve forming images (AT VII 72–73/ CSM II 50–51).

This leaves us with yet another question: In what sense do sensation and imagination involve intellection? It is striking and puzzling that Descartes uses this claim to include sensation and imagination among the modes of the mind in the Sixth Meditation. One would expect that the claim had been prepared earlier in the *Meditations* by an account of how sensation and imagination involve intellection, but it is not obvious that he has given such an account. And the *Meditations* is the only place where he refers to an intellectual aspect for these faculties; elsewhere he relies on the claim that we are immediately conscious of acts of sensation and imagination. Indeed, one wishes that Descartes had been more explicit about what he had in mind—he gives us precious little to go on.

One possibility is that sensation and imagination involve some intellectual *content,* and Descartes does on various occasions express the view that they do, in particular in regard to sensation.[34] In the Sixth Replies he argues that sensation always includes a judgment, which really belongs to the intellect. When we perceive a stick, motions in our body cause a sensation of color and light in the mind, which gives rise to the judgment that the stick is colored. And by reasoning we make judgments about the size, shape, and distance of the stick (AT VII 437/ CSM II 295). We don't realize we make these judgments; we do so almost imperceptibly because we have done so since our childhood. What is particularly important in relation to our present concerns is that Descartes makes similar points in the *Meditations,* namely, in the discussion of the wax. We think we know the wax by the senses, he argues, but in fact we know it by the mind, or intellect, alone, and he contends that this intellectual judgment was there all along, even before we realized it. He provides another example: we think that we see that people walk by outside, but this is really a judgment, and we only perceive their hats and coats (AT VII 31–32/ CSM II 21). So when Descartes writes that sensation and imagination include intellection in their formal concept, he could have in mind his view that these activities involve intellectual contents.

Now one may well find this idea puzzling for various reasons, but perhaps especially on account of what Descartes calls the second grade of sensation, that is "the perceptions of pain, pleasure, thirst, hunger, colors, sound, flavor, smell, heat, cold, and the like" (AT VII 437/ CSM II 294). For these perceptions do not include any judgment and so no intellectual content. Judgment constitutes the third grade, and so only the full three-grade process possesses intellectual content. But surely Descartes wants to include the second grade of sensation among modes of the mind. It is not clear that this is a problem, however, for Descartes could think that sensations are always *accompanied* by judgments rather than that they *contain* them. After all, he does not write that sensation and imagination include intellection, but that their formal concept does. Nevertheless, there are reasons for preferring a different interpretation.

The other obvious candidate to be the answer to our question is provided by Descartes's definitions of thought in terms of consciousness. For example, there is this one in the Geometrical Exposition: "I comprehend by the word thought everything that is in us in such a way that we are immediately conscious of it. So all operations of the will, intellect, imagination and senses are thoughts" (AT VII 160/ CSM II 113).[35] So in the Sixth Meditation he might have in mind that sensation and imagination include consciousness. It is striking that, contrary to his approach in other texts, Descartes never relies on the notion of consciousness in the *Meditations* to include sensation and imagination among thoughts, or at least, he does not do so explicitly. But in the Second Meditation he does rely on a closely related idea. At *Principles* I.9 he connects his identification of thought in terms of consciousness to claims about certainty. He writes that sensation and imagination are thoughts because, even though I may be wrong in believing that I see or walk due to the dependence of these activities on body, it is certain that the sensation or consciousness of seeing or walking does occur. But this kind of certainty also plays a part in the inclusion of sensation and imagination among thoughts in the Second Meditation. So this correlation makes it very plausible that including intellection in the formal concepts of sensation and imagination refers to their relationship to consciousness.

Indeed, this strikes me as the most natural interpretation. But it raises an interesting question: Why does Descartes speak here of intellection rather than consciousness? His doing so implies that he sees a strong connection between consciousness and intellection, but what is that connection supposed to be? Gueroult argues that "to be conscious is to know, and to know is merely to comprehend or understand—*comprehendere, intelligere.*"[36] Now this is an interesting philosophical position, but I see no evidence that Descartes adhered to it. One problem is that, although the notion of consciousness is prominent in his thought, he does not say much about how he understands it. Indeed, I can think of no evidence in his writings that would support any particular answer to this question, and I do not know how to answer it.[37] And this only illustrates the fact that, although Descartes is so much known for his contribution to the modern conception of the mind, much of his view of the mental remains remarkably sketchy.

Finally, one may well wonder whether this interpretation does not reduce the view that the essence of the mind is the intellect to the more familiar view that its essence consists in consciousness. But that conclusion underestimates the asymmetry Descartes sees between intellect on one hand and imagination and sensation on the other hand. The different types of modes of the mind have in common that they are conscious states, but they relate differently to the essence of the mind. The nature of the mind by itself is sufficient to account for intellection, but not for sensation or imagination: these are accidental accretions that arise from and require the union with the body. The sense in which they do will be the subject of chapter 6.

2.3 The Real Distinction Argument and the Independence Thesis

I have argued that the Real Distinction Argument relies only on intellection, and not on sensation and imagination. For Descartes as for his scholastic predecessors, intellection was distinguished from these two other operations by virtue of the Independence Thesis. Let me now turn to the role of this thesis in the argument.

As we saw in the previous chapter, the Real Distinction Argument relies on a conception of the mind as a complete thinking, unextended thing, a substance. And Descartes thinks he conceives of this entity as complete, because he can *deny* extension of the mind. The reason is that each substance has a principal attribute, and its other properties are modes of the substance (or transcendental attributes, like existence and duration). A mode cannot be conceived without its principal attribute so that the fact that we can deny extension of a thinking thing shows that thought is not a mode of extension. One obvious place for criticism of the Real Distinction Argument is Descartes's claim that one can deny extension of the mind. But the Independence Thesis contributes to the plausibility of this claim.

The first thing to note is that the wide-spread acceptance of the Independence Thesis no doubt goes some way towards explaining Descartes's confidence that extension can be denied of a thinking or intellectual thing. But more importantly, given his own conception of the various cognitive faculties, the claim that thought does not presuppose extension is more plausible if this claim is based on consideration of intellection rather than sensation or imagination. For the latter faculties there is a problem with this claim that brings out the importance of the Independence Thesis. I will focus on imagination. We just saw that Descartes presented imagination as an awareness of images, for instance, images of geometrical figures. But this feature of imagination suggests dependence on an image that is actually extended. Indeed, Descartes himself seems to think it does, since in the Sixth Meditation he infers, albeit tentatively, from this feature of imagination to the existence of our body. He speculates that he would understand how imagination works "if some body existed to which the mind is so joined that it applies itself to it in order to inspect it at will, as it were" (AT VII 72–73/ CSM II 50–51). And he writes to Gassendi that imagination involves a species that is a real body—*verum corpus*.

But this line of thought suggests that imagination *presupposes* extension and that it is an activity of an extended thing: its subject of inherence must be extended. Consequently, imagination is unsuitable as a ground for the claim that thought does not presuppose, and thus is not a mode of extension. This is precisely the kind of dependence on body that is at stake in the Real Distinction Argument, and so imagination is unsuitable as a basis for this argument.[38] Indeed, on Descartes's view imagination requires both a mind and a body. But the view that it requires both assumes the real distinction, since it assumes that the mind is distinct from body. The fact that imagination involves a corporeal image could equally well be accounted for by a view on which the subject of imagination is one thing that is both extended and thinking.[39] In this way the importance of the Independence Thesis becomes clear. For the fact that pure intellection does not involve images and lacks this dependence on body enhances the plausibility of the claim that thought does not presuppose extension.[40]

Conclusion

It is natural for us to consider Descartes's defense of dualism just in relation to materialism. But I have argued that proper understanding of this defense requires that we give substantial consideration to its relationship to Aristotelian scholasticism, and that this approach gives us a rather different picture of what he was trying to do. Descartes shared with the scholastics a desire to defeat materialism, but he was more focused on supplanting Aristotelianism. We saw that Descartes's views display important continuities with the scholastics in regard to the intellect. He agreed with them that the intellect is an incorporeal faculty, and like them, he defended the incorporeity of the soul or mind on the basis of its intellectual activity. On the other hand, in several ways he departed from the scholastics in his view of the nature of mind and body, and in his way of drawing the boundary between the mental and the physical. Whereas for the scholastics the mind is just a part of the soul, as Descartes put it, he identified the two. Unlike the scholastics, he held that the soul is only the principle of thought rather than the principle of life. He eliminated various traditional functions of the soul that depend on the body, and which he wanted to explain mechanistically, such as nutrition, growth, and parts or aspects of sensation and imagination. He saw this difference as an advantage in regard to the incorporeity of the soul, and it is important for the Real Distinction Argument. And as he saw it, there is a happy harmony between his view of the scope of mechanistic science and the need to defend the immortality of the soul. In addition, he differed from the scholastics in that he held a mechanistic conception of body, and assigned an aspect or part of sensation and imagination to the mind. The fact that this was a novelty contributes to understanding why he did not rely on those faculties to establish the incorporeity of the mind.

The fact that the Real Distinction Argument relies on claims about intellection rather than sensation and imagination, sets it apart from twentieth-century worries about materialism. Such worries tend to focus on the problem of qualia, a problem that concerns sensation rather than intellection.[41] Its focus on intellection does not, however, make the argument irrelevant to contemporary discussions. As the literature on this argument shows, it continues to engage contemporary philosophers, including ones who are convinced that dualism is false. At the end of chapter 1 I explained the fundamental ideas of the argument that, in my view, are still of interest to our contemporary concerns. They include Descartes's sense that there is a radical difference between the nature of mental and corporeal properties, and his view that a single entity, in his words, a substance, is unified by its nature in regard to the kinds of properties it has. These ideas still stand, even if in our examination of this aspect of the mind-body problem we are likely to part company with Descartes and focus on sensation rather than on intellectual activity.

CHAPTER THREE

Sensible Qualities

In the first two chapters we saw how Descartes argues that mind and body are really distinct. This conclusion serves as support both for the immortality of the soul, and for the view that everything in the physical world can be explained mechanistically. In chapter 2 we saw that in view of this second purpose the conclusion that mind and body are two different substances is a first step, but it is not enough. Descartes also defends a specific view of what belongs to mind and what belongs to body, a view very different from the one held by the Aristotelian scholastics. Interpreters have paid far more attention to his conception of the mind than his conception of body, but Descartes had vastly more to say about body than about mind. In view of his interest in developing a mechanistic conception of body, the question how he defends his view of what pertains to body is of eminent importance. This chapter and the next one will be devoted to this question.

For Descartes the essence of body consists in extension, and its other properties are modes of extension. These modes are all mechanistic qualities, or, in the terminology propagated later by Boyle and Locke, primary qualities. Descartes saw this view as in need of defense in relation to two different, but related points of view. First, he rejects secondary qualities, or, in the terminology common in his time, sensible qualities.[1] This position sets him apart from the common sense as well as the Aristotelian conception of body. His defense of it is the subject of the present chapter. Second, in the next chapter we will see how he rejects certain specifically Aristotelian scholastic entities, namely, real qualities and substantial forms.[2]

Descartes held that sensible qualities are mere sensations in the mind and do not belong to bodies: he thought that ascribing them to body involves a confusion of the mental and the physical. This claim is one of the most important aspects of his reformulation of the notions of mind and body, and it is well known. But in this chapter I will offer a very different view from ones commonly found in the literature on Descartes's strategy for expelling sensible qualities from body. What is more, it will become clear that his strategy for doing so differs in striking ways from those adopted by other major thinkers in the history of philosophy. And in this chapter I will be just as much concerned with the question of how Descarte *does not* argue against sensible qualities as with the question of how he does.

Descartes's first move is to introduce skeptical arguments that are meant to undermine the assumption that there are sensible qualities in the physical world.[3] These doubts are meant to force one to set aside one's beliefs; they generate a need for arguments in favor of any entities one would wish to posit. At the next stage he argues that belief in mechanistic qualities can be justified, but not belief in sensible qualities. Their nature as qualities of bodies is problematic because we have no clear and distinct conception of them, and they are not needed for explanatory purposes. In section 3.1, I will explain the importance of the skeptical arguments for the strength of Descartes's case for a mechanistic conception of body. Section 3.2 addresses the question on what ground he claimed that our ideas of sensible qualities are confused and obscure. Some of the issues of these two sections will be taken up again in the discussion of real qualities in chapter 4.

But just as much needs to be said about how Descartes does *not* argue against sensible qualities. Descartes is widely thought to exclude sensible qualities from the physical world on the basis of the idea that the essence of body is extension. I will argue, however, that this interpretation radically misconstrues the role in his thought of the conception of body as extended (section 3.3). Next I will turn to a pair of arguments that are classics from the literature on sensible qualities. They rely on the idea that such qualities change, or that a body can fail to have them. These arguments do occur in Descartes, but we will find that the place of these arguments in his thought is highly unusual. For he employs these arguments for entirely different purposes than any other major thinkers in the history of philosophy (section 3.4).

Before we begin, it is important to distinguish Descartes's *motivation* from his *arguments*. His mechanistic conception of body is commonly understood to be motivated by his views about scientific explanation. On one interpretation, Descartes was moved by the idea that the qualities of physical objects must be subject to quantification, because this would allow the formulation of precise, quantified physical laws.[4] Alternatively, he may have been inspired by a commitment to mechanistic explanation rather than by an interest in mathematical laws.[5] But in this chapter I will be concerned with his arguments, not his motivation. This distinction is particularly important for our present concerns, since discussions of Descartes's arguments against sensible qualities tend to import suppositions about his motivation at the expense of analysis of his explicit arguments. For instance, his exclusion of such qualities from the physical world is often thought to be based on the idea that qualities of bodies must be quantifiable. But examination of the texts shows that Descartes never relies on that idea.

3.1 Descartes's Skeptical Strategy

The skeptical strategy receives its most elaborate and most sophisticated treatment in the *Meditations*. On the usual reading, the *Meditations* are aimed primarily at refuting skepticism, and the obvious purpose of the deployment of the skeptical arguments is to set up the position that is to be refuted.[6] But in the Synopsis to the *Meditations* Descartes himself makes very clear that the refutation of skepticism is not the sole, or even the primary reason for this deployment:

> In the First Meditation the reasons are expounded for which we can doubt about all things, especially material ones; that is to say, as long as we have no other foundations for the sciences than the ones we have had so far. Although the usefulness of such extensive doubt is not apparent at first sight, its benefit consists most of all in the fact that it liberates us from all prejudices, and provides a very easy way for leading the mind away from the senses; and it also brings about that we can no longer doubt about those things which afterwards we discover to be true. (AT VII 12/ CSM II 9; see also AT VII 171–172/ CSM II 121)

Descartes claims that the *main* benefit of the skeptical doubts is that they liberate us from prejudices and provide a detachment from the senses. And before he subjects himself to the skeptical arguments he describes his epistemological stance as one of faith in the senses: "whatever I have so far admitted as most true, I have accepted either from or through the senses" (AT VII 18/ CSM II 12). This faith is then undermined by these arguments.

The machinery of the skeptical arguments is deployed because Descartes regards our faith in the senses as deeply entrenched and in need of radical measures. As he explains at length in *Principles* I.47, he thinks this faith results from our childhood, during which the mind is deeply immersed in the body. Excessive reliance on the senses results in errors about the nature of the mind and God, but also about the nature of the physical world. Descartes specifically argues that the attribution of sensible qualities to bodies is an error originating in our childhood. During this period we develop the view that the physical world resembles our sensations, in the sense that it has the kinds of qualities it appears to have in sense perception, both mechanistic and sensible ones (*Principles* I.66, 71). But in fact, he holds, bodies have only mechanistic qualities—extension, shape, size, motion, position—and our sensations of sensible qualities are caused by configurations of such qualities. Undermining the naive view of the physical world and promoting his own mechanistic position is an important goal of the *Meditations*. The campaign against trust in the senses, and in particular against the view that bodies resemble our sensations, is an essential tool in pursuing this goal, because he thinks the naive view of the physical world is largely based on the idea that bodies resemble our sensations.[7]

In the *Meditations* the strategy works as follows. The First Meditation generates skepticism about our confidence in the senses and in the existence of the physical world. As a result we need arguments both in favor of the existence of the physical world and for a conception of its nature. Descartes's defeat of skepticism does not simply consist in refuting the skeptical arguments. That approach would result in simply bringing back the views that had been placed in doubt, but he wants to replace them with different ones. It is crucial that anything we accept must be clearly and distinctly perceived and based on good reasons.

This strategy works as follows where sensible qualities are concerned. In the Third and Fifth Meditations Descartes claims that mechanistic qualities are clearly and distinctly perceived. But in the Third Meditation he contends that our perceptions of other qualities "such as light and colors, sounds, smells, flavors, heat and cold and other tactile qualities" are confused and obscure (AT VII 43/ CSM II 30). Accordingly, when he argues for the existence of bodies in the Sixth Meditation, he only concludes that they exist insofar as they have properties we clearly and distinctly perceive, which are mechanistic qualities. Perceptions of sensible qualities should not be regarded as presenting kinds of qualities that characterize the physical world. These ideas are merely sufficiently clear and distinct, he says in the Sixth Meditation, "for informing the mind about what is beneficial or harmful to the composite of which it is a part." And there is no convincing reason [*nulla profecto ratio est quae suadet*], he contends, for believing that there is something similar to our sensation of heat in fire (AT VII 83/ CSM II 57).

Now Descartes's attempt to undermine trust in the senses is directed against what he regarded as a universal tendency towards a naive, misguided attitude. But in addressing this naive attitude, he also sees himself as taking on the Aristotelian scholastics. For he thought that trust in the senses and a naive view of the nature of the physical world were fundamental to Aristotelian scholastic positions—and that these positions were merely philosophical elaborations of commonsense conceptions. In the *Meditations* Descartes does not state his anti-Aristotelian purposes. But he does admit to such purposes for the work to Mersenne (AT III 297–298/ CSM III 173), and they are implicit in his description of his preskeptical self in the Sixth Meditation. Using a slogan of Aristotelian empiricism, he writes: "I easily persuaded myself that I had clearly nothing in my intellect which had not before been in the senses" (*facile mihi persuadebam nullam plane me habere in intellectu, quam non prius habuissem in sensu,* AT VII 75/ CSM II 52).[8]

The view that our sensations resemble bodies was fundamental to a theory of perception, common among Aristotelians, which is often referred to as the species theory. Descartes mentions it on various occasions (*Optics,* AT VI 85, 112, 134, 137/ CSM I 153–154, 165, 169, 170; Sixth Replies, AT VII 437/ CSM II 295). The species theory, as he sees it, is the view that sense perception comes about as a result of physical objects sending images, likenesses of themselves—so-called 'species'—to the perceiving subject. My perceiving a red vase, for instance, is the result of such species reaching my eyes. In vision and other forms of sense perception the representation in me of an object perceived resembles that object. The Aristotelians varied with respect to the details of this theory, but Descartes expressed indifference to variations among their views. Such variations don't matter, he wrote to Mersenne, because "one can easily overturn all of the foundations on which they agree with one another. And once that has been done, all of their specific disputes will appear absurd" (AT III 231–232/ CSM III 156). Moreover, contrary to Descartes's presentation of their views, the Aristotelians did not believe that a single entity was transmitted from the object of perception to the subject.[9] The details of this theory are not important for our purposes, however. What is important is the fact that the theory is committed to the resemblance between bodies and sensations, a commitment Descartes rejects.

In his treatise *The World,* which contains an extensive presentation of his mechanistic view of the physical world, Descartes deploys a strategy similar to the one found in the *Meditations.* Its first chapter is devoted to the claim that we must not assume that the physical world resembles our sensations. He writes: "although we all commonly persuade ourselves that the ideas that we have in our thought are entirely similar to the objects from which they proceed, I see nevertheless no reason that assures us that this is true. On the contrary, I note several experiences that must make us doubt of it" (AT XI 3/ CSM I 81). Unlike the *Meditations, The World* does not rely on the notion of obscure and confused ideas. Instead, Descartes says we should attribute to body only what we know "as perfectly as possible." He rejects a long list of qualities, saying that their nature "contains something that is not known evidently to everyone" (AT XI 33/ CSM I 90–91). And in this work Descartes also argues that sensible qualities lack explanatory value; this contention implies for him that we have no reason to think sensible qualities are out there, although he does not insist on this implication in *The World.* This argument is at most hinted at in the *Meditations,* when Descartes writes there is no reason to think there is anything resembling heat in the physical world. The lack of explanatory value is illustrated in particular by his analysis of heat and fire in the second chapter of *The World.* He argues that our explanations of the burning of wood, or our sensation of heat, do not require believing in anything more than mechanistic qualities. Thus, he implies, we cannot base our belief in such qualities on the idea that we need them for explanatory purposes.

The explanation of sense perception is particularly relevant in relation to the question of sensible qualities. Descartes sometimes attributes belief in sensible qualities to the naive interpretation of sense perception that derives from our childhood, but in the Sixth Replies he supplies a more theoretical source: "the principal reason that has moved philosophers to posit real accidents has been that they thought that without them sense perception cannot be explained" (AT VII 435/ CSM II 293). Real accidents are accidents conceived of as *res,* and as Descartes sees it, that category primarily includes sensible qualities. Furthermore, the connection he sees between sensible qualities and sense perception corresponds to Aristotelian views of these qualities. For, according to their species theory, the causal explanation of our experience of sensible qualities relies on the idea that there are such qualities out there that produce our sensations. So on this view the belief in the external existence of sensible qualities can be justified on the basis of their role in an account of sense perception.

But there is a further reason why explanation of sense perception is of special importance. For on the Aristotelian view, most sensible qualities *only* have the power to produce the species that cause sense perception.[10] Only hot, cold, dry, and wet—which the scholastics referred to as *primae qualitates*—were regarded as having other causal powers as well. In fact, these four qualities alone produce qualitative change in physical objects. For instance, heat in a body can produce heat in another one, but redness can produce only a sensation of red in a sentient being; it cannot make another object red. Thus the question how sense perception works is particularly important for the question of the existence of sensible qualities in the physical world.

Descartes, of course, argues repeatedly that we can explain sensations mechanistically. He uses examples of ordinary cases in which sensations are caused by mechanical processes, such as when a blow to the eye causes sensations of sparks of light (*Principles* IV.198), and he lays out a mechanistic account of vision in the *Optics.* So natural processes, such as the burning of wood, as well as sense perception can be explained mechanistically, and there is no reason to believe in the existence of sensible qualities in the physical world for explanatory purposes.[11] Consequently, we must only accept mechanistic qualities as existing in the physical world.

Descartes was not, of course, at all unusual in his time in removing sensible qualities from the physical world. But his use of skeptical arguments sets him apart.[12] It is an important component of his strategy, and, in particular, it adds considerable force to his use of the claims that ideas of sensible qualities are confused and obscure and that they are not necessary for explanatory purposes. To see its importance it is useful to consider an objection raised by Daniel Garber against Descartes's reliance on this argument from the confusion and obscurity of ideas of sensible qualities. Garber objects that it does not support Descartes's view of bodies as purely mechanistic, because it merely "can lead us seriously to consider the *possibility* that many of the qualities we characteristically attribute to bodies are really just states of mind that we impose on bodies, and don't really exist in the bodies themselves." But this argument does not support "the stronger claim that our idea of body actually *excludes* such sensory qualities."[13]

It is certainly true that ideas of sensible qualities being confused and obscure does not justify the claim that the nature of bodies, or our ideas of bodies, *exclude* sensible qualities. After all, our ideas of these qualities might eventually become clear and distinct, as happens to the idea of the wax in the Second Meditation. One might respond that for Descartes ideas of sensible qualities *cannot* become clear and distinct, not, at least, as long as they are taken to represent qualities of bodies, rather than as mere sensations. Descartes does surely think it is true, but I don't think he wished to rely on it in his rejection of sensible qualities. There are philosophical reasons why doing so would not be a good idea. The claim that ideas of sensible qualities *cannot become* clear and distinct is a much stronger claim than the claim that they are not clear and distinct; it would be even harder to make out, and so it would be hard to base an argument on it. Besides, the fact that *we* can't clearly and distinctly conceive of these qualities does not seem like a good ground for inferring that the world does not contain them. Indeed, whereas Descartes believes it is safe to infer from the clear and distinct perception of a certain proposition to its truth, he never claims that if our perception of a certain proposition lacks clarity and distinctness, we must infer that it is false.[14] Rather, he recommends that we abstain from judgment under those circumstances.

But Garber's objection no longer holds if we see that Descartes's strategy is not to try to establish the conclusion that we *must exclude* sensible qualities from body, and if we also see that the claim that ideas of sensible qualities are obscure and confused is not meant to work by itself as an argument against their existence in the physical world. We must read this claim in the context of the skeptical doubts. Without these doubts it would indeed be Descartes's task to provide arguments that show that there are no such qualities in the physical world. But the skeptical strategy has the effect of shifting the burden of proof: instead we need arguments that show that *there are* such qualities in the physical world. So the proponent of such qualities will have to contend that our ideas of these qualities are clear and distinct, as well as that they are indeed needed for explanatory purposes (or that there is some other argument for their existence in the physical world). Establishing that our ideas of these qualities are clear and distinct is not sufficient to show they exist: after all, it is not obvious that all our clear and distinct ideas are realized in this sense. And Descartes himself distinguishes between arguing that bodies with mechanistic qualities *can* exist—which he does in the Fifth Meditation, on the basis of the relevant clear and distinct ideas—and arguing that they do so exist.

Even so, Descartes's strategy still does not establish with absolute certainty that sensible qualities are not to be found in the physical world. The skeptical arguments question assumptions on which our belief in such qualities is based, and the upshot of the rest of the *Meditations* is merely that we are not justified in claiming that there are. And similar comments apply for *The World.* In chapter 4 we shall see that, where entities whose rejection was politically problematic was concerned Descartes sometimes used the gap between not postulating certain entities and rejecting them outright to his advantage. Sensible qualities, when conceived of as *res*—that is, real qualities—were among such politically sensitive entities. But one may well object that the strategy fails Descartes's own, very stringent demand that truths be derived from first principles.[15] Adequate assessment of the strength of this objection would require examination of the scope of his demand that beliefs be derived from first principles. I wish merely to provide a brief reply to this objection here, but doing so should bring out further the nature of Descartes's strategy against sensible qualities.

In the first place, clearly the skeptical arguments and the withdrawal from sense add considerably to the strength of Descartes's case. His contentions that our ideas of sensible qualities are confused and obscure and that they are useless for explanatory purposes have much more power when we recognize that the skeptical strategy generates a demand for a justification of belief in sensible qualities. Secondly, the objection that Descartes fails to derive the rejection of sensible qualities from first principles implies a surprising demand. For the question at issue is how he rejects a view that is not his. As commentators have often pointed out, it is already asking a lot to demand that one's positive beliefs be derived from first principles. But it is very different, and rather puzzling, to require that one's *rejection* of certain tenets be derived from first principles.[16] This demand becomes even more strained by the fact that the skeptical strategy generates a need for positive arguments. For then it implies that one must derive from first principles the conclusion that there is no good argument for the existence of sensible qualities. In sum, whereas some of Descartes's comments raise the expectation that he will derive his own positive views from first principles (see *Principles* II.64), to my knowledge he never suggests that the rejection of alternative views must also be justified in this way.

In addition to the negative contention that belief in sensible qualities is not justified, Descartes also uses the accompanying positive claim that his own system will commend itself by virtue of its clarity and explanatory power. Indeed, establishment of his own views is an important weapon in his war. At one point he considered refuting an example of scholastic philosophy, namely, Eustachius' work. But in a letter to Mersenne in 1641 he writes that he has given up on this plan because "I see that it is so absolutely and clearly destroyed simply by the establishment of mine, that no other refutation is needed" (AT III 470; for a related comment see the letter to Vatier, February 22, 1638, AT I 563/ CSM III 87). Whatever problems there might be with the details of this strategy—whether or not Descartes's own mechanistic accounts are more intelligible and fruitful than ones that rely on sensible qualities—generally speaking, it is an attractive one. After all, it is more interesting to propose a positive, appealing theory than to spend one's time demolishing a rival one. In fact, in replacing other views, especially Aristotelian ones, Descartes relies far more on the development of his own system than on attempts to destroy alternatives. I will return to this aspect of his strategy in chapter 4.

The skeptical doubts are crucial not only in the negative strategy, but also in the establishment of Descartes's own positive view. For by producing the withdrawal from sense, the doubts are not only meant to lead one to suspend one's belief in sensible qualities, they are also supposed to allow one to see the first principles of Descartes's own metaphysics:

> The first notions that are presupposed for demonstrations in geometry are easily admitted by anyone, since they are consonant with the use of the senses. . . . On the other hand, in metaphysics nothing requires more effort than clear and distinct perception of first notions. For even if by their nature they are no less evident or even more evident than those that are considered by geometers, they are in conflict with many prejudices from the senses to which we have been used since our childhood. As a result they can only be known perfectly by those who meditate very attentively, and who call their mind away from corporeal things as much as possible. (AT VII 156–157/ CSM II 111)

The conflict between the first notions of metaphysics and the senses means that in metaphysics it is not so easy to acquire clear and distinct perceptions of the first notions. We need a special approach that allows us to do so, the analytic method.

I will leave Descartes's analytic method aside here, but the skeptical doubts clearly play a role in achieving its goals, in particular, in virtue of what one might call their therapeutic aspect. Various commentators have argued that the *Meditations* must be taken seriously as a set of meditations.[17] These scholars have pointed to the fact that, although this work is full of philosophical arguments, it also uses other devices. Descartes himself insists on the importance of pondering the work for some time. One reason for this aspect of the strategy is that he thought that the misguided opinions he wanted to supplant resulted from a reliance on the senses that dates back to childhood, and that we are quite attached to the opinions we formed during this period. So there is a need for some strategy for weaning us from these sense-based opinions. But in addition, the meditative, therapeutic aspect serves a specific purpose in the establishment of Descartes's own positive views; by clearing us of our undue dependence on the senses, it allows our minds to grasp the first notions or principles. By virtue of being primary these notions cannot be established by argument, and a different approach is needed.

So Descartes uses the skeptical doubts to force us to consider the questions whether we have clear and distinct ideas of the entities we always believed in and whether there are good reasons, in particular, ones based on explanatory purposes, for believing they exist. Furthermore, he thinks that the withdrawal from sense will reveal the clear and distinct ideas fundamental to philosophy and science.

But what reasons does he give for saying that ideas of sensible qualities are not among them?

3.2 Obscurity and Confusion in Ideas of Sensible Qualities

Descartes claims on various occasions that we perceive mechanistic qualities clearly and distinctly, but sensible qualities only confusedly and obscurely. Whenever he says that some idea is confused and obscure, the question arises on what ground he says so, in other words, what is supposed to convince us of this claim? Unfortunately, where ideas of sensible qualities are concerned, he usually does not say much about this question. It is tempting to think that the obscurity and confusion of our ideas of sensible qualities are a matter of some simple act of introspection. Descartes's explanation of the notion of a clear and distinct idea at *Principles* I.45 invites this approach because of its use of an analogy with vision. But he thinks we can clearly and distinctly perceive conclusions of arguments and mathematical proofs, and it is hard to imagine that he thinks clarity and distinctness there consist in some feature we detect by simple introspection. And indeed, when he does elaborate on the problems with ideas of sensible qualities, a very different picture emerges.

Let me begin with ideas of mechanistic qualities. Descartes sometimes connects the clarity and distinctness of such ideas with the fact that these qualities fall under mathematics. In the Fifth Meditation he writes that the ideas of bodies that are distinct include extension, size, shape, location, and motion. Furthermore:

> Not only are those things, regarded in general, plainly known and perspicuous to me, but in addition, when I pay attention, I perceive innumerable particulars about shapes, number, motion and the like. Their truth is so evident and in harmony with my nature, that when I first discover them, I don't so much seem to learn something new, as to remember those things which I knew before, or to notice for the first time what had been in me for a while, although I had not previously turned the gaze of my mind upon them. (AT VII 63–64/ CSM II 44)

What Descartes emphasizes here is the fact that we can establish various truths about mechanistic qualities with certainty. These truths are obviously mathematical in nature: he considers the example of the geometrical properties one can establish about triangles. A little later in the same Meditation he comments that the truths of mathematics are the ones he always has regarded as the most certain ones (AT VII 65/ CSM II 45).

Similarly, at *Principles* II.64 Descartes identifies the qualities of bodies of which we do have clear and distinct ideas as the objects of mathematics:

> I simply admit that I recognize no other matter in corporeal things than that which is entirely divisible, that can have shapes and move, and which the geometers call quantity and accept as the object of their demonstrations. I consider simply nothing in it except for those divisions, shapes and motions; I admit about them as true only what can be deduced from indubitable common notions with such certainty [*tam evidenter*] that it must be taken for a mathematical demonstration. And because all phenomena of nature can be explained in this way, as will become apparent in what follows, I think that no other principles of physics must be admitted, and that none are desirable. (*Principles* II.64)

Again, the feature Descartes insists on here is certainty: his own explanations have so much of it, he contends, that they can be regarded as mathematical demonstrations.[18] He relies on the possibility of certainty here as the reason for adopting a physics that only relies on mechanistic qualities (in addition to the claim that nothing else is needed).

It is common to think that Descartes thought bodies only have these qualities, and not sensible ones, because the former can be quantified, the latter cannot. But it is important to note that Descartes does not insist on the clarity and distinctness of ideas of mechanistic qualities *on the ground that those qualities are quantifiable.* Rather, his interest in mathematics lies in its high degree of certainty. Naturally, the fact that these qualities fall under mathematics explains at least in part why we can obtain certainty about them. Thus in the Fifth Meditation Descartes describes ideas of mechanistic qualities as clear and distinct, while connecting this claim to the possibility of proofs about these qualities, which mathematics affords.

But it is crucial to see that for Descartes such a connection with mathematics is not *necessary* for clarity and distinctness. It should be clear that he does not regard it as necessary for clarity and distinctness of ideas in general: take the ideas of God or the mind. Moreover, when Descartes claims that ideas of sensible qualities are confused and obscure, he never refers to the idea that they do not fall under mathematics. This point is of philosophical significance: for if he argued that bodies do not have sensible qualities because they do not fall under mathematics, he would have to rely on the premise that all qualities of bodies must fall under mathematics. But that premise is surely not self-evident and would require further argument. The crucial feature that distinguishes our ideas of mechanistic qualities from those of sensible qualities is more basic: the former do, the latter do not result in certainty, and for Descartes clear and distinct ideas are ones that yield certainty (AT VII 58–59, 65, 69/ CSM II 41, 45, 48). Mathematical treatment is just one way in which certainty can be accomplished.

Let us now turn to sensible qualities. Descartes discusses ideas of sensible qualities in the *Meditations,* as well as in sections 66–71 of the first part of the *Principles*. He writes in article 66 that we can have a clear and distinct perception of sensations, emotions, and appetites. In article 68 he explains that "pain and color and so on are clearly and distinctly perceived when they are regarded merely as sensations or thoughts," but not when they are believed to exist outside the mind. So Descartes holds that sensible qualities are mere sensations in the mind and do not belong to bodies. Our ideas are confused if we regard these qualities as pertaining to bodies. This is the view Descartes wishes to defend. But how does he defend it? Why should we think that ideas of pain, color, and the like are confused and obscure when we regard them as existing in bodies; what is the problem?

The *Principles* are not very illuminating on this question. When we think of sensible qualities as existing in the physical world, Descartes claims at *Principles* I. 68, 70, we don't know what it is that we ascribe to bodies. We have a much better understanding of mechanistic properties, he contends in article 69. But he does not explain in what sense we have a better understanding of mechanistic qualities, or what is required for us to know the nature of qualities of bodies. Consequently, it is not at all clear why we should accept his contention that ascribing sensible qualities to bodies is problematic.

In the Third Meditation Descartes says more. He first lists mechanistic qualities, which he claims he perceives clearly and distinctly. They include

> magnitude, or extension in length, width and depth; shape, which arises from the termination of that extension; location, which the various shaped things obtain among themselves; and motion, or change of location; to these can be added substance, duration and number. Others, however, such as light and colors, sounds, smells, flavors, hot and cold, and other tactile qualities are thought by me only very confusedly and obscurely, so that I don't even know whether they are true or false, that is, whether the ideas that I have of them, are of certain things [*rerum*] or of non-things [*non rerum*]. For although just a moment ago I noted that falsity properly speaking, or formal falsity, can only be found in judgments, there is nevertheless a certain other, material falsity in ideas, when they represent a non-thing as a thing. So, for instance, the ideas I have of hot and cold are so little clear and distinct that I cannot learn from them whether cold is only a privation of heat, or heat a privation of cold, or whether each is a real quality, or neither. And since no idea can fail to be as if of things [*tanquam rerum*], if it is true that cold is nothing other than a privation of hot, the idea which represents it to me as something real and positive is not unjustly called false and similarly for the others. (AT VII 43–44/ CSM II 30)

Commentators have seen this passage as concerned with quantifiability.[19] But the first thing to notice about this passage is that there is no mention of mathematics at all. Descartes connects neither the defects of ideas of sensible qualities, nor the virtues of ideas of mechanistic qualities to questions about quantifiability. He connects the virtues of ideas of mechanistic qualities to a conception of them as modes of extension. In regard to ideas of sensible qualities, on the other hand, he insists that they are problematic because they do not allow for certainty. He illustrates this claim by means of the ideas of hot and cold, and unlike in the *Principles,* he now does mention a specific problem—one which scholars have neglected in their analysis of Descartes's rejection of sensible qualities.[20] These ideas, he contends, do not allow us to determine the status of hot and cold in the physical world: they "are so little clear and distinct that I cannot learn from them whether cold is only a privation of heat, or heat a privation of cold, or whether each is a real quality, or neither."

What does Descartes have in mind? Understanding this remark requires consideration of sixteenth- and seventeenth-century discussions of hot and cold. The nature of these qualities was quite controversial.[21]

The standard Aristotelian view of hot and cold was that they are both qualities that exist in the physical world.[22] Among corpuscularians there was disagreement about the nature of hot and cold. Descartes thought that hot is motion of particles and so did Hobbes and Bacon, and later in the century, Boyle.[23] The accompanying view of cold was usually that it is the privation of the local motion that constitutes heat.[24] Bacon, however, apparently thought that cold is instead a different kind of motion.[25] Gassendi held that there are special calorific and frigorific particles: these are particles with specific kinds of mechanistic properties.[26] Furthermore, Gassendi argued that cold is not a privation of hot but a "true and positive quality"—*vera et positiva qualitas*—and that a drop in temperature should not necessarily be understood as a loss of heat but rather as an acquisition of cold and the result of activity of coldness.[27]

Aristotelian and mechanistic conceptions of the physical world were not the only ones around. The sixteenth-century thinker Telesio thought that all phenomena proceed from the interaction of passive matter, hot and cold. Hot, he believed, is the cause of motion, cold, the cause of rest. Cardan, also in the sixteenth century, held a modified Aristotelian view, according to which earth, air, and water are elements, but fire is not. Instead, fire consists in motion, and cold is the absence of heat.[28] Another proponent of this view was William Gilbert, who is better known for his work on magnetism.[29] Thus the idea that heat is motion and that cold is a privation of heat was not confined to thinkers with purely mechanistic systems.

There is good reason to believe that Descartes was aware of the debate about hot and cold. He was intensely interested in the question of the basic nature of the physical universe, and he clearly was informed about contemporary natural philosophy. Thus he discusses views of, for instance, Gassendi and Galileo on other matters in natural philosophy on various occasions.[30] He mentions Telesio in a letter to Beeckman (AT I 158/ CSM III 26–27),[31] and he did, of course, know the Aristotelian views on this issue. So, whereas I know of no evidence that Descartes was familiar with the particular views on the nature of hot and cold I have outlined, it is more than likely that he did know of various such views.

There is a rough correlation between the different views of hot and cold Descartes lists and the ones I have found among his contemporaries and predecessors. Clearly, the Aristotelians held the view that both hot and cold are qualities of bodies. According to Descartes himself, neither hot nor cold are such qualities. Furthermore, there was discussion about the question whether cold is a privation of heat; various thinkers held this view, and Gassendi argues against it. On the other hand, insofar as I am aware, thinkers who regarded cold as a privation of heat had a mechanistic account of heat. I know of no representative of the view that cold is a privation of heat where heat as it appears to us is a quality existing in the physical world. But certainly Descartes means to present precisely that view.[32] Perhaps there were representatives of this view of whom I am not aware. On the other hand, Descartes's list does not read as a careful enumeration of existing views on any account. For I have no reason to believe *anyone* ever adhered to the last view Descartes mentions, namely, the view that hot is a privation of cold. He may have been confused about what views were actually held; he was not particularly careful about what others thought. Given the fact that there were not just straight Aristotelian and mechanistic views, but also positions that combined elements of each, as is the case for Cardan and Gilbert, a proper grasp of the views held by various individuals would have required some care. But, most likely, Descartes simply did not intend to give a precise, systematic list of existing views. His statement of the four views reads as a simple enumeration of the logical possibilities with respect to the question whether hot and cold are real qualities or not: it could be that both of them are, neither is, or just one of them.

So we can now see that Descartes's claim that the ideas of hot and cold are confused and obscure because we cannot determine whether they are real qualities or privations was based on the fact that there was much disagreement about the nature of hot and cold. The existence of this disagreement shows in a very straightforward way that the ideas of these qualities are obscure and confused: we are in a state of uncertainty about what these ideas represent, but clear and distinct ideas are of the sort that yields certainty.

Now on Descartes's view the source of these problems is that these ideas are mere sensations: it is a mistake to project them onto the physical world and ascribe sensible qualities to bodies. But surely one cannot infer from these problems that these ideas are mere sensations. After all, it is in principle possible that we would eventually manage to clear up uncertainties about sensible qualities as qualities of bodies. And indeed, I don't think we need ascribe such an inference to Descartes. Rather, he argues that ideas of sensible qualities are confused and obscure as ideas of corporeal properties, and consequently, we should not ascribe these qualities to bodies. (This conclusion falls short of claiming that they really are not out there.) As a result, what we are left with are sensations in the mind (caused by states of bodies, which he believes to be configurations of mechanistic qualities).

But now an obvious question arises concerning the discussion of hot and cold in the Third Meditation. Descartes thought that ideas of all sensible qualities are confused and obscure, but the problem whether hot and cold are real qualities or privations is specific to these qualities: it does not affect all sensible qualities. Colors and flavors, for instance, were not thought of in terms of privations. So why does he raise this particular issue, since clearly he is concerned with all sensible qualities? One may regard this problem as an objection to my particular interpretation, and a very serious one at that, but doing so does not help. For the fact is that Descartes does refer to the question whether hot and cold are real qualities or privations to explain the confusion and obscurity of the ideas at hand, and that question does not arise for most other sensible qualities.

The first thing to notice is that Descartes mentions this issue as an *example* of problems that affect ideas of sensible qualities: he writes that "for example, my ideas of hot and cold are so little clear and distinct" (AT VII 43/ CSM II 30). So he does not pretend that this particular issue generalizes to other sensible qualities. But if that is so, how should we think of the relationship of this example to the case of other sensible qualities? One possibility is that he assumed that similar problems would arise for those qualities. In the *Principles* Descartes suggests that the problem is pretty obvious for pain or color:

> When [pain, color, and the like] are judged to be certain things existing outside our mind, it can in no way be understood what those things are. But it is clearly the same for someone to say that he sees a color in some body or senses pain in some limb as it is for him to say that he sees or senses something there about which he does not know what it is, that is, he does not know what he sees or senses. For suppose that *not paying much attention* [*minus attendendo*] he persuades himself easily that he has some notion of it, because he supposes that it is something similar to that sensation of color or pain which he experiences in himself; if he *examines* what it is, what that sensation of color or pain represents as if existing in the colored body or in the part that hurts, he notices that he does not know it at all. (*Principles* I.68, emphasis added)[33]

So Descartes suggests that we may think we know what color or pain is in the body when we don't pay much attention, but as soon as we examine the issue, we see that there is a problem. Unfortunately, it does not strike me as obvious what the problem is. Conceivably, Descartes's claim here—that it should be evident what the problems affecting sensible qualities are—is a piece of rhetoric. Alternatively, for his contemporaries the problems in question may have been obvious. We have seen how the discussion of hot and cold in the *Meditations* relates to a debate about those qualities that involved a number of early modern thinkers. There may have been other problems that were easily identifiable to Descartes's contemporaries.[34]

Where his reasoning in the *Meditations* is concerned, however, there is a different and perhaps more promising approach. Hot and cold were particularly important qualities for the Aristotelian scholastics as well as other thinkers. Their special importance comes out in Descartes's presentation of his mechanistic view in *The World*. In chapter 5 he provides an account of the elements, which he distinguishes by virtue of the different mechanistic qualities that characterize the bits of matter that compose them. Then he writes: "If you find it strange that in order to explain these elements I do not use the qualities that are called heat, cold, humidity and dryness, as the philosophers do, I will tell you that these qualities seem to me themselves to need explanation" (AT XI 25–26/ CSM I 89). Descartes does not say here that our perceptions of these qualities are obscure and confused, but that the qualities in question themselves need explanation. To the eye of a twentieth-century reader it is not clear why he mentions these sensible qualities rather than others, or what in particular he has in mind. But for the Aristotelians, these four qualities were their *primae qualitates,* their most basic qualities. The other sensible qualities were in some way supposed to arise from the *primae qualitates* and were explained by them. But the Aristotelians did not offer a clear account of how all the other sensible qualities arise from *primae qualitates,* and this is a problem that Descartes could have had in mind when he expresses dissatisfaction with the understanding of sensible qualities.[35] The *primae qualitates* themselves were not in turn explained by other qualities.[36] So in fact Descartes is here providing a mechanistic alternative to the Aristotelian view of what the *primae qualitates* are. Although there is a difference, in that when the Aristotelians distinguished between *primae qualitates* and *secundae qualitates* all these qualities as they appear to us could be found in the physical world. They did not reduce *secundae qualitates* to sensations or configurations of *primae qualitates*. But setting that difference aside, Descartes's contention is that the Aristotelians are wrong in thinking that hot, cold, dry, and wet are fundamental qualities of the physical world. And as I mentioned above, there was an additional reason why the Aristotelians regarded the *primae qualitates* as particularly important: they also held that all qualitative change in the physical world is brought about by these four qualities. The heat in an object can make something else hot, but the redness in an object does not have the causal power to make another object red. And so the *primae qualitates* are central to questions concerning causal explanations of natural phenomena. Other sensible qualities were thought to be active only insofar as they cause sense perception in sentient beings.

Given the fundamental role of these qualities in the Aristotelian conception of the physical world, it is particularly important for a mechanistic theory to provide an account of natural phenomena that can do without these *primae qualitates*.[37] So one possible way of understanding Descartes's approach in the *Meditations* is this. He uses the example of hot and cold because of their fundamental importance in explaining natural phenomena. He invokes the problem about privations and real qualities to get his readers worried about these qualities, which they might otherwise think they understand best, and argues that ideas of these qualities in fact are not clear and distinct. But, he thinks, if our ideas of some of the most fundamental sensible qualities of the physical world turn out to be problematic, questions arise about all such qualities. And so, whereas the problem about privations and real qualities does not affect all sensible qualities, Descartes can nevertheless use it as a way of creating worries about all such qualities.

It must be admitted, however, that Descartes does not say nearly enough to support his claim that ideas of sensible qualities are obscure and confused: unfortunately, he does not at all make clear what the problem is supposed to be for qualities other than hot and cold. This feature of his argument is the more troubling because without some argument to the contrary it seems not only unproblematic, but very natural to us to ascribe sensible qualities to body. Descartes is very much aware of this problem, and he makes considerable effort to try to address it. He uses the skeptical strategy, which is meant to undermine our ingrained tendency to regard bodies as having colors, flavors, smells, and the like. He also offers an account of our cognitive capacities, according to which they are not meant to result in this tendency. In the *Meditations* he argues that we misuse and misinterpret sensations if we infer from them that bodies have sensible qualities. In the Sixth Meditation he argues that his nature teaches him "to flee those things that bring about the sensation of pain, and to pursue those that bring about the sensation of pleasure, and the like; but it does not appear to teach us to conclude anything more about things posited outside us on the basis of those perceptions of the senses without a previous examination by the intellect, because it seems that to know the truth about them pertains to the mind alone and not to the composite" (AT VII 82/ CSM II 57). So knowledge of the nature of body belongs to the intellect, not to the senses, which are merely supposed to instruct us about practical issues. And of course, on Descartes's view, the intellect would tell us not to ascribe sensible qualities to bodies. Furthermore, in the *Principles* he provides an explanation for our inclination to do so in terms of the state of our mind in childhood. And in article 71 he explains that our tendency to see sensible qualities and states like pain as states of bodies results from an unwarranted assimilation to mechanistic qualities. He seems to think that upon close examination we would see that there is a difference in this regard between ideas of sensible and mechanistic qualities. Ideas of the latter do, but ideas of the former do not represent the qualities in question as if existing outside our thought. This is a remarkable view, although I must confess that it strikes me as rather implausible.[38]

In sum, Descartes says very little to defend his view that ideas of sensible qualities are confused and obscure when we regard them as representing qualities of bodies. He is most explicit in his discussion of hot and cold in the *Meditations,* but it remains difficult not to feel dissatisfied with the sketchiness of his remarks.

But some of the negative results of my discussion are equally significant. In light of the common tendency to regard Descartes as rejecting sensible qualities because they are not quantifiable, it is important to note that he does *not* say that ideas of these qualities are confused and obscure because they do not fall under mathematics. One might think that nevertheless this is how his argument should be filled out. But we saw that in the Third Meditation he supports his claim that ideas of hot and cold are obscure and confused by pointing to an entirely *different* issue, the impossibility of settling whether they are real qualities or privations. It is also important that Descartes does *not* say these ideas are obscure and confused because we do not think of hot and cold as modes of extension. And this observation leads us to the topic of the next section.

3.3 Principal Attributes and Modes

Descartes's mechanistic conception of body is frequently connected with his view that the essence of body is extension. Scholars sometimes regard this view of the essence of body as an expression of his exclusion of sensible qualities, and they frequently claim that it is the basis for an argument for this exclusion.[39] Descartes's rejection of sensible qualities has not received too much attention from historians of philosophy. When it is addressed, scholars often claim that he based it on his conception of body as extended, but generally without providing any textual support. I will contend that Descartes never offers such an argument and that there is good reason to believe he did not wish to do so. I will propose that in fact things are the other way around.

At first blush, excluding sensible qualities on the basis of the view that the essence of body consists in extension seems puzzling, since even if the essence of body is extension, sensible qualities might be among its accidental properties. But the idea that Descartes excludes sensible qualities in this way gains considerable plausibility when one takes into account his mode-attribute conception of substance, which we discussed in some detail in chapter 1. On this conception, the nature or essence of a substance consists in a principal attribute, which determines what kinds of modes that substance can have. All modes must be understood through and referred to the principal attribute of the substance to which they belong. A thinking substance can only have modes that presuppose and are understood through thought. An extended substance has only modes that presuppose and are understood through extension. A mode can belong only to a substance that has the right kind of principal attribute.

This conception of substance could be used to eliminate sensible qualities from body in two different ways. One obvious strategy would be to contend that sensible qualities do not presuppose extension and thus are not modes of body. But alternatively, one could rely on the idea that sensible qualities presuppose thought and thus are modes of the mind rather than of the body. Both strategies have been ascribed to Descartes. I will consider them in reverse order.

The second strategy is ascribed to Descartes by Daniel Garber. He writes that Descartes uses his conception of substance "to eliminate sensible qualities from bodies and geometrize the material world," and that his view of conceptual dependency "leads him to view bodies as extended things that exclude all mentality."[40] Some of Garber's remarks suggest that he ascribes the first strategy to Descartes—which consists in eliminating sensible qualities from body on the ground that they do not presuppose extension. But when he turns to a detailed discussion of the rejection of sensible qualities, he argues that Descartes relies on the idea that sensible qualities presuppose thought and thus are modes of the mind. He finds this line of argument in the Sixth Meditation, right after the conclusion of the Real Distinction Argument:[41]

> Moreover I find in me faculties for certain special modes of thinking, namely the faculties of imagination and sensation. I can clearly and distinctly understand myself as a whole without them, but not *vice versa* them without me, that is, without an intelligent substance in which they inhere [*insint*]. For they include some intellection in their formal concept; hence I perceive that they are distinguished from me as modes from a thing. Also I recognize certain other faculties, such as those of changing place, being endowed with various shapes and the like, which can no more than the faculties just-mentioned be understood without some substance in which they inhere, and which, consequently, cannot exist without it. But it is manifest that these, if they exist, must inhere in a corporeal or extended substance, not in an intelligent substance. For their clear and distinct concept certainly contains some extension, but clearly no thought. (AT VII 78–79/ CSM II 54–55)

It is true that Descartes's claims in this passage are based on his view that the modes of a substance cannot be understood without that substance and its principal attribute. But he plainly makes no claims about sensible qualities in this passage. He does not say that *they* belong to the mind, instead he says that *the faculties of imagination and sensation* belong to the mind. This claim is quite different. For, of course, even if sensation and imagination belong to the mind, the sensible qualities that we seem to experience in those mental activities might well belong to physical objects.[42] Indeed, rather than being concerned to deny sensible qualities for bodies, Descartes is here concerned with his reconceptualization of the mind, which, as we saw in chapter 2, involves assigning these faculties to it.

Nevertheless, Descartes's view that sensation and imagination are modes of the mind is important for his mechanistic program. This view was certainly unusual, at least from an Aristotelian perspective, and his conception of the mind formed an integral part of his attempt to provide metaphysical underpinnings for his contention that everything in the physical world could be explained mechanistically. To see this point we need to remind ourselves of two comparisons, which were discussed in chapter 2, between the Aristotelian scholastics and Descartes concerning the mind. Like Descartes, the Aristotelians generally regarded the mind as the incorporeal part of the human being. They saw the mind as the subject of intellectual operations, including the will—the intellectual appetite. These operations they did not regard as part of the physical world. But unlike Descartes, they thought that sensation and imagination belong to the ensouled body, or to the body-soul composite, and that their activities take place in the physical world. So Descartes proposes a clearly different view in claiming that sensation and imagination belong to the mind. That is the issue he is concerned with in the passage in question from the Sixth Meditation.

From Descartes's mechanistic point of view there are obvious reasons for regarding sensation and imagination as belonging to the mind rather than to the body. In these activities we have experiences as of sensible qualities. Now according to the Aristotelians these activities occur in virtue of species, likenesses of such qualities being produced in the body. But how can a purely mechanistic conception of the body account for these experiences? On such a view it is not at all clear how there is room for anything like sensible species in the sensing body. All the occurrences in our bodies consist in mechanical processes, and so for Descartes our experiences of such qualities take place in the incorporeal mind.[43]

So although concerns with mechanism are at play in the passage in question, Descartes there assigns sensation and imagination, not sensible qualities, to the mind. He does not turn to the claim that sensible qualities belong only to the mind until later in the Sixth Meditation. Right after the passage just discussed he argues for the existence of bodies, and he writes that his proof only establishes the existence of bodies insofar as they have mechanistic properties. He expresses uncertainty about whether in bodies we can find "light, sound, pain and the like," sensible qualities, as well as objects of what he calls inner sensations (AT VII 80/ CSM II 55). He then turns to addressing this question. These observations might strike one as amounting to a minor claim about a short passage. But Descartes's strategy in the *Principles* is similar. In part I, article 53 he describes mind and body, identifying their principal attributes and assigning the same sets of modes to them as in the Sixth Meditation, and the issue of sensible qualities is not addressed until later in part I.[44] In fact, I know of no place where Descartes argues that sensible qualities are confined to the mind on the basis of the idea that they presuppose thought.

Let us now turn to the other way in which Descartes might use the mode-attribute conception of substance to exclude sensible qualities from body; he could argue that they do not presuppose extension and thus are not modes of body. Then, assuming his dualism, they must be modes of the mind. More specifically, Descartes could argue that bodies do not have sensible qualities on the basis of the following three claims: (1) the essence of body is extension, (2) all the accidents of body are modes of extension, ways of being extended, (3) sensible qualities are not ways of being extended. Descartes certainly holds all these claims, but he never argues this way. He does explicitly state (1) and (2) at *Principles* I.53, where he lays out his conception of substance. Descartes comes close to presenting (1) and (2) in the Sixth Meditation, just after he has argued that mind and body are really distinct. But on this occasion he does not claim that *all* the properties of body are modes of extension. On *neither* of these occasions does he add the third claim; that is, he does not contend that sensible qualities are not modes of extension. This is noteworthy; the mere absence of an explicit statement of the argument in question would seem to be compatible with Descartes's relying on it. But these are surely occasions where one would expect him to offer the argument, and he conspicuously fails to do so. This strikes me as a virtue of Descartes's strategy. After all, it certainly seems natural to think that at least some sensible qualities, such as color, cannot be conceived without extension and so presuppose extension. But then on the Cartesian scheme such qualities would seem to be modes of extension.[45]

So far I have considered arguments that rely on the idea that a mode cannot be understood without its principal attribute. But there is another way of looking at the notion of a mode, from the perspective of the principal attribute, so to speak. That is to say, being a mode of body does not just imply presupposing extension, but it also means being nothing over and above a modification, a way of being of extension.[46] In the Third Meditation Descartes presents mechanistic qualities from this perspective, although without using the technical vocabulary of mode and attribute. He lists the properties of body we clearly and distinctly perceive: "magnitude or extension in length, breadth and depth; shape, which arises from the limitation of this extension; location, which the various shaped things obtain among each other; motion, or change of position" (AT VII 43/ CSM II 30). That line of thought offers a more promising way of ruling out sensible qualities. It is plausible that we cannot think of sensible qualities in this way: it seems hard to conceive of color as arising in a way similar to the ones described here for the mechanistic modes of body. Nevertheless, when Descartes next turns in this passage to his claim that our ideas of sensible qualities are confused and obscure, he does not rely on this line of thought. Instead he turns to the question whether hot and cold are real qualities or privations. This is important, for surely if he wished to argue that our ideas of sensible qualities are confused and obscure on the ground that they are not modes of extension, this is the place where one would most expect him to do so. But whereas we find him willing to present ideas of mechanistic qualities as clear and distinct because we think of such qualities as modes of extension, he refrains from using the corresponding negative claim for sensible qualities.

So Descartes does not *use* his mode-attribute conception of substance to exclude sensible qualities from the physical world and confine them to the mind. The *Meditations* and the *Principles* are works where both the mode-attribute conception of substance is present (although more implicitly in the case of the *Meditations*) and the question of the status of sensible qualities is addressed. In these works Descartes does use the mode-attribute conception of substance to support positive aspects of his conception of body and mind and their modes. But he defends the negative claim that sensible qualities cannot be found in the physical world on different grounds, which we discussed in sections 3.1 and 3.2.

There are historical reasons why Descartes should have been reluctant to argue that bodies do not have sensible qualities on the ground that they fail to be modes of extension. For his principal opponents on this issue, the Aristotelian scholastics, would not have accepted it. The argument requires the claim that *all* the properties of body are modes of extension, but the scholastics did not accept this claim. They regarded sensible qualities as "real qualities," as Descartes put it. These qualities were supposed to be more than mere modes; they were thought to be *res,* things, having their own reality or, in Suárez' words, *entitas.*[47]

This is not to say that his rejection of sensible qualities has nothing to do with his conception of body as characterized by extension and its modes. Perhaps Descartes's rejection of sensible qualities was *motivated* by his commitment to the claim that bodies are just characterized by extension and its modes, although there is at least as much reason to think that it was motivated by a commitment to mechanistic explanation. But what I have wished to establish is that he does not rely on that claim to argue against these qualities. As I see it, the view that he does rely on that claim gets the picture backwards: instead, the claim that *all* the qualities of body are mechanistic modes of extension is meant to *emerge from* the rejection of sensible qualities. By way of the skeptical arguments Descartes creates a situation where we need a justification for any beliefs concerning the existence and nature of bodies. He then argues that we are justified in believing in the existence of bodies as having mechanistic qualities, but that there is no justification for belief in sensible qualities—or, for that matter, for belief in other undesirable entities, such as real qualities and substantial forms. Consequently, what we are left with is a mechanistic conception of body, according to which its essence is extension, and all its other properties are modes of extension.

Finally, it is plausible that for Descartes the claims that the essence of body is extension and that all its other properties are modes of extension *express* his purely mechanistic conception of body. For, as we shall see in chapter 4.1, within scholasticism we find the view that mechanistic qualities are modes of quantity, but sensible qualities are real qualities. In that kind of historical climate Descartes's claim that all the properties of body are modes of extension could convey his purely mechanistic conception of body to many of his readers.

3.4 Elimination, Change, and the Essence of Body

When arguing against sensible qualities, philosophers have often invoked the idea that bodies can lack such qualities, or that such qualities are subject to change. When John Locke introduces the distinction between mechanistic and sensible qualities, or in his terms, primary and secondary qualities, he identifies the former as those qualities that bodies always have.[48] In the *Assayer* Galileo argues that whenever we conceive of a body we feel the need to think of it as having various mechanistic qualities, but not as having sensible ones. He concludes that sensible qualities are "mere names so far as the object in which we place them is concerned, and that they reside only in consciousness."[49] This line of argument can also be found in Lucretius' *De rerum natura*. He contends that some bodies lack smell, sound, color; thus we can conceive of bodies that lack such qualities.[50] Following Garber, I will label this argument the Argument from Elimination. Lucretius also relies on a different line of thought, which I will call the Argument from Change: he argues that atoms don't have colors on the ground that colors *change*.[51] Both arguments appear in Descartes's writings, in particular, in the wax passage in the Second Meditation and in the second part of the *Principles*. Interpreters commonly do not distinguish between these arguments. They are easily confused, and some of Descartes's statements seem to present them as just one argument. Nevertheless, as we shall see, there are some important differences.

One would expect that, like Lucretius, Galileo, and Locke, Descartes also uses these arguments for distinguishing sensible and mechanistic qualities, and commentators have duly interpreted him in this way. Close examination of the texts reveals, however, that he does not do so: interestingly enough, Descartes employs these arguments in the service of completely different goals. This is a striking result, not only because it departs from the views proposed by various interpreters, but even more so because it means that Descartes departs in interesting ways from other major thinkers in the history of philosophy. I will first discuss the wax passage, then turn to the *Principles*.

In the Second Meditation Descartes famously considers what the nature of a particular piece of wax is:

> It was taken out of the honeycomb very recently. It has not yet lost all the flavor of the honey; it retains some of the smell of the flowers from which it was gathered; its color, shape, size are manifest; it is hard, cold, can easily be touched, and, if you strike it with a finger, it emits a sound; everything is present that seems to be required in order for a body to be known as distinctly as possible. But see, while I speak, it is brought closer to the fire: the remainders of flavor are removed, its smell vanishes, its

> color changes, its shape is lost, it increases in size, it becomes liquid, warm, it can hardly be touched, and no longer will it emit sound when you knock on it. Does the same wax still remain? We must believe that it does: no one denies it, no one thinks otherwise. What was there in it that I comprehended so distinctly? Certainly none of those things that I reached by way of the senses; for whatever falls under taste, smell, sight, touch or hearing has changed. Yet the wax remains. (AT VII 30/ CSM II 20)

Descartes claims here that all the qualities initially observed in the wax change, but the wax itself remains. He infers on this ground that none of these qualities pertain to the nature of the wax. Instead, the piece of wax is merely "something extended, flexible and changeable." He goes on to conclude that the wax is not known by the senses, nor by the imagination, but "by an inspection of the mind alone," that is, the intellect.

This is an instance of the Argument from Change. Descartes may seem to rely also on the Argument from Elimination, since he writes about some of the qualities of the wax that they change, about others that they disappear. But in fact he *relies* only on the observation that the qualities of the wax *change*. Nothing in the passage depends on the idea that the wax loses some property entirely.

The wax passage is usually interpreted as meant to support the view that bodies do not have sensible qualities, although some commentators have argued to the contrary.[52] What seems to have escaped notice, however, is that there is a very obvious reason why it can be said that this passage has nothing to do with the issue: for Descartes treats mechanistic properties, shape and size, *in exactly the same way* as sensible qualities, such as flavor, smell, color! When the wax is brought closer to the fire, he says "the remainders of flavor are removed, its smell vanishes, its color changes, its shape is lost, it increases in size, it becomes liquid, warm, it can hardly be touched, and no longer will it emit sound when you knock on it." Since Descartes presents *both* mechanistic and sensible qualities as changed or lost, he cannot mean to argue that bodies do not have sensible qualities while maintaining that they do have mechanistic qualities. Accordingly, he writes in the Third Replies that in the wax passage he meant to prove that "*color, hardness, shape* do not pertain to the formal concept—*ratio formalis*—of the wax itself" (AT VII 175/ CSM II 124, emphasis added). So, clearly, the wax passage has nothing to do with the rejection of sensible qualities.

The tendency to regard the passage as concerned with the distinction between sensible and mechanistic qualities derives to some extent from misunderstanding of Descartes's conclusion that the nature of the piece of wax is that it is "something extended, flexible, changeable—*extensum quid, flexibile, mutabile*" (AT VII 31/ CSM II 20). The term *mutabile* (*muable* in the French) is often understood to mean "mobile."[53] The supposition that Descartes means changeable only with respect to motion suggests that the passage is concerned with the distinction between sensible and mechanistic qualities. But the term is much broader than that and should be translated as 'changeable.' This text is sometimes compared to *Principles* II.23, where Descartes expresses his mechanistic conception of body, saying "all the properties which we clearly perceive in [matter] are reducible to its divisibility and consequent mobility in respect of its parts." But the terminology is clearly different here: Descartes does not use the term *'mutabilis,'* but he speaks of *"mobilis secundum partes"*—movable in regard to its parts.

Moreover, the argument of the wax passage does not in the least support the idea that Descartes meant changeable only with respect to motion. He discusses all sorts of change in the piece of wax. Indeed, although he moves the wax closer to the fire, he does not at all discuss that change in motion directly in the argument. Instead, the passage emphasizes changes with respect to other qualities of the wax that result from the closer proximity to the fire.

I do not wish to give a full account of the wax passage here, but the following observations should reveal how Descartes does use the Argument from Change in this passage. As he himself says, he is concerned here with the entirely different purpose of arguing that body is not known by the senses, but by the intellect, and that mind is better known than body (AT VII 34/ CSM II 22–23).[54] In the Third Replies he writes that the passage is not concerned with the *ratio formalis*, formal definition, of body, but of the wax. It is essential to Descartes's purpose here that he is concerned with a *particular* body rather than with the essence of body in general, and he insists on this point at least twice in the wax passage (AT VII 30, 31/ CSM II 20). For his purpose is to argue that even a *particular* body is known by the intellect, not by the senses. The reason is that Descartes is defending his view that the intellect is the true source of knowledge, and that we know our minds better than body against the objection that particular bodies—which are the objects of the senses—are best known. He responds to this objection by pointing out that the qualities of the wax that we sense change while the piece of wax remains the same. Consequently, our *sensory* grasp of the wax does not tell us what it is: for by means of our senses we only know the qualities a body has at the moment when we perceive it, and those qualities change while the wax remains. So we need some other faculty to tell us what the wax is. The next candidate is the imagination, which cannot handle the great range of variation we conceive in the wax, and Descartes concludes that we know the wax by means of the intellect, which alone can grasp this range of variation.

Let us now turn to the *Principles*. In part II, articles 4 and 11 we find arguments that are similar to the one in the wax passage, but there are some important differences. In the *Principles* we find the Argument from Elimination rather than the Argument from Change, and here, unlike in the discussion of the wax, Descartes is now clearly and explicitly focused on the question of the essence of body. The title of article 4 is: "The nature of body consists not in weight, hardness, color, and the like, but only in extension." It is worth quoting this article in full:

> If we do this [use only our intellect, not our senses], we will perceive that the nature of matter or body regarded in general does not consist in the fact that it is a thing that is hard, heavy, or colored, or that affects the senses in any other way; but only in the fact that it is a thing extended in length, width and depth. For, with respect to hardness, sense perception indicates nothing else to us about it than that the parts of hard bodies resist the motion of our hands when they encounter them. For suppose that whenever our hands move in some direction, all bodies there existing would recede with the same speed by which the hands approach. In that case we would never feel any hardness. And it is not in any way intelligible that bodies that so recede would thereby lose their corporeal nature; consequently this nature does not consist in hardness. By the same reasoning it can be shown that weight, color and all other such qualities that are sensed in corporeal matter, can be removed from it, while it remains in its entirety; from this it follows that its nature depends on none of them.

So Descartes argues that we can think of a body of which we never have a sensation of hardness, and that doing so leaves intact the idea that it is a body. Similarly, he suggests, for other sensible qualities, and he infers that they are not part of the essence of body. This is the Argument from Elimination.

It is very tempting to think that now Descartes is concerned to exclude sensible qualities from body, and various scholars have interpreted the passage this way.[55] But as Garber points out, there is a very serious problem with this argument in relation to the rejection of sensible qualities: for the argument completely fails to establish the desired conclusion that *no* bodies have sensible qualities.[56] At best, it establishes that *some* bodies do not have certain sensible qualities. That is enough to show that the essence of body does not contain these qualities, but the argument does not establish that bodies *only* have mechanistic properties.

Garber is right to raise this objection. But Descartes is not guilty of the misstep it implies, for in fact the argument of *Principles* II.4 is not concerned to establish that bodies have only mechanistic properties and no sensible ones. The first thing to notice is that Descartes himself does not claim that the argument establishes that conclusion. His stated purpose is to argue that hardness and the like do not belong to the *essence* of body. The argument that bodies can fail to have hardness, color, and the like is a good strategy (whether or not it is successful in its details),[57] and an obvious, standard one for showing that they do not belong to the essence of body. Descartes himself clearly believed that inseparability was *necessary* for a quality being essential (cf. AT VII 219/ CSM II 155), although he did not regard it as sufficient.[58] So for him the argument from elimination would be adequate to *exclude* properties from an essence, even though, as Garber points out, arguing that extension is inseparable would not be enough to *include* it in the essence of body. But Descartes is not trying to establish that second point by means of this argument.

But now a different problem arises. For why does Descartes merely try to argue that these qualities do not belong to the *essence* of body rather than that they do not belong to bodies at all?

The reason is that Descartes is here not at all concerned with the rejection of the Aristotelian and common sense view that bodies have sensible qualities as they appear to us, but with a completely different issue. This becomes clear in article 11, where he picks up the argument again. There he argues that not only hardness, but also color, heaviness, cold, and hot are not essential to body, because some bodies lack these qualities.[59] But the article is entitled: "How [space] does not differ in reality [*in re*] from corporeal substance." At the beginning of this article he writes that "the same extension constitutes the nature of body and the nature of space," and he closes it saying "the same [extension] is contained in the idea of space, not only of space full of bodies, but also of that which is called empty." The real aim of the argument is to defend the view that there is only a distinction of reason between body and space, and that there is no void, empty space. The Aristotelians did not believe in the void any more than Descartes did and so they are not his target in articles 4 and 11. In this part of the *Principles* Descartes is concerned to defend his view that the essence of matter is extension and that there is only a distinction of reason between matter and space. Defending this view does require addressing the Aristotelian scholastics, but in articles 4 and 11 he is after a different target: believers in empty space such as the atomists. Let us look again at *Principles* 4, and now also 11 in light of this purpose.

The idea that the essence of body is just extension is instrumental in Descartes's rejection of empty space. For he uses the idea that the essences of body and space are identical to argue that there is no difference in reality between body and space, and so that there is no empty space.[60] But now how does the Argument from Elimination address this issue? First, it is important to distinguish between the positive claim that the essence of body is extension and the negative claim that the essence of body does not also include hardness, color, and the like. Article 4 gives the impression that it means to establish both claims. But it argues explicitly only for the negative claim that the essence of body does not include hardness, color, and the like: nothing is said in favor of the positive claim that extension is inseparable from body or essential to it.

Indeed, Descartes's purpose in this article is merely to defend this negative claim. He specifically wants to eliminate what he regards as an important source of the belief that there is empty space, namely, the view that bodies are essentially sensible. A proponent of this view, he envisions, would infer that there are empty spaces from the observation that there are spaces in which we do not sense anything. Thus when explaining the *ordinary* use of the term 'empty' in article 17 he writes: "Space is empty when there is nothing sensible in it, although it is full of created, self-subsisting matter."[61] The belief in the void, he thinks, is another result of the faith in the senses that we grow up with. In the *Meditations* Descartes lists, among ill-considered judgments, the belief that "any space in which simply nothing is occurring that stimulates my senses is empty." He rejects this prejudice, saying "even though there is nothing in some given space that stimulates the senses, it does not follow that there is no body there" (AT VII 82, 83/ CSM II 56, 57; see also *Rules,* AT X 424/ CSM I 48; and *The World,* AT XI 16–17/ CSM I 85).

We can now understand why Descartes merely wants to argue that the essence of bodies does not include hardness, color, and the like. For this point is sufficient to resist the defense of the void on the basis of the view that bodies must affect our senses. Descartes wants to show that even when we find a space in which we sense nothing, it does not follow that this space is empty. He does so by trying to rule out any particular source of sensory effect (hardness, color, hot, cold) as essential to body. He implies that, consequently, no quality that produces such effects is essential to body. One may well object that it does not follow that a body can lack *all* such qualities. Perhaps something could be a body without having color or hardness; but it might still be the case that a body must be sensible in *some* way. Margaret Wilson responds to this objection—and I agree—that here the burden of proof lies with Descartes's opponent.[62]

There is a further, very important point to be made about Descartes's use of the Argument from Elimination: there is yet another sense in which it has absolutely nothing to do with the distinction between sensible and mechanistic qualities. For Descartes is not even concerned with the question whether the *essence* of bodies includes *sensible qualities as they appear to us,* and the question whether bodies can be understood mechanistically is not at all at stake. There are two reasons. First, what Descartes needs here is not just the conclusion that sensible qualities as they appear to us are not essential to bodies. In order to defend his view that there is no empty space he needs to rule out that bodies are essentially sensible *on any account of what in bodies causes our sensations of them.* Even on a mechanistic conception of body one might still believe that it is part of the essence of body that it be capable of producing sensations in us, and that under certain particular circumstances it will exercise that capacity. So on such a conception of body Descartes needs the claim that a body does not necessarily have a configuration of mechanistic properties that make it sensible to us. This leads us to the second reason why he is not concerned with sensible qualities as they appear to us. He is addressing supporters of the void, which include the atomists. But the atomists shared his view that there are no sensible qualities in the physical world. The Aristotelians, on the other hand, thought there were such qualities, but they did not believe in the void.[63]

A closer look at the texts makes clear that the view that there are sensible qualities in bodies that resemble our sensations is not at stake. For instance, in article 4 Descartes argues that hardness is not part of the essence of body. But the argument he gives is not directed against a specific conception of what hardness is in bodies, or, to put the point differently, what it is in bodies that gives us a sensation of hardness. He describes hardness by saying that "sensation indicates nothing more to us about [hardness] than that the parts of hard bodies resist the motion of our hands when they encounter them." The reason he gives why hardness is not essential to bodies is that bodies could fail to cause this sensation by always receding without thereby losing their corporeal nature. Similar observations apply to the argument in article 11. So Descartes does not even try to establish that sensible qualities as they appear to us belong to the essence of body. Rather, he tries to establish that it is not essential to bodies that they produce sensations in us, regardless of the question of what it is in them that allows them to do so.

Nevertheless, it is striking that in the *Principles* Descartes applies the Argument from Elimination just to sensible qualities. This is an interesting difference with the wax passage, where he treats mechanistic qualities, such as size and shape, and sensible qualities in the same way. So why would he only apply the argument to sensible qualities, if he is not concerned to defend the mechanistic conception of body?

The reason is that the thesis the argument is meant to support—that there is no distinction in reality between body and space and thus no void—is related to the two types of qualities in different ways. I have explained how, for Descartes, the rejection of the void requires that the essence of body does not include that bodies produce sensations of sensible qualities. For, he believes, we commonly hold that there is a void because there are spaces that do not stimulate our senses. But the case of mechanistic properties is different: we do think of parts of space, including empty space, as having shape and size, even position, in spite of the fact that we do not think that we sense space. So we don't think of these qualities as distinguishing bodies from space, and they do not bear on the question whether a space is empty, and so they pose no problem for the identity of space and body. There is one mechanistic quality that is different in this respect: motion. We ascribe motion to bodies, but not to space. And indeed, Descartes duly addresses this issue in article 12: he writes that when we think of a stone as being moved, we think of its extension as being moved, and the extension of its place as staying behind. His solution, briefly, is that there is a distinction of reason between body and space.

Let me conclude this section by briefly comparing the Argument from Change to the Argument from Elimination. The distinction between these arguments is significant, as they differ in what they can establish about the relationship between the essence of body and the senses. These differences correspond to the concerns of the contexts in which Descartes uses them. For if the color or shape of a body changes, as is the case with the wax, that does not by itself show that the essence of body—or the essence of *that* body—does not include that it have *some* color or shape. But the idea that a particular color or shape is not essential to a particular piece of wax is enough for the purposes of the wax passage. For there Descartes wants to establish that the piece of wax is known by the intellect, and not by the senses, which can only detect particular colors or shapes. For this reason the Argument from Change is appropriate in the wax passage. On the other hand, if there are bodies that have *no* color, as Descartes contends in the *Principles,* that does establish that being colored is not part of the essence of body. This stronger point, expanded to all qualities that stimulate our senses, is what he needs for his defense of the view that there is no empty space, which is his concern at *Principles* II.4 and 11. So in the *Principles* he needs the Argument from Elimination, and indeed it is what he relies on there.

We can now distinguish several ways in which Descartes places the intellect over the senses for knowledge of the essence of body. For one thing, the senses mislead us into thinking that bodies have sensible qualities. In addition, in the wax passage he wants to show that we do not grasp with the senses what the essence of body is—even in the case of a particular body, because of the changeability of both sensible and mechanistic qualities. The wax passage leaves open the possibility that body does essentially have qualities (whatever those qualities are in themselves) that make it sensible. But in the *Principles* Descartes wants to rule out the idea that it is essential to body that it can be sensed. And as we saw, this contention is aimed at yet another mistake that is due to the senses: the mistake of thinking that where nothing is sensed, there is no body.

Conclusion

In this chapter I have considered a central component of Descartes's enterprise of redrawing the boundary between the mental and the physical, namely, his defense of the view that bodies only have mechanistic qualities and that sensible qualities are mere sensations in the mind. I have argued that his defense of this view is very different from what scholars have believed, and also that it departs in interesting ways from strategies followed by other opponents of sensible qualities. Descartes uses the skeptical doubts to undermine our commitment to sensible qualities by detaching us from our reliance on the senses. They generate a demand for a justification of belief in sensible qualities, which he believes is not forthcoming: our ideas of sensible qualities are confused and obscure, and such qualities are not needed for explanatory purposes. His reliance on the method of doubt is distinctive of his strategy, and it sets him apart from other thinkers who have dealt with the issue of mechanistic and sensible qualities. In addition, it forestalls, or at least blunts, certain types of objections to his arguments. Finally, the skeptical arguments don't only play a role in this negative argument, they are also essential to a positive side of Descartes's strategy. For in his defense of a mechanistic picture of the physical world he counts on both the explanatory power and the perspicuousness of that picture. The skeptical doubts are supposed to clear our minds of various kinds of prejudices and allow us to see the ideas basic to his own theory.

I have discussed various arguments that are often ascribed to Descartes, but that he does not use. Thus, unlike other philosophers, he does not rely on the Argument from Change or the Argument from Elimination. Speaking more generally, his strategy is not to argue that there is something about the nature of bodies that makes it impossible for them to have sensible qualities. Thus he does not reject sensible qualities from the physical world on the ground that qualities of body must be quantifiable. Nor, contrary to what scholars often believe, does he exclude sensible qualities from the physical world on the basis of his view that the nature of body is extension. In fact, in regard to this last argument, things are the other way around. His view that the qualities of bodies only include extension and its modes emerges *as a result of* his strategy for eliminating such undesirable entities as sensible qualities. Broadly speaking, Descartes's strategy does not rely on specific *a priori* views about the nature of body and scientific explanation. He argues that his mechanistic approach is the right one because of its intelligibility and explanatory power. But in principle these criteria could be used to defend a very different position.

CHAPTER FOUR

Real Qualities and Substantial Forms

Descartes's enterprise of generating properly cleaned-up notions of mind and body does not only include the rejection of sensible qualities. Also quite prominent in this undertaking is his elimination of two specifically scholastic notions, those of substantial forms and real qualities. Descartes regarded these entities as the products of confusions of the mental and the physical. But this is not the only thing he saw wrong with them. An important criticism he voices is that the notions of substantial forms and real qualities involve inconsistencies regarding the notion of substance. He objects with particular vigor to the notion of real accident in this regard, and its dismissal is part and parcel of his development of the mode-attribute conception of substance. Furthermore, he argues that real qualities and substantial forms are useless for explanatory purposes and should be dropped in favor of his mechanistic account of the physical world.

An important goal of this chapter is to do away with a pervasive and rather serious misunderstanding of Descartes's treatment of substantial forms and real qualities. For the scholastics these notions stand for radically different types of entities, but in the scholarly literature on Descartes they are nearly always run together. Some commentators claim that he did not distinguish between them, others fail to grasp the distinction themselves.[1] From a scholastic point of view a failure to distinguish between real qualities and substantial forms constitutes a very basic and very serious error. If Descartes makes this mistake, he fundamentally misunderstands these notions. Now he does sometimes encourage the expectation that he did not have a very good grasp of scholastic thought, as in a letter to Mersenne of September 30, 1640, where he claimed he had not read their works in some 20 years (AT III 185/ CSM III 153).[2] But over the course of this chapter it will become clear that, whatever misconceptions he harbored about scholastic views, he did distinguish quite clearly between real qualities and substantial forms. The distinction between these two types of entities is relevant not only to Descartes's rejection of them, but also to his views of the union of mind and body, as we shall see in chapter 5.

Section 4.1 is devoted to the questions of how real qualities and substantial forms were understood in late scholasticism and how Descartes thought they were understood. In section 4.2, I turn to his overall strategy for eliminating substantial forms and real qualities. Section 4.3 is concerned with the argument that these entities are not needed for explanatory purposes, and I argue that there is an interesting relationship between this argument and the opposition from religious quarters to the rejection of these entities. In section 4.4 I turn to the conceptual problems Descartes raises for real qualities and substantial forms. I conclude in section 4.5 with discussion of a surprising line of argument against sensible qualities and substantial forms, which relies on an appeal to the senses.

4.1 Real Qualities and Substantial Forms in Scholasticism

In Aristotelian categorial theory the most fundamental distinction is the one between substance and accident. Intuitively, that is the distinction between things and, very loosely speaking, properties of things. Accidents are further subdivided into nine different species: quantity, quality, relation, place, time, position, condition, passion, action. For the Aristotelian scholastics, substances are composed of prime matter and substantial form. That is to say, corporeal substances are—which are the ones that will concern us. Spiritual ones, angels and God, don't contain any matter. In addition, a substance has various accidents. I will first discuss the notion of substantial form, then turn to real qualities.

The scholastic notion of substantial form is rich and complex, but I will focus on aspects and versions of this notion that are particularly relevant to Descartes. One very important role for the notion of substantial form derives from an analysis of substantial change that goes back to Aristotle. In substantial change, corporeal substances, such as living things, come into and go out of existence. By contrast, in a case of merely accidental change, such as a human being acquiring a tan, a substance continues to exist while its accidents change. The notion of substantial form is essential in the analysis of the generation and corruption of substances: these processes consist in the union and separation of matter and substantial form.[3]

Descartes never refers to this role of the notion of substantial form. Instead, he says that such forms: "were introduced by philosophers for no other reason than to account for [*ratio reddi*] the actions proper to natural things, of which this form is the principle and root" (AT III 506/ CSM III 208). He ascribes to the scholastics the view that these actions were supposed to proceed from such forms, and indeed, this view was quite prominent in late scholasticism, as is illustrated by this passage from the Coimbra Commentary on Aristotle's *Physics:*

> Singular natural things have certain proper and peculiar functions, for instance human beings reason, horses neigh, fire heats, etc; but such functions cannot arise from matter, which, as we have shown above, has no effective power; therefore they arise from the substantial form. And it is not sufficient to say that they arise from matter supplied with accidents. For, I ask, why are these accidents rather than other ones found in this matter; why does heat rather than cold belong to fire? (*Physics* 1.9.9.2, pp. 179–180)

So the substantial form determines what proper accidents a substance has, that is to say, those accidents that are characteristic of a particular kind of substance.[4]

Suárez gives a number of arguments for substantial forms. These include the argument from substantial change, but also several that are very close to the argument quoted from the Coimbra Commentators. One of these arguments begins with the idea that the human being has a substantial form and then infers the need for substantial forms in other composite substances as well:

> From the same composition of the human being it is gathered that the aggregation of a number of faculties and accidental forms in a simple substantial subject is not sufficient to constitute a natural thing. For in a human being there are such faculties and accidental forms, and perhaps

> in greater number and more perfect than in other natural things. Yet they do not suffice to constitute some complete natural being, and require in addition a form which, as it were, presides over [*praesit*] all those faculties and accidents, and is the source of all the actions and natural motions of such a being. In this form that whole variety of accidents and powers has its root and a kind of unity; so for the same reason it is necessary that in other natural things there is some substantial form distinct from accidents, which is also more intimate and more perfect than they are. (DM XV.I.7)

Here the idea is not just that the substantial form determines what accidents a substance has, but also that this form *unifies* them.[5] Suárez adduces several other arguments, which all concern an account of what accidents a substance has and how these accidents behave. This type of argument for substantial forms, he writes, is taken from "various indications that spring from the accidents and operations of natural things, which indicate that there is a substantial form that underlies them [*latere sub*]." One such indication he explains by means of the example of water. After water has been heated and the source of heat has been removed, it returns to being cold. He argues that water must have a substantial form to explain this tendency to revert to cold instead of retaining the temperature it had acquired.[6]

Substantial forms were classified under the category of substance, although they were regarded as incomplete substances. On the scholastic view they could not be accidents: rather, as we just saw, accidents presuppose a substantial form. The scholastics did also refer to accidental forms, but those are fundamentally different.[7] One crucial difference is that a substantial form is a component of a substance. With matter, another incomplete substance, such a form (or, as some thought, several such forms) constitutes a genuine individual, a substance. An accident, on the other hand, belongs to a substance, but it is not a constituent of it, and it cannot be combined with anything else to make a substance. The combination of a substance with an accident is not a genuine individual; it is not, as the scholastics said, an *ens per se,* but an *ens per accidens.*[8]

Let us now turn to real qualities. Descartes mostly used the broad term 'real accident', and he means to reject that entire category. But in fact his treatment of this issue was specifically concerned with qualities, which are just one type of accident, and I will confine my discussion accordingly. Now Descartes uses the terms 'real quality' and 'real accident' in a sense that did not seem to be at all common among the scholastics.[9] But it is quite clear what he had in mind: he was concerned with the view that various kinds of accidents are *res,* things—as the scholastics themselves put it. There was much discussion among the scholastics about the ontological status of accidents, and the issue was not always understood in the same way, since it was embedded in theories of distinctions, which varied with different thinkers. In relation to Descartes's discussion the most relevant thinker is Suárez, as they both saw the issue in the same way.[10]

The question for these two thinkers was whether certain qualities are *res* or modes. The relevant notion of a mode was a late scholastic creature. Suárez was its most systematic expositor, and, perhaps, the progenitor of the notion relevant to Descartes. He distinguishes modes from "things, [*res*], or forms having proper entity from themselves—[*formae habentes ex se proprias entitates*]."[11] He explains the notion of mode as follows: "there are in created entities certain modes affecting them, whose nature [*ratio*] seems to consist in this that they do not suffice by themselves to constitute a being or entity in the nature of things, but they intrinsically require some entity that they affect, without which they can *in no way* exist" (DM VII.I.18; emphasis mine). And he writes that: "[modes] do not from their proper concept have sufficient entity in which they are conserved, but they are conserved only by way of a kind of identity with those things in which they inhere; therefore whatever is separable in the aforesaid manner, even by [God's] absolute power, is not a mode, but a distinct thing [*res*]" (DM VII.II.10). So modes cannot in any way be separated from their subject of inherence, not even by God's power. They do not have sufficient 'entity', and they are not really distinct from their subject of inherence. In this respect they differ from *res.* If an accident is a *res,* it is really distinct from its subject and can be separated from it. It is crucial in this context that for Suárez, as for other scholastics, the term *res* is a technical term, and that modes are not *res* in this sense. Descartes sometimes uses the term in this sense too. On other occasions, however, he calls both substances and their modes *res.*[12]

Suárez and Descartes agree that the question is whether qualities are modes or *res,* but they give different answers to this question. Suárez allows that some qualities are not modes, but *res.* Descartes held that there are just two types of entities in the world: substances and modes. Substances exist in their own right and can be separated from anything else; modes exist by belonging to substances and cannot be separated from them. On his view all qualities, indeed all accidents, are modes.

Among the scholastics the question what qualities or what accidents are *res* was subject to debate.[13] Qualities were classified into four species: (1) dispositions (*habitus* and *dispositiones*); (2) natural capacities and incapacities; (3) passions and passive qualities, which include sensible qualities; (4) shape and form, curvature, straightness, and so on.[14] For our purposes, qualities of the third and fourth kind are of most interest. They include sensible and mechanistic qualities and are at stake in Descartes's rejection of real qualities in favor of modes. According to one view, which can be found in Ockham, sensible qualities are *res,* but qualities of the fourth kind, and so mechanistic qualities, are not. Ockham rejected the view, held by others, that *all* qualities are *res.*[15] Suárez also thought that only some qualities are *res,* for instance, heat, but not others, such as shape, which is a mode of quantity.[16] I have not found Suárez give an exhaustive answer to the question what qualities he regards as *res* or modes, but the examples he cites suggest that, like Ockham, he thought qualities of the third kind are *res,* qualities of the fourth kind are not.[17]

The view that *no* qualities are *res* was rare and condemned in Paris in 1347, probably at least in part because this view was regarded as inconsistent with the doctrine of transubstantiation.[18] It is tempting to suppose that the scholastics were motivated to think that qualities are *res* solely in order to account for the miracle of the Eucharist. This issue was clearly important and a major obstacle to the rejection of real qualities. Transubstantiation was thought to require the reification of various kinds of qualities as well as the accident of quantity, on the ground that this miracle requires the separability of these entities. Thus Suárez writes that non-Christian philosophers *(philosophi gentili),* including Aristotle, held that the nature of accidents consists in actual inherence. But that view, he continues, is not open to Christian philosophers because the Eucharist requires their separability.[19] Consequently, the scholastics commonly defined accidents in terms of an *aptitude* to inhere.[20] Transubstantiation clearly posed problems for Descartes. Various of his correspondents asked how, on his view of qualities, the miracle of the Eucharist should be understood. Indeed, the perceived implications of his views for this miracle played a central role in the persecution of his views in France after his death and contributed significantly to his works being placed on the Index in 1663.[21]

But this should not obscure the fact that within scholasticism there were also considerations of a purely philosophical nature. This is suggested by the fact that the scholastics frequently regarded accidents not clearly relevant to the Eucharist as *res* as well. As I mentioned some thought that all accidents are *res*. Others were less ontologically generous. Ockham, for instance, thought that the question whether an accident is a *res* depends on considerations about the nature of change. He believed that all change is due either to some *res* being produced or ceasing to exist, or local motion, and that a quality is a *res* if it can not be produced by local motion. For this reason figure is not a *res*, heat is.[22]

For us it is not only important what items the scholastics themselves classified among qualities that are *res*, but also what Descartes thought they included in this category. He never provides a comprehensive answer to this question, but he clearly thought sensible qualities were included. They are prominent in the discussions of the Eucharist, and in a letter to Elizabeth he mentions heat—an example that is used also by Suárez and by Ockham (AT III 667/ CSM III 219).[23] In fact, sometimes he seems to think that all real qualities are sensible ones, although the example he discusses most frequently is heaviness. But the scholastics did not include heaviness among sensible qualities; it was not regarded as one of the qualities that produce species and thus sensation in us.[24] Descartes himself, however, did at least sometimes present heaviness as a sensible quality, as in the Fourth Replies, where he cites color, flavor, and heaviness as examples of qualities that move the senses (AT VII 254/ CSM II 177; see also *Principles* IV.191). He there cites sense perception as the only source of belief in real qualities. But it is perhaps rather a function of the context that he does so on this occasion, since he is focusing on the explanation of sense perceptions in relation to the Eucharist. And the reason why real qualities were crucial in regard to the Eucharist is that the transubstantiated bread and wine continue to affect our senses in the same way despite the presumed change in substance.

I am inclined to think that Descartes is simply not being careful when he gives the impression that he thinks heaviness is a sensible quality.[25] More importantly, in his analysis of heaviness he treats it quite differently from sensible qualities, as we shall see later in this chapter. For he thinks that the commonsense view that sensible qualities exist in the physical world wrongly projects sensations onto body.

But the naive notion of heaviness, on his view, involves a projection of a different idea of the mind onto the physical world, our idea of the action of the soul on the body.

What does Descartes regard as the source of the belief in real qualities? In the Sixth Replies he writes: "No one has ever thought that they exist, unless because he believed he sensed them." *(Quis autem unquam existimavit illa esse, nisi quia putavit sentiri.)* But a little later in the text, he gives a more theoretical explanation, which sounds rather different: "the principal reason that has moved philosophers to posit real accidents has been that they thought that without them sense perception cannot be explained" (AT VII 434–435/ CSM II 293).[26] Here the connection between real qualities and transubstantiation is again in the background. Descartes is responding to questions prompted by his contention that the sense perceptions of the Eucharist pose no problem for his theory, because they can be explained in terms of the surfaces of bodies, which are merely modes.

In fact, on Descartes's view the notion of real qualities derives from a combination of two sources. For he regards this notion as a philosophical conception of types of qualities that are also admitted by common sense. He does not clearly spell out the relationship between the philosophical sources and common sense, but it is easy to see what he has in mind. As we saw in chapter 3.1, *Principles* I.71 describes our belief in the existence of sensible qualities as a prejudice from childhood. And in the Sixth Replies he presents heaviness as an example of a confusion that results from childhood (AT VII 441–442/ CSM II 297). But his view must be that the idea that they are *res* is due to philosophers. After all, it is hard to imagine that he regarded the belief in their separability as commonsensical, and in fact, their status as *res* had been defended on philosophical grounds.

Indeed, in the Fourth Replies Descartes expresses the view that philosophical activity resulted in this aspect of the notion. There he addresses the question of whether transubstantiation motivated belief in real qualities and suggests that the source of this belief lies in philosophy rather than religion. He makes a point of denying that the teachings of the Church require this notion or even that it was, in the first instance, motivated by transubstantiation:

> In so far as I know at least, the Church has never taught anywhere that the species of the bread and wine remaining in the Sacrament of the

> Eucharist are certain real accidents, which miraculously subsist alone when the substance in which they inhered is removed. It may be, however, that the first theologians who attempted to explain this question in philosophical fashion were so firmly convinced that the accidents that stimulate our senses were something really distinct from substance that they did not notice that there could ever be any doubt on this matter, and they supposed without any examination and without just reasoning that the species of the bread are such real accidents. And subsequently they applied themselves to explain how they could be without a subject. (AT VII 252–253/ CSM II 175–176)

So as Descartes sees it, when theologians first tried to provide a philosophical explanation of transubstantiation, they already thought of sensible qualities as *res,* entities really distinct from substances, and they immediately assumed that the species of the bread in the Eucharist are real accidents.

Given Descartes's polemical purposes, however, we may want to be cautious in regarding this statement as entirely sincere. He clearly had a stake in convincing his readers that theological issues, in particular transubstantiation, do not require belief in real qualities, and this interest is likely to influence his claims about the motivation of the supporters of real qualities. As Suárez' comments about the difference between Christian and non-Christian philosophers make clear, he for one would certainly deny Descartes's suggestion that the miracle of the Eucharist does not require real accidents. Nevertheless, as we saw, the scholastic commitment to these entities was also based on other considerations.

Descartes's rejection of real qualities is complex because it involves not only the question whether a quality can be a *res,* but also the issue of sensible qualities. Both problems are brought out clearly by Arnauld, who is also quite clear about the theological difficulties raised by Descartes's dismissal of real qualities:

> What I see as likely to be most offensive to theologians is that according to the author's doctrines it seems that the Church's teaching concerning the sacred mysteries of the Eucharist cannot remain completely intact. For we believe on faith that when the substance of the bread is taken away from the bread of the Eucharist, only the accidents remain. These are extension, shape, color, smell, taste and other sensible qualities. The author thinks, however, that there are no sensible qualities, but merely various motions in the bodies that surround us by which we perceive the various impressions which we then call 'color', 'taste' and 'smell'. Hence

> only shape, extension and mobility remain. But the author denies that these faculties can be understood without some substance in which they inhere, and hence he denies that they can exist without such a substance. (AT VII 217/ CSM II 152–153)

First Arnauld recognizes that Descartes rejects the idea that bodies have sensible qualities as they appear to us, even without referring to the question whether they would be *res* or modes. He also sees clearly that in addition for Descartes no qualities are separable from their subjects, and that they are all modes. So the qualities he does accept, mechanistic ones, are modes.

Since most real qualities are also sensible qualities, Descartes's arguments against the latter also count against the former, but the dismissal of the idea that *any* accidents are *res* is an additional contention, which I will address specifically in this chapter. Furthermore, I will devote particular attention to the quality of heaviness. It deserves special treatment because it is the real quality Descartes discusses most, and it is different in interesting ways from sensible qualities.

4.2 Descartes's Strategy

Descartes's contemporaries were well aware of the importance of the rejection of substantial forms and real qualities to his mechanistic program, and his writings as a whole leave no doubt about his position on these entities. Nevertheless, in his major works he hardly ever even mentions substantial forms and real qualities, let alone reject them outright. This may seem surprising. But there are two reasons that provide a straightforward explanation.

First, the stiff opposition to the rejection of real qualities by contemporary Aristotelians gave Descartes ample reason to be evasive about his criticism of these entities, especially given that concerns with transubstantiation infused a religious element into this opposition. His rejection of substantial forms also gave rise to religious objections quite early on, which first emerged in disputes about Cartesianism in The Netherlands. The most famous of these erupted in the early 1640s at the University at Utrecht and pitted Descartes and his disciple Regius, a professor of medicine, against Voetius, who taught theology and became rector of the University. Voetius charged that the elimination of substantial forms undermines the immortality of the human soul. The problem was not local to Utrecht, however, because the

Lateran Council had commanded that one hold that the human soul is the substantial form of the body.[27]

The second, connected reason why Descartes does not argue much against real qualities and substantial forms stems from his main strategy of substituting his own view for Aristotelian scholasticism. On January 28, 1641, he writes to Mersenne: "I will tell you, between you and me, that these six Meditations contain all the foundations of my Physics. But please do not say so; for those who favor Aristotle would perhaps cause more trouble for their approval. And I hope that those who read them, will get used to my principles without noticing and recognize their truth before realizing that they destroy those of Aristotle" (AT III 297–298/ CSM III 173). So Descartes saw the *Meditations* as contributing to the abolition of Aristotelianism. But in this letter to Mersenne he makes quite clear that the method employed is indirect and covert, and indeed, he does not take on real qualities and substantial forms explicitly in the *Meditations.* He never mentions substantial forms at all. He does talk about qualities in the Third and Sixth Meditations, but does not focus on the question of regarding them as *res* versus modes (see chapter 3.2). There is a hint at his rejection of real qualities in the argument for dualism in the Sixth Meditation, when he claims that it makes no difference by what power mind and body are separated; separability entails that there are two different things (AT VII 78/ CSM II 54). The implication is clearly that separability entails that there are two different substances, and so, that there are no real qualities. But his strategy primarily consists in developing his own system, which does without substantial forms and real qualities. The *Meditations* is just an example of this pattern, which he also follows in his earlier writings.

Descartes did, at one point, intend to write a work in which he would discuss Aristotelianism explicitly and extensively. He expresses this intention in a letter to Mersenne of November 11, 1640, when envisioning writing the *Principles.* He says he plans to write a philosophy textbook, and adds "in the same book I will have an ordinary course of philosophy printed, such as perhaps the one by Father Eustachius, with my notes at the end of each question, where I will add the different opinions of the others, and what one should think of them all. And perhaps at the end I will draw a comparison between the two philosophies" (AT III 233/ CSM III 157). But Descartes did not entertain this idea for long. He again refers to this plan in December 1640 and January 1641 (AT III 259–260/ CSM III 161 and AT III 286), but he wrote to Mersenne on December 22, 1641, that he did not find it necessary to refute the Aristotelians because he expected that the establishment of his own system would be enough (AT III 470). And indeed, again in the *Principles* he does not discuss substantial forms and real qualities at any length, although views expressed in that work certainly count against them. This is specifically so for his claim that real distinction properly only obtains between substances (*Principles* I.60), which implies a rejection of real qualities. But he speaks of real qualities and substantial forms only at *Principles* IV.198.

Descartes does, however, offer several arguments against these entities. He is cautious in his major writings and does not offer them spontaneously. But in response to questions from his interlocutors, in letters as well as in the Replies to the Objections, he is more forthcoming.[28] Two sorts of arguments in particular appear on a number of occasions. Roughly speaking, the idea of the first type of argument is that our conceptions of these entities are problematic. I will call it the Conceptual Argument. The second type of argument I will refer to as the Argument from Explanatory Power, of which we have already had a glimpse. It exploits Descartes's claim that these entities are not necessary and in fact are useless for explanatory purposes. Both arguments are really clusters of considerations, which vary in subtle but sometimes significant ways. Most importantly, there are meaningful differences in the way in which Descartes applies them to real qualities and substantial forms, respectively, differences that reflect the conceptual and theoretical distinctions between these entities in scholastic thought.

4.3 The Argument from Explanatory Power

Descartes claims that he can provide explanations for natural phenomena without relying on real qualities and substantial forms, and that he relies on fewer types of entities than the Aristotelian one. This greater parsimony, he claims in the *Geometry,* is a virtue that should recommend his view to the reader: "in order to keep the peace with the philosophers, I do not at all wish to deny what they imagine in bodies in addition to what I have said about them, such as their substantial forms, their real qualities and the like. But it seems to me that my reasons are more deserving of approval as I make them depend on fewer things" (AT VI 239; see also *The World,* ch. 2, and AT II 199–200/ CSM III 107). But not only does his theory rely on fewer entities, it is also more fruitful. In fact, Descartes goes so far as to claim that real qualities and substantial forms have been *useless* for purposes of explanation. He contends in a letter to Voetius that "no one has ever gotten anything useful from prime matter, substantial forms, occult qualities and the like" (AT VIII-2 26/ CSM III 221). He goes further in a letter to Dinet, where he claims these entities are in fact harmful to students: "we have seen that those pitiful entities (namely substantial forms and real qualities) are simply useless, except for blinding the minds of students, and thrusting upon them some arrogant form of ignorance, instead of that learned form of ignorance that you recommend so strongly" (AT VII 592; see also AT III 500/ CSM III 207).

Now the fact that substantial forms and real qualities are useless for explanation is in principle compatible with their existence. This point may strike one as a weakness in the argument,[29] since surely Descartes is firmly convinced that there are no substantial forms (other than the human soul) or real qualities. But he is clearly aware of this feature of his strategy, and what is more, he sometimes makes it work in his own favor. For it constitutes a loophole that allows him to avoid the politically charged conclusion that substantial forms and real qualities do not exist. Thus when Descartes claims that he does not rely on these entities for explanations, he often simply leaves open the question whether they exist. On other occasions he claims that although he does not rely on these entities, he does not reject them. We saw that in the *Meteors* he points out that in order to keep the peace with the philosophers he does not deny substantial forms and real qualities, although he does not rely on them. He reiterates this stance in the Fourth Replies, and even goes so far as to say: "from the fact that I said that modes cannot be understood without any substance in which they inhere, it must not be inferred that I deny that they can be placed apart from it by the divine power, because I simply affirm and believe that God can bring about many things which we can not understand" (AT VII 249/ CSM II 173). This comment actually suggests that separable accidents cannot be ruled out as contradictory, contrary to what he argues elsewhere, as we shall see in section 4.4.1 below.[30] Next Descartes writes that if he speaks more frankly he will admit that our sense perceptions are produced simply by the surface of the object of perception, which is a mode. He proceeds to argue that even transubstantiation can be explained in terms of modes and does not require real accidents. It is, of course, difficult to escape the conclusion that Descartes does not believe in real accidents, and the Fourth Objections show that Arnauld had certainly made that inference. Still, although Descartes says he will be frank here, he again does not admit to rejecting real accidents.

In a letter to Regius of January 1642, however, Descartes is finally forthright about his view. For now he argues that the explanatory uselessness of real qualities and substantial forms automatically leads to their rejection. The reason is that philosophers had accepted the existence of these entities precisely because they thought they were necessary for explanation:

> I fully agree with the view of the learned Rector [Voetius] that those "harmless entities" called substantial forms and real qualities should not be rashly expelled from their ancient territory. Indeed, up to now we have certainly not rejected them absolutely; we merely claim that we do not need them in order to explain the causes of natural things. We think that our arguments are to be commended especially on the ground that they do not in any way depend on uncertain and obscure assumptions of this sort. Now in such matters, saying that one will not make use of these entities is almost the same as saying one will not accept them; for indeed, they are accepted by others for no other reason than that they are thought necessary to explain the causes of natural effects. So we will be ready enough to confess that we do reject them entirely. (AT III 500/ CSM III 207)

So Descartes does now admit that he rejects substantial forms and real qualities. But in the same letter he admonishes Regius for not following the procedure he himself had adopted in the *Meteors*—that is, the strategy of not relying on substantial forms and qualities without eliminating them explicitly. That strategy, he claims, would have avoided the hostile reactions from Regius' colleagues, whereas in fact "no one in your audience would have failed to reject them, when noticing that they were of no use" (AT III 492/ CSM III 205; see also AT III 506/ CSM III 208–209). So he thinks it is simply not necessary to dismiss these entities publicly in order to get their supporters to drop them. Once it becomes clear that they are useless for explanatory purposes, the justification for believing in them is completely undermined, and they will be abandoned. Explicit rejection in public is impolitic and unnecessary.[31] Nevertheless, it is worth pointing out that where real qualities are concerned Descartes's conceptual objections make quite clear that he rejects them. And he does voice these objections in the Replies, which were meant for publication. I will return to this issue at the beginning of section 4.4.2.

So it would seem that there is a nice fit between Descartes's need to be cautious about rejecting real qualities and substantial forms and his method for rejecting them. But where real qualities are concerned we have only addressed one of the two explanations of why they were accepted. Descartes also saw the belief in such qualities as rooted in our childhood prejudices. The presence of this source means it is hard to get rid of belief in these qualities, as such belief is a matter of well-entrenched habit. But in chapter 3 we saw that the skeptical arguments are important for dealing with that source: they serve as a way to wean us from our attachment to the senses and our long-held childhood beliefs.

It is clear, however, that the rejection of real qualities and substantial forms depends significantly on the virtues of Descartes's mechanistic explanations, which make these scholastic entities superfluous. In this very general way his treatment of both kinds of entities is the same. But we saw that in scholastic thought substantial forms and real qualities fulfilled different theoretical roles, and that Descartes was well aware of this. Consequently, there are interesting differences in the way in which he supplants them. Descartes believed that heaviness can be accounted for mechanistically, in terms of bits of matter in motion (AT VII 440/ CSM II 297 and *Principles* IV. 20–27), and the same goes for sense perception. With regard to substantial forms matters are somewhat more complex. In the letter to Regius of January 1642 he had written that substantial forms "were introduced by philosophers for no other reason than to account for [*ratio reddi*] the actions proper to natural things, of which this form is the principle and root." But these forms are useless for this purpose, he comments, "whereas by those essential forms which we explain, we give manifest and mathematical accounts [*rationes*] for natural actions, as is apparent about the general form of salt in my *Meteors*" (AT III 506/ CSM III 209; Descartes is referring to *Meteors,* AT VI 251–252). So substantial forms in entities other than human beings are supplanted by mechanistic qualities because the latter do explain natural phenomena, like the behavior of salt. This is a point about specific types of bodies and physical phenomena. But in another sense, the role of substantial forms in scholasticism is taken over by Descartes's notion of principal attribute. He described substantial form as the source or principle of the forms and activities characteristic of a substance. But on his own view principal attributes play this kind of role. As we saw in chapter 1, the principal attributes of extension and thought determine the kinds of modes found in bodies in general and in minds (*Principles* I.53). So at this more general level the principal attribute is the successor of substantial form. In fact, this point relates to one of the most fundamental differences between Descartes and the scholastics. For the latter thought there are many different kinds of substances in the world, each with its own nature and kind of substantial form. But for Descartes there are only two types of substances, minds and bodies, and their natures consist in the two kinds of principal attributes.

Now we can see another shift with respect to scholasticism. For Descartes also holds that the principal attribute of the mind, thought, determines what kinds of modes the mind has. That is striking from a scholastic perspective in a different way. For the scholastics thought the soul (which includes the mind) is itself a substantial form, which determines what activities are characteristic of the substance that is a human being. But we see now that for Descartes the mind *has* a principal attribute, something analogous to a substantial form in that it determines the mind's modes. Yet he does sometimes call the soul a substantial form. But the fact that the principal attribute is something analogous to such a form means that we must be careful in determining the content of Descartes's description of the mind as a substantial form. That question is the subject for chapter 5.

4.4 The Conceptual Argument

Often the Conceptual Argument occurs by itself, but on some occasions Descartes connects it to the Argument from Explanatory Power. Unsurprisingly, he criticizes explanations in terms of real qualities and substantial forms on the ground that they use entities we don't understand or explain the obscure through the more obscure (AT III 506, 507/ CSM III 208–209). The Conceptual Argument sometimes takes the form of the simple contention that we have no conception of the entities in question (AT II 367/ CSM III 122 and AT III 649/ CSM III 216). On other occasions, Descartes argues that our ideas of substantial forms and real qualities are confused, and he specifies two different sorts of confusion. First, he thinks that in ideas of both substantial forms and real qualities we mix ideas that pertain to the mental with ones that pertain to the physical. Thus he writes in the Sixth Replies that once he had distinguished the notion of the mind from the notions of body and corporeal motion he saw that "all the other ideas, of real qualities and substantial forms which I had before, had been put together and made up by me from [these notions]" (AT VII 443/ CSM II 298; see also AT III 420/ CSM III 188). Secondly, he contends that problems arise because the scholastics conceive of these entities as substances. In the case of real qualities this renders our ideas inconsistent. In the case of substantial forms Descartes's objection is different. He gives what I will call the Theological Argument. I will begin with real qualities, then turn to substantial forms.

4.4.1 The Conceptual Argument and Real Qualities

Descartes gives his most explicit analysis of an idea of a real quality as confused in a very interesting discussion of heaviness in the Sixth Replies:

> I conceived of heaviness as some real quality, which inheres in a solid body; I called it a *quality,* insofar as I referred it to bodies in which it inhered, but because I added that it is *real,* I really thought that it was a substance: in the same way clothing, considered in itself, is a substance, although when it is referred to a clothed man, it is a quality. And the mind also, even though it really is a substance, can yet be called a quality of the body to which it is joined. Although I imagined heaviness to be spread through the entire body which is heavy, I did not, however, attribute the same extension to it which constitutes the nature of body. For the real extension of body is such that it excludes any penetrability of parts; but I thought that there is the same amount of heaviness in a mass of gold or some other metal of one foot as in a piece of wood of ten feet; and so I thought that it can all be contracted to one mathematical point. I also saw that while heaviness remains extended throughout the heavy body, it could exercise its whole force in any part of it; for if the body were hung from a rope attached to any of its parts, it would pull the rope down with all its heaviness, just as if this heaviness was only in the part touching the rope instead of also being spread through the other parts. This is exactly the way in which I now understand the mind to be coextensive with the body: whole in the whole, and whole in any of its parts. But what makes it especially clear that my idea of heaviness was taken partly from the idea I had of the mind is the fact that I thought it carried bodies towards the center of the earth, as if it had some cognition of it

> within itself. For this surely could not happen without knowledge, and there can be no knowledge except in a mind. Nevertheless, I attributed to heaviness various other things which cannot be understood about the mind in the same way, for example, being divisible, measurable, and so on. (AT VII 441–442/ CSM II 297–298)

So Descartes's charge is that the notion of heaviness contains both corporeal and mentalistic elements. It contains something corporeal insofar as it depicts this quality as divisible and measurable.[32] On the other hand, it includes the mentalistic idea of knowledge, as well as the sense in which the mind, but not body, is extended—that is, whole in the whole body and whole in each part.

It is important to note that Descartes does not merely discuss the notion of heaviness in order to offer criticisms. In letters to Elizabeth and Arnauld he claims that this notion, in particular, the special sense of extension it includes, is in fact the one to turn to for thinking of the action of the mind on the body. The way in which heaviness is believed to move a body towards the earth, he proposes, derives from the idea that really represents the way in which the mind moves the body (AT III 667, 694/ CSM III 219, 228; AT V 222–223/ CSM III 358).[33] This positive use for the notion of heaviness is clearly the reason why it, among all real qualities, gets special attention.

In its details this analysis of heaviness as a confusion of the mental and the physical is clearly specific to heaviness and does not generalize to other real qualities. It contains an interesting mixture of common sense and scholastic elements. Descartes presents the idea of heaviness as one we develop during our childhood, and what he says does indeed reflect aspects of our ordinary notion of heaviness—even if one may quarrel with the adequacy of the analysis. But his use of the expression "whole in the whole and whole in the parts" is clearly a reference to scholasticism. In relation to the scholastics the analysis is rather peculiar.

In the first place, insofar as I know, they did not use the idea of being whole in the whole, whole in the parts to analyze heaviness, whereas they did use it to refer to the union of the human soul to body. Now Descartes also proposes that the notion applies to the union of mind on body, and that it is a misapplication of a notion that we are supposed to apply to this union. But now it would seem that, insofar as his analysis of this notion of extension is meant to address the scholastics, it entirely misses its target, since they did already use it for the union of mind, or rather soul, and body. And Descartes's position seems much more like the scholastic one than he seems to recognize. There is truth in this assessment, and this is a point where he did not seem to be nearly careful enough in his discussion of a scholastic notion. But, in fact, matters are more complicated.

First, Descartes could respond that this objection does not imply that his analysis is entirely inappropriate. For he could say that the scholastic notion of heaviness also incorporates this notion of extension insofar as their notion of heaviness derives from a childhood projection of this special sense of extension onto body. He might go on to argue that the notion of being whole in the whole and whole in the parts is just a philosophical version of that sense of extension. Second, and most interestingly, Descartes and the scholastics used this notion for entirely different aspects of the soul-body union. Descartes used it to explain union insofar as it concerns action of mind on body, but the scholastics clearly did not do so: in fact, they seemed to think that precisely in this respect the soul can be said to be in only one part of the body rather than whole in the whole and whole in the parts.[34]

So the relationship of Descartes's analysis of heaviness to scholastic thought is very complex. It is particularly noteworthy that despite superficial similarities he uses the idea of the mind being whole in the whole and whole in the parts quite differently. His use of that idea merits further discussion in view of his account of the action of mind on body. I will briefly return to it in chapters 5.5 and 6.1, but the topic of mind-body interaction I will mostly leave for another occasion.

We have seen in what sense Descartes claims that our notion of heaviness is a confusion of the mental and the physical. But how about other real qualities? He does not specifically answer this question when focusing on the notion of a real quality, but his general treatment of sensible qualities fills the gap. For he claims that such qualities as they appear to us are mere sensations, which we project onto bodies (AT VII 440/ CSM II 297). Thus our conceptions of heat and heaviness have their source in ideas of different aspects of the mind. But it is striking that for Descartes ideas that pertain to mind-body interaction are such prominent sources for confused ideas of real qualities.

Descartes's other conceptual objection to the notion of a real quality is that it amounts to conceiving of qualities as substances. Even though he usually formulates it in relation to heaviness, this objection clearly applies to all such qualities. It is directed at the scholastic view that some or all qualities are *res* and separable by God from a substance they inhere in. Descartes writes to Elizabeth that conceiving of qualities as real means thinking of them "as having an existence distinct from that of body, and consequently as substances, although we called them qualities" (AT III 667/ CSM III 219). But mostly he explains this notion of reality by claiming that their presumed separability entails substancehood (AT V 223/ CSM III 358 and AT VII 253–254, 434–435/ CSM II 176, 293).[35]

The charge that conceiving of qualities as real amounts to regarding them as substances is a very serious objection, since, on the Aristotelian scheme, no entity is both a quality—or any other kind of accident—and a substance. They are mutually exclusive categories. Indeed, Descartes explains very clearly in the Sixth Replies that the notion of such qualities is inconsistent:

> It is entirely contradictory that there should be real accidents, because whatever is real, can exist separately from any other subject; but whatever can exist so separately, is a substance, not an accident. It makes no difference to say that real accidents cannot be separated from their subjects naturally, but only by the divine power. For it is nothing else for something to happen naturally, than to come about by God's ordinary power, which differs in no way from his extraordinary power, and which posits nothing different in things. Therefore just as anything that can exist without a subject naturally is a substance, whatever can be without a subject through some extraordinary power of God, must be called a substance. (AT VII 434–435/ CSM II 293; see also AT VII 253–254/ CSM II 176)

Descartes addresses the notion of real quality again a little later in the Sixth Replies in a passage that I quoted at the beginning of this section. What he says there might seem to contradict his charge that the notion of a real quality is inconsistent, and it seems to have confused some interpreters.[36] For in this later passage he claims that something can be both a substance and a quality, and he invokes an analogy with clothing, which can be thought of as a substance as well as a quality. But, in fact, Descartes does not contradict himself. For he continues the passage just quoted with a perfectly lucid explanation of the analogy with clothing: "I do admit that one substance can pertain to [*accidere*] another substance; yet when this happens, it is not the substance itself that has the form of an accident, but only the mode in which it pertains to *(accidit)* the other substance does. Just as when clothing pertains to *(accidit)* a man, it is not the clothing itself, but the being clothed that is an accident *(est accidens)*" (AT VII 435/ CSM II 293; see also AT VIII-2 351/ CSM I 299).[37] So Descartes does not admit the possibility of something being both a substance and a quality: he does believe that a substance *belonging to something else* can be a quality.

From a scholastic point of view, Descartes's charge that the notion of a real quality constitutes a confusion of qualities and substances is certainly a very serious objection, and it strikes me as philosophically pretty devastating: the idea of a separable quality does indeed seem incoherent. It is also interesting to note that although Descartes was much concerned to overthrow Aristotelianism, in this regard he is much closer to Aristotle's position than the scholastics were. As we saw, Suárez pointed out that for Aristotle accidents could not exist without belonging to something. Only substances can. But this is simply one issue among others in which there is a considerable difference between Aristotle and the scholastic Aristotelians.

The scholastic background suggests a very interesting question about Descartes's view of the full import of this objection to real qualities. For, as I explained in section 4.1, at least some scholastics regarded sensible qualities but not mechanistic ones as *res*. Ockham argued that qualities that don't change as a result of local motion must be *res*. Given this background, Descartes may have thought that if sensible qualities exist in the physical world, they are *res* and not modes. In that case, he may have believed that the incoherence of qualities being *res* entails by itself that there are no sensible qualities in the physical world. Indeed, I find it extremely likely that he did or would have accepted this line of argument. But he does not seem to want to rely on it to convince his readers to eliminate sensible qualities. Some texts are sufficiently unclear so as to leave open the possibility that this line of thought should be used to supplement what he says, in particular when he calls ideas of sensible qualities obscure and confused. But it is significant that in the Third Meditation he offers a different argument instead and focuses on the problems for determining whether hot and cold are real qualities or privations. That question has nothing to do with the distinction between *res* and modes.

Finally, before turning to substantial forms, it is worth paying attention to one accident that underwent an entirely different fate at Descartes's hands. This is the accident of extension, which the scholastics often referred to as continuous quantity, and which in fact had special importance in light of the explanation of transubstantiation.[38] Descartes does not eliminate the accident of quantity in any sense: on the contrary, he makes it the principal attribute of body. Furthermore, unlike in the case of real qualities, given the choice between mode and *res,* in effect he opts for *res*. For, as I discussed in chapter 1.5, Descartes tends to identify substances with their principal attributes. Insofar as he does so, extension turns out to be identical with corporeal substance.

4.4.2 The Conceptual Argument and Substantial Forms

It is common to assume that Descartes rejects the notion of substantial form entirely. But as I will discuss at length in chapter 5.3, in the letter to Regius of January 1642 he writes that the human mind is "a real substantial form" and that it is "the only substantial form" (AT III 503, 505/ CSM III 207–208). Now when Descartes calls the soul a substantial form in this letter, he is engaged in instructing Regius about how to respond to his enemies, and so one might discount this letter as not necessarily evidence of what he really believed. But it is important to note that he never argues that the notion of substantial form is inherently contradictory. This is an interesting difference from his treatment of real accidents, not only philosophically but also politically. For the Lateran Council had demanded in so many words that one hold that the rational soul is a substantial form, whereas the formulations of the Church concerning transubstantiation had left open the possibility of denying real qualities. As we saw, in the Fourth Replies Descartes made use of this possibility to deny that the Church demanded belief in real qualities.

Elsewhere in this letter to Regius Descartes specifies the sense in which he does reject substantial forms: "To prevent any terminological ambiguity, it must be noted here that when we deny that there are substantial forms, we understand by the term some substance joined to matter and composing some merely corporeal whole with it, and which, not less or even more than matter, is a real substance, or thing subsisting *per se,* since it is said to be act, matter mere potency" (AT III 502/ CSM III 207). So he objects to the possibility of a substantial form that is a substance that, when combined with matter, constitutes *a merely corporeal whole*. It is not surprising that Descartes raises this objection, given that he calls the human soul the only such form, and that he regards it as an *in*corporeal substance. Clearly, on his view the combination of matter and substantial form constitutes a composite that is not merely corporeal. On other occasions he describes the notion of substantial form as a confusion of the notions of soul and body. Now in the case of real qualities we have seen in what sense Descartes regards them as confusions of mentalistic and corporeal elements. But the situation is less straightforward for the notion of substantial form. Whereas he made quite explicit why heaviness is such a confusion, he does not do the same for such substantial forms.

How apt is Descartes's criticism of substantial forms? From a scholastic point of view his objection to regarding composites of matter and substantial form as merely corporeal wholes is on target to the extent that the scholastics did indeed regard most such composites as corporeal. According to them, since they ascribed such forms to all sublunary substances, the human soul is just one among many substantial forms. Thus this category includes human souls, animal souls, the souls of plants, as well as the forms of inanimate substances—mixed substances, such as wood or bronze, and the elements, fire, air, water, and earth.[39] But the scholastics generally regarded only the human soul as spiritual or incorporeal, and they did so on account of its ability to exist without matter, which they often defended on the basis of its intellectual capacity. And they regarded the human soul as a mental substance insofar as they either regarded it as consisting in the mind or considered the mind to be a part of the soul, as we shall see in chapter 5.1 below. As we shall see in the next section, other substantial forms they called 'material', because they could not exist without matter without divine intervention. So there is a sense in which most hylomorphic substances are indeed corporeal wholes for the scholastics.

Matters are complicated, however, by the fact that the division between the corporeal and the incorporeal in scholastic thought is simply not the same as for Descartes. Indeed this is what much of their most interesting differences with Descartes are about, including those concerning qualities and substantial forms. The scholastics did not have the clean form of dualism he adopted, nor did the category of the incorporeal simply coincide with the mental. Thus Aquinas argued that substantial forms that are part of composite substances have degrees of immateriality. The lowest degree is that of the forms of the elements, the highest degree belongs to the human soul:

> the nobler a form is, the more it dominates corporeal matter, the less it is immersed in it, and the more its operation or power exceeds it. Hence we see that the form of a mixed body has some operation which is not caused by the qualities of the elements. And the nobler the form, the more one finds that its power exceeds elemental matter, so that the vegetative soul does so more than the form of a metal, and the sensitive soul more than the vegetative soul. The human soul, however, is the most noble among forms. Hence its power exceeds corporeal matter so much that it has some operation and power in which corporeal matter in no way participates. And this power is called the intellect. (ST I.76.1; see also SCG II.68)[40]

Be that as it may, clearly the appropriate viewpoint from which to evaluate Descartes's claim of confusion of the corporeal with the incorporeal and the mental is not the scholastic one. He clearly meant to make his charge in terms of his own view of how those categories are distinguished. For he claims that he sees that the notions of real qualities and substantial forms are confused in this way, once he has recognized the distinction between the notions of body and soul, a recognition that he thought was precisely absent in scholasticism (letter to Arnauld of July 29, 1648, AT V 222–223/ CSM III 358).

One might expect Descartes to provide an explanation of this charge when he calls the soul a substantial form. But as we shall see, whereas he does explicitly connect the status of the soul as substantial form with its being a *substance,* he does not say what about its *mental* nature qualifies it as a substantial form. In other words, he does not make clear in what sense substantial forms are necessarily mental—contrary to the scholastic view that the intellectual soul is just one type of substantial form. Scholars have sometimes seen the answer to this question in Descartes's analysis of heaviness.[41] But this approach relies, of course, on a failure to distinguish between real qualities and substantial forms. For the moment, Descartes's charge that the notion is a confusion of the mental with the physical will have to remain unexplained. I will, however, return to it at the end of the next section.

4.4.3 The Theological Argument

In Descartes's view, both real qualities and substantial forms are conceived of as substances. In the case of the notion of real qualities he infers that the notion is incoherent, but for substantial forms he argues that inconsistency arises in a more indirect way. In the letter to Regius of January 1642 he formulates what he calls a Theological Argument and claims it is the *main* argument against substantial forms.[42] This claim about the importance of the argument must, however, be approached with some caution given its context, the heated dispute at Utrecht. In particular, Descartes is responding to Voetius' charge that his view is theologically unacceptable because it threatens the immortality of the soul. In light of the seriousness of such objections, it is natural for Descartes to respond by emphasizing theological advantages of his rejection of substantial forms. So his contention that the Theological Argument is the main one can not be taken at face value, especially given that other considerations are more frequent in his writings.

The Theological Argument begins by raising the question how substantial forms come into existence:

> The physical reasons or demonstrations against substantial forms, which we think clearly compel the mind avid for truth, lie primarily in the following *a priori* metaphysical or theological consideration. For it is clearly contradictory that any substance come into existence from nothing [*de novo existat*], unless it is created from nothing [*de novo*] by God. We see daily, however, that many of those forms which are called substantial begin to exist from nothing, although those who believe that they are substances do not believe that they are created by God; therefore their view is deficient [*ergo male hoc putant*]. This is confirmed by the example of the soul, which is the real substantial form of the human being. For the soul is thought to be directly created by God for no other reason than that it is a substance. Furthermore, since other substantial forms are not regarded as created in the same way, but as only educed from matter, they must also not be regarded as substances. From this it is clear that not those who deny substantial forms, but rather those who affirm them "can be driven by solid reasoning to become beasts or atheists." (AT III 505/ CSM III 208)

Descartes claims that in scholasticism substantial forms are conceived of as substances, and substances, he contends, can only come into existence by creation. But the scholastics are inconsistent, because on their view many forms they call substantial are not created. Furthermore, he charges that the scholastics actually accept the view that substances are created, because it explains their view that the human soul is created rather than educed from matter. Finally, he infers from the confusion about creation that a commitment to substantial forms can lead us to become beasts or atheists.

Descartes never uses this argument against real qualities. Insofar as he contends that real qualities are qualities conceived of as substances, he should be willing to apply it to them as well. Their coming into existence should, on his view, also require an act of divine creation, and the scholastics certainly did not think so. Now one reason why Descartes might not feel inclined to apply this objection to real qualities is that his contention that the notion of a real quality is contradictory in fact makes this objection superfluous. But more importantly, there are historical reasons why he would not use this argument against real qualities. For the Theological Argument refers to an existing discussion that specifically concerns the production of substantial forms, and that bears on the issue of the immortality of the human soul. Descartes refers to this issue in the last sentence of the argument, when he says that "not those who deny substantial forms, but rather those who affirm them can be driven by solid arguments to become beasts or atheists." This is a rather cryptic remark. What does it mean?

Descartes is taking the phrase from Voetius, to whom he is responding. Voetius had put forth a long list of dire consequences of a denial of substantial forms. One of these is that young people, led astray, "will be forced, through solid reasoning, to become beasts or atheists" (AT III 515). The list includes the rejection of the rational soul, because it is supposed to be a substantial form (AT III 488). In response, Descartes offers the Theological Argument; he claims that the rational soul is the *only* substantial form, and he charges that really Voetius' own view will lead one to become a beast or atheist.

Given that in the middle of the argument Descartes claims that the human soul is a substantial form, the commitment to such forms he rejects is clearly one that ascribes substantial forms not only to human beings, but also to other entities. The problem he sees is that this view makes it hard to distinguish between beasts and human beings in such a way as to maintain the immortality of the human soul. As a result, this view might lead one to become a beast (because humans turn out to be no different from beasts) or an atheist (because one ceases to believe in immortality). In this vein Descartes writes earlier in the same letter to Regius:

> from the opinion that affirms substantial forms it is very easy to slip into the opinion of those who say that the human soul is corporeal and mortal; when it is acknowledged that [the human soul] alone is a substantial form, and that the others consist of the configuration and mo-

> tion of parts, this very privileged status it has over the others shows that it differs from them in nature, and this difference in nature opens a very easy road to showing its immateriality and immortality, as can be seen in the recently published *Meditations on First Philosophy.* (AT III 503/ CSM III 207–208)

So on Descartes's view, the immortality of the human soul is more easily established if other substantial forms are denied.

We have seen this line of argument before: for it also occurs in the analysis of the difference between animals and human beings in the *Discourse,* which I discussed in chapter 2. There Descartes argues that only human beings have souls and that animals are just machines. Recognition of this radical difference generates support for the immortality of the human soul, he contends, because it abolishes the idea that human and animal souls are at all of the same nature. That idea is potentially problematic because it might make one imagine that "we have nothing to fear or hope after this life, nothing more than mosquitoes and ants. Whereas, when we know how much they differ, we understand much better the reasons that prove that our soul has a nature entirely independent from the body, and that, consequently, it is not subject to death with it. Furthermore, since we see no other causes that might destroy it, we are naturally brought to judge that it is immortal" (AT VI 59–60/ CSM I 141). The upshot of the discussion in the *Discourse* is that the human soul is the only soul there is. Similarly, in the letter to Regius Descartes claims that the human soul is the only substantial form.[43] The main point on both occasions is that recognition of the radically different nature of the human soul supports its immortality: it is the only soul or substantial form, none can be found in other parts of the physical world—which can be described entirely mechanistically. And so there is no risk of assimilating the human soul to entities that are not immortal.

In the *Discourse* Descartes focuses on the view found in Montaigne and Silhon that animals are not so different and that one cannot prove the immortality of the human soul. In the letter to Regius he is addressing the scholastic view that the human soul is not the only kind of substantial form. But most scholastics did in fact argue that the human soul is importantly different from other substantial forms and that it is the only one that is immortal. So Descartes must think we need to reject this position in order to save the immortality of the human soul. But why?

The answer to this question lies in scholastic views about how substantial forms come into being. In the Theological Argument Descartes focuses on this issue, and on the idea that the soul is created, that it is not "educed from matter." In the *Discourse* he also mentions this issue, and indeed, it was important for the scholastics in relation to the question of immortality. Now Descartes claims that the soul is regarded as created by God because it is a substance. This is in accord with his own view of substances, which he identifies with things created by God (AT VII 14/ CSM II 10). But the claim would have surprised the scholastics, who allow for complex substances—composites of matter and form—that are generated by natural processes.

The way to understand Descartes's point, however, is to relate it to their treatment of substantial forms. The scholastics thought that the human soul is created by God, but that other such forms are educed from matter. It is not necessary to go into the details of this notion here, but the basic idea is that these forms come into existence by way of natural processes. This difference in their production was connected to a difference in their fate when the organism dies: whereas human souls were regarded as immortal, other substantial forms go out of existence when their substances cease to be. Thus the Coimbra Commentators wrote that the claim that the soul is not created is against the faith and that "those who assert it are convicted in public of denying the immortality of the soul."[44]

These views about the production of substantial forms were routinely expressed in scholastic writings. For instance, Suárez writes:

> The true and Peripatetic opinion is that among substantial forms some are spiritual and independent from matter, although they really inform it; others, however, are material and inhere in matter, so that they depend on it in being and coming-to-be—*esse et fieri.* Only human souls (for we deal here only with informing forms) are of the first kind, and about them the consequence inferred concerning the difficulty in question must be conceded, namely that they certainly come to be from nothing through real creation. (DM XV.II.10)[45]

He explains that the body does not contribute to bringing the soul into being, but merely provides an occasion for its creation. The reason is the soul's independence from matter: "It is clear that body or matter does not result of itself [*non influat per se*] in the coming-to-be or being of the soul. This is clear from the fact that the rational soul retains its being when separated from the body; therefore it does not depend on a sustaining subject in its being; therefore neither does it so depend in its coming-to-be; for the coming-to-be of a thing is like its being." The issue of the production of substantial forms involves an important distinction between two kinds of substantial forms: spiritual ones and material ones.[46] Only the human soul is a spiritual form and does not depend on matter for its existence. It survives the demise of the body and it is created—these features are aspects of its independence from matter. Suárez did think that other substantial forms can exist separately, but, unlike the human soul, they cannot do so naturally, only by God's power.[47]

At this point we are in a position to understand something important about the Theological Argument: for we can now see why for Descartes there is a connection between the question whether a substantial form is created and whether it is immortal. But we don't yet have an answer to the question why he thinks the view that there are substantial forms other than human souls is a threat to the immortality of the soul. Why couldn't Descartes accept Suárez' distinction between spiritual forms, which are created and immortal, and material forms, which are not?

Descartes himself does not tell us, but there is an obvious reason, which lies in his views about the connection between substance and separability. For on his view the ability to exist by itself, whether naturally or by God's power, is a sufficient indication for substancehood. As we saw in our discussion of real qualities, for Descartes the power by which an entity can exist apart is entirely irrelevant to its ontological status (AT VII 78, 170, 434–435/ CSM II 54, 120, 293). By this criterion substantial forms (and real accidents) as understood by the scholastics are substances. Now the scholastics generally did regard substantial forms as substances, albeit incomplete or partial ones. But the reason was not their separability, which was simply not regarded as sufficient for substancehood: many accidents were supposed to be separable. As we shall see in chapter 5.2, substantial forms were regarded as incomplete substances on account of the fact that by their nature they require combination with matter to constitute an entire substance. They fall under the category of substance reductively, not directly. Furthermore, unlike for Descartes, it was important for them in what sense an entity was separable. They thought the human soul is *naturally* separable, but all other substantial forms, as well as real accidents, can exist apart only by God's power. This difference with respect to power, we saw, is quite important in relation to the distinction between material and spiritual substantial forms. But Descartes's denial of the significance of this difference undermines the scholastic distinction between the human soul and other substantial forms. Consequently, for him all substantial forms are on a par, and so it should not surprise us that he accuses the scholastics of inconsistency in treating the human soul and other substantial forms differently with respect to creation.

Furthermore, there are clearly two ways of treating all substantial forms equally in regard to their coming-to-be, both of which Descartes addresses in the Theological Argument. On one hand, one could assimilate the human soul to other kinds of substantial forms: this would deprive it of its immortality. He warns against this approach when he writes that admitting substantial forms other than the human soul leads us to "become beasts or atheists." The other option is to assimilate all substantial forms to the human soul, and this is what he has in mind when he claims all substantial forms must be regarded as created on the basis of their status as substance. This possibility does not generate problems for the view that human souls are immortal, rather it would follow that the souls of animals are also immortal. But clearly, this consequence was also considered unacceptable.[48] So the assimilation of human souls to other substantial forms is problematic on either account, and we can see why Descartes saw his view, that the human soul is the only substantial form, as having theological advantages. As when he rejects souls of animals in the *Discourse,* he envisages that his view that everything except what pertains to the human soul can be explained mechanistically is a view that is particularly favorable to the immortality of the human soul.

It is clear how in this argument Descartes sees the notion of substance as a stumbling block for the scholastic position on substantial forms. But I think that in addition the argument can also provide us with a hypothesis about his view that the notion of a substantial form is a confusion of the notions of body and soul. I pointed out in the previous section that Descartes does not explain what mental features are included in the notion of substantial form. But he may have had the following in mind. We have seen now that for Suárez, as well as for other scholastics, all substantial forms are separable from matter, but for forms other than the human soul this requires God's power: they are not naturally separable. Since for Descartes this distinction has no force, these forms are all independent from matter in the same way. Thus whereas the scholastics called the human soul a spiritual form on account of its natural separability, Descartes might say that this label should be applied to all substantial forms. Furthermore, on his own view, in fact only the human soul is independent from matter in this sense. So as he saw it, these scholastics ascribed a feature to all substantial forms that really only belongs to the soul or mind. Consequently, what he may have in mind when he says that the notion of substantial form is a confusion of the notions of body and soul is the separability of substantial forms from matter. In addition, he may have thought that separability from body could only belong to such a form in virtue of an ability to think. And so the scholastics ascribe to substantial forms a feature that requires that they be minds. If this is right, then Descartes's view that the notion of substantial form is a confusion of the mental and the physical is intimately connected to his view that it is the notion of a full-fledged substance. But whether or not he actually did have this idea in mind it is not possible to say with certainty.

We have now seen how Descartes criticizes the scholastics' use of the notions of real qualities and substantial forms on the ground that they conceive of these entities as substances. Before closing this part of my discussion I wish to comment on the strength of this line of objection, because it has sometimes been misunderstood. Gilson argues that Descartes objects to a conception of real qualities and substantial forms that simply did not exist in scholasticism. For, he claims, "In Aristotelian scholasticism the form of a body, even a substantial one, is only an abstraction; it can be thought apart by the mind; but it cannot subsist apart, except in the unique case of the rational soul."[49] Gilson states his point in terms of substantial forms, but in fact he does not distinguish, at least not adequately, between real qualities and substantial forms. His discussion is a classic in the literature on Descartes's relationship to scholasticism, but as we have seen, he unjustly accuses Descartes of misrepresenting his target. Gilson is right insofar as Aquinas thought that among substantial forms only the human soul is separable, the other ones are abstractions. But his criticism does not take into account the fact that many other scholastics, and certainly the late scholastics, held that substantial forms generally, as well as real qualities, are separable—by God.

In a different sense, however, Descartes does impose his own views on the scholastics, since the latter did not admit that the ability to exist apart is sufficient for substancehood. But this imposition does not make his criticisms irrelevant. For his objection is really that, like it or not, separability implies that an entity is a substance, and that, consequently, the scholastics did in fact think of substantial forms and real qualities as substances. Descartes himself makes this point quite clearly about real qualities in a letter to Arnauld: "It does not matter that they say that this heaviness is not a substance; for when they claim that it is real and can exist without the stone by some power (namely, Divine power), they really conceive of it as a substance" (AT V 223/ CSM III 358).

4.5 Explanatory Power and Sense Perception

Descartes's writings are pervaded by his view that trust in the senses is an important source of error, for the Aristotelians as well as others. But interestingly enough, on some occasions he does also appeal to the senses, as well as the imagination, *in support* of his own mechanistic view. He sometimes adduces as an advantage of his own theory that it only relies on types of entities we already know exist *on the basis of sense experience.* This is a striking argument, given his usual criticisms of the senses.

An instance of this line of argument can be found in a letter to Morin of July 13, 1638. Descartes lists various reasons that count in favor of his mechanistic approach, including the claim that his own theory will be found to be more convincing than others "when the suppositions made by others—that is to say, all their real qualities, their substantial forms, their elements and the like, whose number is almost infinite—are compared to mine, that is, with this alone that all bodies are composed of parts, *which is something that one sees with one's eyes in many bodies,* and which one can prove with an infinite number of reasons to be true in other ones" (AT II 200/ CSM III 107; emphasis mine). The same line of thought can be found in *The World,* chapter 2:

> When fire burns wood or some other similar material, *we can see with our eyes* that it moves the small parts of this wood and separates them from one another, thus transforming the more subtle ones into fire, air

> and smoke and leaving the larger ones as ashes. Someone else may imagine, if he wants, in this wood the form of fire, the quality of heat, and the action that burns it as entirely different things; as for me, who fear making a mistake if I suppose there is anything more in it than what I see must necessarily be there, I am content to conceive in it the motions of parts. (AT XI 7/ CSM I 83; emphasis mine)

Descartes also cites the senses in support of his view in the *Principles,* when he argues that many natural phenomena should be explained in terms of the properties of subvisible particles. He begins with a deprecation of the senses: "I consider many particles in particular bodies that are not perceived by the senses; those who take their senses as the measure of what can be known do not, perhaps, approve of this approach." His point here is that particles that are too small to be sensed should not be dismissed on this account. But shortly afterwards he lines up the senses on *his* side, against his opponents:

> I do not think that those who use their reason will deny that it is much better to use the example of those things about which we perceive by the senses that they happen to large bodies to make judgements about what happens in very small corpuscles, which escape our senses only because they are small. They will not deny that this is much better than to explain these things by inventing [*excogitare*] some new unknown things which have no similarity with those things that are sensed. (*Principles* IV.201)

The French edition specifies that such unknown things include "prime matter, substantial forms and this great collection of qualities that many customarily suppose to exist, each one of which is more difficult to know than all the things that one proposes to explain by means of them." So on one hand, we would rely excessively on sense if we denied subvisible phenomena on the ground that we cannot perceive them with our senses. On the other hand, Descartes thinks his own theory is superior to alternative accounts that rely on real qualities and substantial forms because he only relies on types of entities we already know exist on the basis of the senses. All we need to do is expand our view of how many phenomena can be explained in terms of these kinds of things. We need not expand our ontology.

This argument is not one that Descartes appeals to explicitly on many occasions. But it is significant in that it does reflect an important aspect of his scientific practice, which contains numerous attempts, for instance, in *The World* and the *Principles,* to specify mechanisms that can account for particular natural phenomena. Frequently Descartes's approach is to assume observations of mechanistic phenomena by the senses, and then, in effect, to use his imagination to postulate subvisible ones.[50]

It is easy to see how this argument from sense perception has force against substantial forms. For they were not regarded as perceptible by the senses but functioned as theoretical entities introduced for explanatory purposes. The matter is more complicated for real qualities. On one hand, the conception of these qualities as *res* would seem to have its source in philosophy. But since the ones that interest Descartes are mostly reified sensible qualities, belief in them derives from the senses, as he himself agreed. So a scholastic could respond to Descartes's argument from sense perception by setting aside, at least for the moment, the claim that the qualities in question are *res*. He could reply that we do sense such qualities: we perceive by our senses that bodies are colored, hot, cold, and the like, just as much as we sense that they have mechanistic qualities. Thus this argument from the senses would seem to have no hold on the view that bodies do have these qualities. Next, the scholastic could go beyond the senses and argue on philosophical grounds that sensible qualities must be *res*. Descartes clearly does not accept that any qualities could be *res*, and so now he could adopt either of two choices. First, he could accept the argument and then contend that there cannot be any sensible qualities in the physical world—since they must be *res*. Second, if he does not accept the argument, he would have to establish on different grounds that there are no sensible qualities. But notice what happens: in either case at this point the discussion leaves behind the senses as the source for determining whether these qualities exist. The question whether these qualities are *res* or modes is not a matter of sense perception. Descartes's objection to the idea that they are *res*, and his claim that qualities must be modes, is based on the idea that the notion of quality that is a *res* amounts to thinking of a quality as both a substance and a quality, which is contradictory. Consequently, the argument from the senses does not by itself have any force against real qualities. Descartes may well have thought that it did because the view that a quality cannot be a *res* is quite commonsensical. But it does not follow that this view is based on the senses.

In addition, there are two different but related arguments in *The World* and the *Principles*. For Descartes is not just interested in what kinds of *entities* there are. Central to his commitment to mechanism is his stance on what *causal processes* can be found in the physical world. Indeed, in chapter 2 of *The World* Descartes's point is in part that we simply see mechanistic processes at work: we see that in the burning of the wood motion of particles produces the effects of fire. The passage suggests that the postulation of entities or processes over and above the mechanistic ones we witness is not necessary. The issue of causal processes is quite explicit again at *Principles* IV.198, but this time in a different way:

> We understand very well in what way the various local motions of one body are brought about [*excitentur*] by the different size, shape and motion of the particles of another body; but we can not at all understand in what way those very same things (namely size, shape and motion) can produce something else that is entirely different from them in nature, as are those substantial forms and real qualities, which many suppose to be in things; nor in what way those qualities or forms then have the power to bring about [*excitandi*] local motions in other bodies.[51]

Now Descartes claims that we *understand* causal interaction among mechanistic qualities. But he contends that we do not understand interaction between mechanistic qualities on one hand and real qualities and substantial forms on the other hand.

This last contention is certainly not without its difficulties, given the fact that the early modern period yielded considerable worries about the nature of most types of causation. In fact, Descartes's own view of causal interaction between bodies has generated much discussion. Many commentators have thought he did not think bodies have any real causal efficacy, and that he regarded them as entirely passive. Consequently, his claim that interaction between mechanistic qualities is intelligible is a rather problematic basis for an argument.[52] But more importantly, we have again left behind the senses: the claim that some types of causal interaction are more intelligible than others constitutes an appeal to the intellect. And this fact is in line with the earlier observation that in regard to real qualities an appeal to the senses by itself won't do.

It is not clear whether, where real qualities are concerned, Descartes himself thinks an appeal to the intellect is necessary to complete his argument from sense perception. Nevertheless, given his general tendency to deprecate the senses, it is very important to note that he does appeal to the senses in favor of mechanistic explanation, especially since this appeal corresponds to much of his scientific practice of postulating unobserved mechanistic processes by analogy with observed instances.

Conclusion

In his main published works Descartes avoids discussing real qualities and substantial forms, which was certainly a prudent strategy. But when prompted by his contemporaries, he does make it clear that he rejects these entities. This is not to say that the major works make no contribution to the rejection of these entities. In the previous chapter we saw that Descartes relies on skeptical arguments to force one to come up with arguments for clear and distinct perceptions of whatever entities one wishes to adopt. The skeptical arguments are no doubt particularly important as a tool for weaning us from our belief in sensible qualities. After all, as Descartes sees it, since it dates from our childhood, this belief is quite entrenched. But, clearly, the positive views he develops in the wake of the skeptical arguments omit not only sensible qualities, but also substantial forms and real qualities—and his contemporaries did notice. Also, he does not rely only on criticisms of scholastic views, but also very much on the virtues of his own position in his elimination of these entities. As he himself said, the development and presentation of his own, alternative system carries an important part, perhaps the most important part, of the weight in edging out Aristotelianism.

Furthermore, over the course of this chapter we have seen that there are significant differences between substantial forms and real qualities, both within scholasticism and in Descartes's treatment of these entities. Consequently, we must conclude that the common perception that he did not distinguish between these notions is unwarranted. The distinction between them will again be important in the next chapter, which concerns the question whether Descartes thought the union of body and soul should be understood in terms of the soul being the substantial form of the body.

Insofar as Descartes regarded the notions of real qualities and substantial forms as confusions of the corporeal and the mental, his rejection of these notions is an aspect of his dualism. In this chapter I have discussed some of the ways in which his view of the boundary between the corporeal and the spiritual was different from the scholastic view. But it is also worth noting that Descartes's effort to remove confusions of the mental and the physical primarily concerns the physical world: it essentially amounts to purging notions he regards as useless, undesirable, and mentalistic from the scholastic conception of *body.* He is willing to say that the human soul is a substantial form, but he insists that the physical world contains none. Furthermore, the real qualities he discusses are all examples of qualities that the scholastics ascribed to bodies. Descartes never discusses qualities of the mind, which were also regarded as *res* by at least some scholastics.[53] He charges that the notions of real qualities and substantial forms are confusions of the mental and the physical; but that complaint takes the form of saying that the scholastics postulate entities in the corporeal world that incorporate mentalistic elements.

Having completed the discussion of sensible qualities, real qualities, and substantial forms, we are now in a position to state the essentials of the transformation of the scholastic conception of corporeal substance into the Cartesian one. A scholastic corporeal substance has prime matter, at least one substantial form, the accident of quantity, and a variety of other accidents, in particular, qualities. At least some of these accidents are *res.* Descartes collapses matter and quantity into one thing: the corporeal substance. This result is accomplished by his elevation of the accident of quantity, or rather extension, to the status of principal attribute, and his rejection of the notion of prime matter.[54] Furthermore, in chapters 3 and 4 we saw how he argues that none of the qualities of body are *res,* and that they do not include sensible qualities. As a result, they only include mechanistic qualities, which are modes of extension. On the conception of body that emerges extension takes over an important function of the notion of substantial form. It constitutes the nature of body and determines what kinds of properties bodies have.

CHAPTER FIVE

Hylomorphism and the Unity of the Human Being

One of the most important questions for understanding Descartes's dualism concerns the union of mind and body. We tend to think of ourselves as single entities, genuine individuals that include both the mental and the physical. But it is difficult to see how on Descartes's conception of mind and body a composite of these two can constitute such a unified individual. Nevertheless, a number of his interpreters have claimed that he held that mind and body together constitute a genuine unity, in particular, a substance. For Descartes an important candidate for an answer to the question how mind and body do so is the possibility that he accepted the hylomorphic solution. That is, he may have followed the scholastic Aristotelians in regarding the human mind or soul as the substantial form of the body. After all, on various occasions Descartes says that the soul or mind is the form of the body or of the human being, or that the soul informs the body.

Nevertheless, at first sight the idea that he regarded the human soul as a substantial form of the body is very surprising: his dualism seems diametrically opposed to a hylomorphic account of the human being. Dualism presents mind and body as two distinct substances and raises the possibility that the human being is simply an aggregate, an entity that is no more unified than a heap of stones. On the other hand, on a hylomorphic conception of the human being, it is a single substance. Soul and body are interdependent in a very strong sense, as matter and form are on the Aristotelian scheme, and perhaps even mere abstractions. Consequently, commentators have often thought that Descartes's use of hylomorphic phrases holds no water. Gilson commented: "We don't forget Descartes's ability to pour new wine in old bottles."[1] Other interpreters, however, have taken his hylomorphic language seriously, such as Geneviève Rodis-Lewis, Paul Hoffman, and Marjorie Grene.[2] Hoffman in particular has argued in great detail for the hylomorphic interpretation of Descartes's conception of the union of mind and body.

I disagree with this interpretation, which I will address in this chapter. Now some readers might doubt the value of doing so, since the hylomorphic interpretation would appear to be a minority position, or at least this is clearly so in the English-speaking world. But there is much to be learned from an examination of its plausibility. Hoffman's analysis shows that there is more similarity between Descartes's dualism and at least some versions of scholastic hylomorphism than is often recognized. For this reason it is well worth comparing these positions in some depth, and doing so allows us to gain a much better understanding of the complex relationship between the notions of the soul and the human being found in the scholastics and those found in Descartes. This relationship is quite subtle in interesting ways and in some respects rather different than is often thought.

It is tempting to compare Descartes and the scholastics on the union of mind and body by focusing entirely on the question of the separability of mind and body. Comparison in regard to this issue constitutes an important component of Hoffman's discussion, and there is indeed considerable similarity with scholastic positions in this regard. But I will argue that there are important relevant questions that go beyond this similarity, and that Descartes's differences with the scholastics on these questions mean that he rejects views that for the scholastics are essential to the soul's status as a substantial form of the body. Nevertheless, Descartes himself might still have regarded hylomorphism as the solution to the problem of the union of mind and body. But I will argue that a close examination of his writings reveals that he does not. Furthermore, Descartes's rejection of hylomorphism as the solution for the problem of the union of mind and body leaves open the possibility that he holds that the human being is a substance. I will conclude, however, by contending that he does not. The question of the union of mind and body is also the subject of the next, and final chapter.

5.1 Problems for the Unity of the Human Being in Scholasticism

The Aristotelian scholastics regarded the soul as the form of the body and its actuality, and they used this conception of the soul to argue that the human being is a genuine unity and not a mere aggregate. I will not attempt to give a full account of the scholastic position, but focus on those aspects of it that bear on the question of the unity of the human being and that are particularly relevant to Descartes. The scholastics did not define the notion of unity at issue, but one can get an intuitive sense of what is at stake. They contrasted genuine unity, as is found in a substance, with the type of unity found in an aggregate, like a heap of stones, and with the unity of a substance with an accident.[3] The former is a genuine unity, in their terms, an *unum per se* and an *ens per se*. Each of the latter is an *unum per accidens* and *ens per accidens*. The question of what is a genuine unity—*unum*—and what is a genuine being—*ens*—are answered together, since, in Suárez' words, the scholastics held that *unum consequitur ens*—unity follows being.[4]

It will be important for our purposes that the scholastics already struggled with serious obstacles for the unity of the human being. These obstacles arose from two directions. In the first place, there were problems specific to the question of the unity of the human being as opposed to other hylomorphic substances, that is, other composites of matter and substantial form. As we saw before in chapters 2 and 4, the medieval Aristotelians generally held that the human soul is separable from the body and that it can exist after the demise of that body. They argued that the human, rational soul is an incorporeal, spiritual substance created by God, whereas other substantial forms are not created but educed from matter: they come into existence by way of natural processes. This difference in production corresponds to a difference in their fate when the organism dies: whereas human souls are immortal, other substantial forms go out of existence when substances of which they are constituents cease to be.

This conception of the human soul was clearly motivated by a commitment to Christianity and the immortality of the human soul. In addition, medieval scholastics often referred to passages in Aristotle's *De anima* where he seemed to allow that the rational soul, or perhaps just the intellect, is separable from the body.[5] In general, however, for

Aristotle a form is not something that is separable from the substance to which it belongs: a form is the actuality of a body. As the scholastics themselves saw it, there is considerable tension between their view that (1) the soul is the form of the body, and that (2) it is the principle of an operation, intellection, that does not take place in the body, which indicates that the soul itself is incorporeal and separable from the body. Indeed, in his commentaries on Aristotle Averroes argued that these two ideas are incompatible. He regarded the soul as the form of the body and inseparable from it and concluded that the intellect does not belong to the human soul, but that it is a separate entity, which is not a part of the human being, and which is one for all people, eternal and immortal. Aquinas and other scholastics, however, eagerly made use of the relevant passages in Aristotle to defend the view that the human soul can exist apart from the body. These scholastics, who included Suárez, Eustachius, and the Coimbra Commentators, argued for the separability of the soul on the basis of the nature of intellection. The argument was based on the claim that the subject of inherence of intellectual activity includes only the soul and not the body.[6] Both Averroes and Aquinas had their followers on this issue.

There was yet another important line of thought. Aquinas and Averroes agreed that the nature of the intellect showed that it belonged to an incorporeal entity—whether this entity be the soul or a separate entity. But Scotus and Ockham thought that it was not possible to show by natural reason or by experience that the principle of intellectual activity is an incorporeal entity. On their view, and they also had their disciples, one's commitment to the incorporeity of the human intellectual soul had to come entirely from faith. Like others, Ockham sensed the tension between the soul's incorporeity and its status as form of the body, as the following remark suggests: "Perhaps if we experienced that this intellection [the kind that is proper to an immaterial substance] is in us, we could conclude nothing more than that its subject is in us as a motor, but not as a form."[7]

These problems for the unity of the human being are due to the special nature of the rational soul. But for many scholastics problems arose for the unity of *all* substances that are composites of matter and form. The most important source of trouble was that, unlike Aquinas, many scholastics held that prime matter is not pure potentiality, but has an actuality of its own. For Aquinas it was essential for the unity of a composite substance that it contains only one component with actuality, the substantial form, which complements matter, which is pure potentiality. Others held, however, that such a substance contains more than one such component. Scotus and Ockham were of this opinion, and so were Eustachius and Suárez. Prime matter must be actual, they argued, because it must exist. Its theoretical roles, for instance, that of being a component of a substance and of being the ultimate substratum of change, require that it has existence in its own right. And they contended that a purely potential being is unintelligible.[8]

The scholastics who granted some actuality to matter gave up an important component of Aquinas' account of unity—that matter owes its existence entirely to form. For him the idea that matter is pure potentiality was essential to the unity of a composite substance, because it allowed him to say that matter and form exist by the same act of existence. Ordinarily the act of existence belongs only to the composite, not to either of the component parts. In the case of the human being, Aquinas held, this act of existence adheres to the soul, which it retains when separated from the body, but communicates to matter when joined to it.[9] This is not the place to draw a full-fledged comparison between the two views at issue. A number of arguments on either side would need discussion. But whatever the overall merits of either view, I think it is fair to say that Aquinas' position provides a stronger account of the unity of hylomorphic substances than the view of those who regarded matter as having an actuality of its own.[10]

The scholastics generally adhered to the view that form and matter together form a genuine unity, an *ens per se,* because they complement each other as potency and act. This view goes back to Aristotle. To save this Aristotelian idea and solve the problems resulting from their conception of matter as actual, the philosophers in question distinguished between two types of actuality, and they denied that prime matter has the kind of actuality characteristic of form, which they sometimes regarded as the most proper sort of actuality. For instance, Ockham wrote that matter does not have 'informing actuality': in that sense it is pure potency. On the other hand, it has actuality insofar as it does exist. Much later Suárez made a similar distinction: he wrote that matter lacks formal actuality but does have entitative actuality.[11] To put the point more intuitively, on this view prime matter is actual insofar as it exists, but it does not have actuality in the sense of having a nature of its own. For this it needs form, and prime matter is something like a bare particular.

In Descartes's thought the language of actuality and potentiality is not important, although it is worth noting that he certainly held that mind and body are each actual in their own right, and in fact, that they each had formal actuality. On the other hand, clearly significant in relation to Descartes is the question whether matter and form can exist without one another. The notion of actuality is relevant to this question in scholasticism because philosophers who held that matter has its own actuality also held that it can exist separately. Aquinas, on the other hand, believed that matter cannot exist separately, *even by God's power,* because this would mean "speaking of an actual being without actuality," which is contradictory. He also thought that substantial forms other than the human soul cannot exist without matter, even by God's power, because, he claimed, a separated substantial form would be intellectual.[12] But other scholastics tended to think that both form and matter could exist without the other by God's power. Suárez and Eustachius, for instance, are quite explicit about it. Furthermore, for them mutual separability, regardless of the nature of the power required, establishes real distinction.[13]

There was yet a third important source of pressure on the unity of composite substances. Many scholastics, including Ockham and Scotus, thought that a substance can contain more than one substantial form; they were 'pluralists'. So they held that a substance can contain several constituents with formal actuality. For instance, Ockham thought the human being contains a form of corporeity, a sensitive soul and an intellectual soul. On his view, the rational soul is only the principle of intellectual activity and volition and really distinct from other substantial forms in a human being, such as the sensitive soul. Functions of life other than intellection and volition are exercised by virtue of the other substantial forms in the organism. Aquinas, Suárez, and the Coimbra Commentators, however, were 'unitarians': they held that a substance can contain only one substantial form.[14]

The pluralist position is very interesting in relation to Descartes, because in scholastic terms he believed that matter has not just entitative but also formal actuality, since it has its own nature: extension. So the Cartesian human being consists of several components with formal actuality. In addition, his view of the mind bears an intriguing similarity to Ockham's, since the latter regarded the intellectual soul as the principle of intellectual activity, but ascribed other manifestations of life to other substantial forms. For Descartes manifestations of life other than thought pertain to the mechanistic body.[15]

In fact, Descartes's position bears most resemblance to the pluralist version of Aristotelianism. But I will discuss the comparison only briefly, because it is quite easy to see that such a comparison does not support a hylomorphic interpretation of his conception of the union of mind and body. In the first place, the pluralist conception of the rational soul makes it quite hard to conceive of it as the form of the body in any robust sense. That is to say, it is hard to do so if, as was common, the operations specific to the intellectual soul are regarded as not being located in the body. For a unitarian at least the intellectual soul also has operations that do take place in the body, and those give content to the idea that it is the form and actuality of the body. But the pluralist conception of the rational soul bears a striking similarity to Averroes' position, according to which the incorporeal intellect does not belong to the human soul, that is, a substantial form. Indeed, it is significant in this context to remember that Ockham displays hesitation towards the idea that the intellectual soul is both a subject of an incorporeal activity and the form of the body.[16]

Secondly, the pluralists saw very well that their position raised questions about the unity of a substance, and so they addressed the questions what substantial forms can be found together in a substance, and how their number is compatible with the unity of the substance. Their solution was that these forms must be subordinated to one another and constitute a hierarchy.[17] But there is simply no mention of this idea in Descartes. As we shall see, we can find in his writings traces of a scholastic solution to the problem of the unity of the human being, in terms of the idea of incompleteness. But this solution was common to pluralists and unitarians for substantial forms, and it does not address the specific problems posed by a plurality of substantial forms. So Descartes's view suffers from the more extensive threat to the unity of the human being that affects the pluralist view, but he does nothing to meet this more serious threat. Consequently, when compared with the pluralists on the issue of the unity, Descartes's account does not fare well. So in the end, given what he says about the union of mind and body, the most appropriate comparison for our purposes is with scholastics who held that a substance can only have one substantial form.[18]

Hoffman focuses on Ockham and Scotus on the ground that they held that a substance can contain more than one actual component. This is a very important virtue of his analysis, since the view—held by many, in fact most, scholastics—that a substance can have several actual separable components had been completely overlooked in the literature on Descartes and hylomorphism. But in that respect Suárez and Eustachius are no different, since they regarded matter as having actuality and as separable from form, and for the reasons provided, they are more relevant to Descartes than the pluralists.

5.2 Scholastic Accounts of the Unity of the Human Being

So in Aristotelian scholastic thought there were already serious problems for the unity of the human being and for the soul's status as substantial form. Most interestingly, in relation to Descartes, for most scholastics the soul, but for many also matter, can exist apart. The scholastics themselves were quite aware of these problems and worked hard and ingeniously to try to solve them. Aquinas displays a keen awareness of these difficulties, and components of his attempts at reconciliation can be found time and again in later scholastics, including Suárez, the Coimbra Commentators, and Eustachius.

As we saw, these later scholastics thought that not only the human soul, but all substantial forms as well as matter can exist apart in virtue of God's power. What will become clear is that for these scholastics, as for Aquinas, separability is compatible with entities constituting *entia per se*. They regarded various kinds of entities that normally they exist together as separable by God: matter, substantial form, and what Descartes called real accidents. But the question of separability was not considered decisive for genuine unity: some but not others of these types of entities were thought to combine to form *entia per se*, and the question which ones can combine depends on other aspects of their natures. This point is crucial for a comparison with Descartes, because it is tempting to focus completely on the question what entities can be separated from one another and by what power. But that approach misses the essence of the scholastic accounts of *per se* unity.

When discussing the union of body and soul, the Coimbra Commentators write that when a union is *per accidens* it is so "because of the nature and condition of the things that are joined, since they are such that they cannot come together in an *unum simpliciter*—which does not happen in this case. For soul and body are act and potency of the same kind, which have a natural disposition [*habitudo*] and proportion to one another for constituting one substantial thing, as we have said above" (*De anima* 2.1.6.3, p. 100). This passage is representative of the Aristotelian scholastic view that matter and substantial form constituted an *ens per se* because they complement each other as potency and act of the right genus.[19] As I pointed out, the notions of potency and act were central to their account of the unity of substances. This is important, because the fact that Descartes does not use these notions to account for the unity of the human being already constitutes a significant difference between his account and that of Aristotle as well as the medieval Aristotelians.

Descartes does use another idea central to the account found in Aquinas and other scholastics, namely, the idea that the soul is only an incomplete substance:

> It must be said that an entity in the proper sense of the term is an individual in the genus of substance. . . . Now to be an individual in the genus of substance does not simply mean to be that which can subsist *per se* but also to be complete in a given species and genus of substance. Whence the Philosopher . . . says that a hand, a foot and things like that are parts of substances rather than first or second substances. For although they are not in another as in a subject, and this is essentially what we mean by substance, still they do not share fully in the nature of a species; hence they do not belong to a species nor to a genus except by reduction. (Aquinas 1968b, qu. 1)[20]

So the soul is an incomplete substance in that by itself it does not fall under the category of substance, which is a claim that has its place in the scholastic classification of entities under the categories. And the incompleteness of the soul means that by its very nature it properly belongs in the union with the body. This is so, according to Aquinas, even though the soul is separable from the body, and thus, strictly speaking, its union with the body is not essential to it. He is well aware that the soul's separability poses a problem for its status as form, as his formulation of this objection makes clear:

> What belongs to something according to itself [*secundum se*], always belongs to it. But it belongs to a form according to itself to be united to

> matter. For it is the act of matter not in some accidental manner, but by virtue of its essence, otherwise matter and form would not be one substantially but accidentally. Therefore, a form can not be without matter. But since the intellective principle is incorruptible, as has been shown above, it remains when it is not united to the body, when the body is corrupted. (ST I.76.1, sixth objection)

He replies:

> it belongs to the soul by virtue of itself to be united to the body, just as it belongs to a light body by virtue of itself to be up. And just as a light body remains light even when it has been separated from its proper place and retains nevertheless its aptitude and inclination for its proper place, so the human soul retains its being *(manet in suo esse)* when it has been separated from the body, and it still has the aptitude and natural inclination for union with the body. (ST I.76.1, ad 6)

The idea that the soul has an aptitude and inclination for union with the body was frequently adopted by other scholastics, including Suárez, the Coimbra Commentators, and Eustachius. And they routinely wrote that separation from the body is beyond its nature—*praeter naturam*—a label that applies to a state intermediate between one that is natural to an entity and against its nature.[21]

On this view the human soul is an unusual substantial form. It exists in matter, but it can also exist without it; unlike other substantial forms, it is not *immersed* in matter. It straddles the realm of substantial forms that are entirely dependent on matter and the realm of purely spiritual substances that do not exist in matter at all.[22] In a wonderful application of the great chain of being Suárez argues that there *must* be such a thing as a form that informs matter, but that is also a spiritual substance. The perfection of the universe demands, he claims, that it contain all grades of beings and that higher beings are connected to lower ones by way of an intermediate kind of entity. God must create the kinds of beings we are, composites of spiritual substances and matter, because we occupy the middle position on a scale of entities that ranges from purely corporeal ones to purely spiritual ones.[23]

Although Aquinas' attempt to reconcile the two opposing aspects of the human soul by describing the soul as inclined to union with the body is ingenious, it strikes me as unsatisfactory where the question of separability is concerned. When neither form nor matter can exist apart from the other their union is essential and unproblematic. But since the soul can exist apart on Aquinas' view, its union with the body is simply not essential, but accidental to it, and it becomes unclear in what sense soul and body are one. To stay within the scholastic context, the union of the soul and body is not clearly greater than that of a substance plus accident, but the latter type of unity is a paradigm example of accidental unity for the scholastics. Aquinas' comparison with the tendency of light bodies to go up is interesting. It suggests that the connection between soul and body is strengthened by their tendency towards this union, just as it requires force to hold down a light body. But this analogy does not show how soul and body constitute a genuine unity, one substance. Rather it seems that they are two completely distinct things, although both have a tendency towards togetherness and require some intervention to pry them apart.

It was important to the scholastics that matter and form are supposed to be incomplete and together form an *ens per se,* because it is part of their very nature or essence that they belong together. Eustachius writes, for example, that matter and form cannot be understood without one another because they "involve an essential ordering [*ordinem*] to each other." Speaking of the intellectual soul in particular, the Coimbra Commentators observe: "the rational soul obtains its being in view of [*in ordine ad*] the body, of which it is the form. Hence it is essentially defined through its disposition [*habitudinem*] to it."[24] The idea that the essence of the rational soul demands the union with the body was a standard topic of discussion because of the rational soul's unique status as a form that can exist apart naturally and not merely by God's power. But why does the soul demand this union? The scholastics gave content to this idea in an interesting way.

Unitarians, such as Aquinas, Suárez, the Coimbra Commentators, Eustachius, regarded the rational soul not just as the principle of intellectual activity, but also as the principle of other manifestations of life, in particular, nutrition, locomotion, sensation, imagination. These latter functions have their root in the soul, but could clearly only be exercised in the body. Thus these activities give a clear sense to the idea that the soul is essentially incomplete without the body, and that it is the form of the body.[25] The situation is different for the intellect. As I mentioned before, many scholastics thought that the intellect could be shown to be a faculty that is not corporeal, in the sense that it does not take place in the body and is a faculty of the incorporeal mind. As we saw, this idea is what prompted Averroes to conclude that the intellect does not belong to the soul, the form of the body. Along the same lines one might object that the rational soul is only the form of the body with respect to functions other than intellectual ones, namely, nutritive and sensitive ones, which depend on and inhere in matter. The Coimbra Commentators noted this objection (referring to Cajetan). Their response was:

> The human soul is truly and properly the form of the human being not only with respect to the grades of sensing and vegetative and other functions of the above variety, but also with respect to the grade of intellection. This is proved as follows. Since we recognize the forms of things from their operations and it is proper to the human being to understand and reason, it is necessary to believe that the rational soul is the true and proper form of the human being even with respect to that grade from which such actions emanate. Secondly, in this life the intellectual soul takes all cognition from the senses, and for the use of species also—at least for the most part—it depends on the body insofar as it is necessary for someone who uses the intellect to contemplate phantasms. (*De anima* 2.1.6.2, p. 98)[26]

The second argument in this passage is the most interesting one, given that the scholastics often attempted to account for the unity of the human being in terms of a tendency, appetite, or inclination of the soul to be united with the body. We can now see how the soul would have such an inclination even with respect to the intellect, for the scholastics thought that the human intellect depends on the imagination in two ways. First, they held that intellectual representations, the so-called intelligible species, are derived from sense perception by way of the imagination. Secondly, they thought that a human being must always use the imagination when thinking. But they regarded the imagination as a faculty that resides in the (ensouled) body. So even to exercise the intellect, the human soul needs the body.[27] The idea that intellectual activity requires the body clearly has special significance in this context. For it is the activity proper to human beings and distinctive of the human species. One important aspect of the notion of substantial form is that such a form locates an entity in a species.

Let me summarize the significance of scholastic views on the unity of the human being. Two points are especially important. First, clearly for the medieval Aristotelians the unity of the human being was already problematic as a result of their conceptions of the human soul. And for many, their views of matter and substantial forms in general generated further problems. This unity is threatened by the fact that most scholastics regarded both the soul and matter as separable. So the conception of the late scholastics is clearly quite similar to Descartes's conception of the human being in regard to the question of separability, and so in terms of this question they all faced the same difficulty in explaining the unity of the human being. But second, a central component to the scholastic solution to these problems was the idea that the constituents of the human being are essentially incomplete. As we shall see, although Descartes does call body and soul incomplete, the sense in which he does so is crucially different. Indeed, in the end he clearly does not accept the scholastic analysis of the unity of the human being based on incompleteness.

5.3 The Soul as Substantial Form in Descartes

We have now seen that there are some important similarities between Descartes and the scholastics that bear on the question of the union of mind and body. For us, his view that mind and body each can exist without the other may seem incompatible with the unity of the mind-body composite and with a hylomorphic interpretation of that unity. But it is clear that from a scholastic point of view this is not so. So we cannot reject a hylomorphic interpretation of Descartes on the ground that he regards mind and body as separable. That is to say, his commitment to their separability is not sufficient to rule out that he himself really understood their union hylomorphically. Still, we could deny that his view amounts to a genuine form of hylomorphism. For it is certainly arguable, and in fact I think it is true, that various aspects of his view, as well as of the views of most scholastics, stretch hylomorphism beyond recognition. I must confess that I agree with Averroes that the view that the human intellect is an incorporeal activity, and that its subject is separable from body, constitutes an abandonment of the conception of that subject as form and actuality of the body.

I will not, however, attempt to establish that claim. The question at hand is whether Descartes himself proposes to solve the problem of soul-body union by means of the solutions that can be found within scholastic hylomorphism. I will argue that he does not, but before I do so let me briefly mention one objection to a hylomorphic interpretation of Descartes that can be disposed of easily. It is tempting to reject such an interpretation out of hand given his famous opposition to substantial forms. However, as Paul Hoffman has pointed out, and as should be clear from chapter 4, Descartes's arguments against substantial forms apply only to substantial forms other than the human soul.[28] In his long letter to Regius of January 1642 Descartes argues that one should reject all substantial forms *except* for the human soul. Furthermore, one type of argument against substantial forms relies on the charge that the notion of such forms is anthropomorphic. But that objection obviously does not apply to the human soul. Finally, Descartes argues that he need not appeal to such forms, since he can explain everything in the physical world mechanistically. Again, this argument has no bearing on the realm of the human mind. We experience that we have one, and Descartes does not think he can explain the mental mechanistically.

The primary evidence for ascribing hylomorphism to Descartes is simply that he sometimes says that the mind is the form of the body, or of the human being (AT VII 356/ CSM II 246; AT III 503, 505/ CSM III 207–208; and AT IV 346/ CSM III 279), or that the soul or mind informs the body (*Rules for the Direction of the Mind,* AT X 411/ CSM I 40; *Principles* IV.189). But what content does he give to such statements? The mere occurrence of Aristotelian language is certainly not sufficient to support a hylomorphic interpretation. In this context it is interesting to note Suárez' introduction of the rational soul: "by the words 'rational soul' is understood that principle of understanding and reasoning that we experience in ourselves."[29] The question is then, he continues, *what kind* of entity the rational soul is. This introduction should serve as a warning that the occurrence in Descartes of labels like 'principle of thought' cannot be assumed to indicate a hylomorphic conception of the soul (cf. AT VII 356/ CSM II 246).

To begin determining the content of Descartes's Aristotelian language, we must note the contexts in which it occurs. The most important observation is this: although his interpreters never seem to notice this, Descartes simply *never* proposes that the mind is the form of the body *as an account of their union.* Surely this fact is extremely surprising, if in fact he thought that hylomorphism constitutes the solution to the problem of the union. And he certainly was confronted on several occasions with questions about the union. For instance, he does not offer this solution to Arnauld, who questions him about the unity of the human being in the Fourth Objections.

A particularly important but complicated source for Descartes's views about the union of mind and body is his correspondence with Regius. Regius had been attacked at the University of Utrecht for claiming that the human being is only an *ens per accidens*. His opponents at the University, most notably Voetius, took him to task about this claim. As a consequence, the problem became Descartes's, since Regius was an advocate of his views. In the letter of January 1642 Descartes does actually claim twice that the soul is the form of the body. His doing so might seem to support a hylomorphic interpretation of the union. But the opposite is true. I will examine this letter to Regius at some length.

One important observation about this letter is that Descartes calls the soul a substantial form when he is explicitly engaged in advising Regius about how to respond to his opponents. Given this purpose, one must be cautious in interpreting what he says as reliable information about what he really believed. One may simply infer that Descartes's advice in this letter cannot be regarded as expressing his own views, but this is not the strategy I want to adopt. For even if we take him to say exactly what he thinks, we will still have to conclude that he did not regard hylomorphism as the solution to the problem of the union of mind and body.

In this correspondence with Regius Descartes does address this problem extensively. But even in these letters he never offers as the solution the claim that the soul is the substantial form of the body. When he does call the soul a substantial form in this correspondence, he is concerned with a different issue, namely, the question whether *there are any substantial forms*. This feature of the correspondence is quite striking: Voetius was an Aristotelian, and so it would have been most appropriate for Descartes to offer the hylomorphic solution to the problem of the union if he thought it was the right one. The fact that he does not do so, precisely when this would have been exactly the right thing to pacify his opponents, makes it extremely unlikely that he believed hylomorphism to be the solution to this problem.

Furthermore, what Descartes says in the letter of January 1642 to Regius when he does claim that the soul is a substantial form does not support, but rather strains against the idea that he saw hylomorphism as the solution to the problem of the union. For the characteristics he connects with the notion of substantial form are precisely those that for the scholastics distinguished the rational soul from other substantial forms, characteristics that they rightly regarded as in tension with the soul's status as a substantial form and with the unity of the human composite.

When Descartes first calls the soul a substantial form in this letter to Regius, he is responding to the claim that rejection of substantial forms in purely material things will lead to doubts about there being such forms in human beings and from there to skepticism about the immortality of the soul. Descartes replies:

> on the contrary, from the opinion that affirms substantial forms it is very easy to slip into the opinion of those who say that the human soul is corporeal and mortal; [but] when it is acknowledged that [the human soul] alone is a substantial form, and that the others consist of the configuration and motion of parts, this very privileged status it has over the others shows that it differs from them in nature, and this difference in nature opens a very easy road to showing its immateriality and immortality, as can be seen in the recently published *Meditations on First Philosophy.* (AT III 503/ CSM III 207–208)

So here Descartes says that on the view that the soul is the only substantial form it is easier to show that it is *incorporeal* and *immortal,* a claim I discussed in chapter 4.4.3 in relation to the Theological Argument. This argument occurs later in the same letter, and it is worth quoting again:

> it is clearly contradictory for any substance to come into existence from nothing [*de novo existat*], unless it is created from nothing [*de novo*] by God. We see daily, however, that many of those forms which are called substantial begin to exist from nothing, although those who believe that they are substances do not believe that they are created by God; therefore their view is deficient [*ergo male hoc putant*]. This is confirmed by the example of the soul, which is the real substantial form of the human being. For the soul is thought to be directly created by God for no other reason than that it is a substance. Furthermore, since other substantial forms are not regarded as created in the same way, but as only educed from matter, they must also not be regarded as substances. From this it is clear that not those who deny substantial forms, but rather those who affirm them "can be driven by solid reasoning to become beasts or atheists." (AT III 505/ CSM III 208)

This time Descartes calls the soul a substantial form because it is *created.* We saw how this idea is connected to the immortality of the soul in this argument, and that this connection explains the prediction that the believers in substantial forms other than the human soul will "become beasts or atheists." But what is important now is that for the scholastics the ideas that the soul is created and immortal are precisely the features that generate tension with the view that the soul is the substantial form of the body. These features are part of the conception of the soul as spiritual substance as opposed to form, and they do not distinguish the scholastic or Cartesian conception of the soul from a purely Platonistic one.[30]

In sum, Descartes's descriptions of the soul as substantial form in this letter to Regius do not at all suggest that he regarded the view that the soul is the form of the body as the solution to the problem of their union. On the contrary.[31]

5.4 Incompleteness

Descartes does sometimes employ other aspects of scholastic attempts to defend the *per se* unity of the human being, in particular he uses the notion of incompleteness. So we need to ask ourselves whether he uses this notion to defend the unity of the human being in anything like the way the scholastics did.

The Fourth Replies contains Descartes's most important use of this notion. Arnauld had charged that the argument for dualism leads to a Platonistic view of the human being as a soul using a body. In his reply Descartes appeals to the notions of incomplete and complete substances, which earlier in the Fourth Replies he explains as follows:

> I know that certain substances are ordinarily called incomplete. But if they are called incomplete because they can not exist *per se* alone, it seems contradictory to me that they are substances, that is, things that subsist *per se,* and that they are at the same time incomplete, that is, unable to subsist *per se*. They can be called incomplete substances in a different way, namely in the sense that in so far as they are substances they have nothing incomplete, but only insofar as they are referred to some other substance with which they compose something one *per se.* Thus the hand is an incomplete substance, when it is referred to the whole body of which it is a part; but it is a complete substance when regarded alone. And in the same way, mind and body are incomplete substances when they are referred to the human being that they compose; but regarded alone, they are complete. For insofar as to be extended, divisible, endowed with shape etc. are forms or attributes from which I recognize that substance that is called body; so to be intelligent, willing, doubting etc., are forms from which I recognize the substance

> that is called mind; and I no less understand that a thinking substance is a complete thing, than that an extended substance is one. (AT VII 222–223/ CSM II 156–157)

Descartes here distinguishes two versions of the complete-incomplete distinction. The first one has nothing to do with the scholastic distinction used for *per se* unity, and he himself does not rely on it for the question of the union. In his own terms, it is just the distinction between substances and modes.[32] The second one is relevant to our purposes, and it is the one Descartes employs in the service of the union. He claims that in this sense mind and body are complete by themselves, but incomplete in relation to each other: they need each other to form the human being.

This analysis might sound at first hearing just like the one found among the scholastics. Nevertheless, Descartes's use of these notions is different in a subtle but crucial way. First, the scholastics regard matter and form as incomplete *by their very nature:* it is part of *their very essence* to belong to a composite. Thus the soul's essence all by itself contains a demand for union with matter. But Descartes's view is genuinely different, since he did not regard soul and matter as incomplete in and of themselves. Second, the scholastics thought that *qua* substances, matter and form, including the human soul, are incomplete. By themselves they do not fall under the category of substance, and this was crucial for their account of *per se* unity. Thus Suárez writes that "because one being is complete and whole in its genus, what is added to it belongs to it accidentally, and therefore it is said to compose an *unum per accidens* with it."[33] But Descartes explains the relevant notions of incompleteness for substances by saying that "in so far as they are substances they have nothing incomplete." Consequently, mind and body are not incomplete *qua* substances, but only insofar as they need each other *to form a whole human being.* So in fact Descartes entirely abandons the sense in which the scholastics regarded matter and form as incomplete.

In other texts the difference with the scholastic distinction comes out even more clearly. In the long letter to Regius of January 1642 Descartes considers the objection that the union is part of the essence of mind and body. He tries to be diplomatic, but in fact he simply refuses to accept this view:

> It may be objected that it is not accidental to the human body that it should be joined to the soul, but its very nature; since, when a body has

> all the dispositions required to receive the soul, without which it is not a human body, it cannot be without a miracle that the soul is not united to it. And also that it is not accidental to the soul to be joined to the body, but only accidental to it that after death it is separated from the body. All these things should not be denied in every respect, so that the theologians are not again offended. But it must be responded nevertheless that those things can be said to be accidental because, *when we consider the body alone we simply perceive nothing in it because of which it desires to be united to the soul; just as we perceive nothing in the soul because of which it must be united with the body;* and for this reason I said a little earlier that it is *in some sense* accidental, but not *absolutely* accidental. (AT III 460–461/ CSM III 200; emphasis mine)

So unlike the scholastics, Descartes thinks that when regarded on their own, body and soul are complete; *nothing* in their essences, which consist in their being thinking and extended things, respectively, requires the presence of the other. Accordingly, in the Fourth Replies he writes that the argument for dualism relies on a perception of the mind that does not include the union with the body, which is not part of its essence (AT VII 219/ CSM II 155).

Descartes does sometimes write that the union is *in some manner* accidental to mind and body. But when he explains what he means it becomes quite clear that the union is not accidental in the different sense that it is essential *to the human being:*

> we have not said that the man is an *ens per accidens,* except in relation to the parts, that is, soul and body; we certainly indicated that it is in some manner accidental to each of these parts that it is joined to the other, because it can exist apart and that is called an accident, which is present or absent without the corruption of the subject. But insofar as the man is considered in himself [*in se*] as a whole, we say that he is entirely one *ens per se,* and not *per accidens,* because the union by which mind and body are joined to each other, is not accidental to him, but essential, *since without it a man is not a man.* (AT III 508/ CSM III 209; emphasis mine)

In sum, Descartes simply did not think that the union is essential to mind or body themselves. But he does clearly commit himself to the idea that the union is essential to the entire human being. A mind or a body alone doesn't constitute a human being, which requires a union of both.[34]

So Descartes does not adopt the scholastic solution to the problem of body-soul union in terms of the essential incompleteness of these two entities.[35] His claim that mind and body are incomplete and that the union is essential in relation to the human being is of no use where an account of *per se* unity of the human being is concerned and is surely a clever verbal manœuvre meant to pacify his opponents. But there is more to this claim, and it does convey something important about his conception of the human being. For it implies that a human being includes the body, and so it constitutes a denial of the Platonic view that a human being consists in just the mind. And that was an important point. Arnauld had objected that Descartes's argument for dualism proves too much and leads to "that Platonic opinion (which the author refutes, however), that nothing corporeal belongs to our essence so that the man is just the mind, the body nothing but the vehicle of the mind; hence they define the man as a mind using a body" (AT VII 203/ CSM II 143). As commentators have pointed out, Arnauld's question echoes scholastic rejections of Platonism.[36] Descartes vigorously denies that he is committed to such a Platonic view of the human being:

> I do not see, however, why this argument proves too much. . . . And it seems to me that I have taken sufficient care that no one would think as a result [of the real distinction of mind and body] that the man is only a mind using a body. For in this same sixth Meditation in which I dealt with the distinction of the mind from the body, I also proved at the same time that it is substantially united to it; and I have used stronger reasons than any I remember having read elsewhere for proving the same conclusion. Furthermore, someone who would say that the arm of a man is a substance really distinct from the rest of his body, would not therefore deny that that same thing belongs to the nature of the entire man; and it is not the case that whoever says that the same arm pertains to the nature of the entire man therefore gives occasion for suspecting that it cannot subsist *per se*. Similarly, it does not seem to me that I have proved too much by showing that the mind can be without the body, nor have I proved too little in saying that it is substantially united to it, because that substantial union does not prevent that there is a clear and distinct concept of the mind alone as a complete thing. (AT VII 227–228/ CSM II 160)[37]

Descartes's answer to Arnauld's objection is that the real distinction of mind and body is compatible with the view that body belongs to the nature of the whole man: mind and body are both parts of the whole human being and, in this respect, incomplete. Nevertheless, Arnauld's objection is certainly appropriate, not only because of the questions raised by Cartesian mind-body dualism, but also because the way Descartes expresses himself often suggests that for him the human being is just the mind. In the *Meditations* (and, in fact, often elsewhere) he does not state dualism by saying that *mind* is really distinct from body, but that *he* is really distinct from body. And these statements are in tension with his response to Arnauld that the human being includes the body. Descartes could perhaps remove this tension by distinguishing between himself as the person and the human being, and he could hold that in this life he is accidentally a human being, a mind-body composite. But this strikes me as a rather unintuitive position.[38]

So what does Descartes's claim that the body is a part of the human being tell us about his conception of the union of mind and body? Not much; for this claim is not nearly enough to determine the nature of this union. It is important to be clear about the relationship between the question what is the human being, and the question how are mind and body united.[39] Dualism raises concerns about both, and they are connected, but different. The view that the body is a part of the human being does not entail an answer to the question how are mind and body united. This view does not make clear, for instance, how the relationship of mind and body differs from the one that obtains between two people who form a couple. Each is complete *qua* human being, but they are incomplete in so far as they need each other to form a couple. But nothing very strong follows about the metaphysical status of the couple. Thus Descartes's appeal to the idea that mind and body are incomplete in relation to the human being does not at all entail that the human being is a single individual as opposed to an aggregate.

Let us now return to the comparison of Descartes and the scholastics on the union of body and soul. We saw that Descartes did not accept the scholastic view that the soul is essentially incomplete. For the scholastics the idea that the human soul is incomplete and constitutes a genuine unity with matter meant that it has an aptitude or inclination to the union in virtue of its essence. Now we already saw that in a letter to Regius Descartes rejects this claim and denies that mind and body, taken by themselves, demand the union. A further examination of his conception of the mind shows why he would reject it and reveals the depth of his differences with the scholastics.

The scholastics relied on the view that the functions of the soul require the union with the body, but Descartes did not hold that view. First, he clearly rejected the idea that the intellect depends on the body. He was an innatist and did not believe that all our ideas are derived from sense experience. Nor did he accept the scholastic view that understanding cannot take place without imagination. Thus he claims in the Sixth Meditation that one can grasp the figure of a pentagon either by means of the intellect alone or by imagining it as well (AT VII 72–73/ CSM II 50–51). Second, Descartes confined the soul to the mind, that is, the soul as principle of thought. Consequently, vegetative functions clearly cannot give content to the idea that the soul needs to be united to the body. Matters are more complicated for sensitive operations. On one hand, for Descartes sensation, imagination, and other functions involve both mind and body. Whereas he describes sensation and imagination as modes of the mind, he also believes that they require that the mind be joined to the body. In chapter 6 we will see that he relies on the nature of sensation to argue that mind and body are genuinely united. But that defense of the union is very different from the teleological one that is relevant here. For Descartes does not defend the union by arguing that the corporeal dependence of sensation means that the mind needs the body and 'desires' union with it, or that union with the body is its natural state. In light of the fact that he regarded sensation and imagination merely as *modes* of the mind and not as part of its essence or nature, this is as it should be. Thus on Descartes's view the mind does not need the union by virtue of its very essence or nature.[40]

In the Sixth Meditation Descartes does bring teleological considerations to bear on sensation. He argues there that sensation is good for the union of mind and body (AT VII 83/ CSM II 57). But in this context he is not trying to defend the idea that there is a genuine union of mind and body. Instead he is arguing that sensation is good for something despite its inaccuracy about the nature of the physical world. Sensation serves a different purpose, namely, that of preserving the union.

One might respond that this implies that the union is a good and that, consequently, Descartes does agree with the scholastics to the extent that he could give content to the idea that the mind 'desires' the union. But it is important that he never does so, and one would have to reconcile this claim with his denial to Regius that mind and body 'desire' the union. Besides, unlike the scholastics, he does not present sensation and the union as a good *for the mind* here. I think that Descartes simply did not wish to rely on this kind of teleological consideration to defend the union, and in my view he was right. For, as I noted when discussing Aquinas' proposal of this teleological solution, this attempt to explain the union does not strike me as satisfactory.

Nevertheless, Descartes does occasionally refer to a natural aptitude of mind and body for the union. He does so in the letter to Dinet while describing theses defended at the University of Utrecht, in particular, the thesis that "from mind and body does not arise an *unum ens per se*, but *per accidens*." He explains this thesis by saying that its proponents call "an *ens per accidens* everything that consists of two plainly different substances, and therefore they did not deny the substantial union by which mind and body are conjoined nor a natural aptitude of each part to that union, as was clear from the fact that immediately afterwards they added: 'those substances are called incomplete by reason of the composite which arises from their union'" (AT VII 585).[41] Now this passage is a problematic source for attributing views to Descartes because he is describing theses defended by others. But in addition, he supports his view that the theses in question do not rule out an aptitude for union by pointing to the claim by their proponents that mind and body are incomplete. So what is meant by that claim is crucial. Descartes reports that they are called incomplete "by reason of the composite," as was his own view. But we saw that his own view is that mind and body are incomplete simply in the sense that both are needed to constitute a human being. Consequently, the aptitude for the union seems to amount to no more than the ability of mind and body to be combined to form a human being. We have already seen that this claim is really different from the scholastic view, and that it does not do anything to explain the nature of their union. So even if we take Descartes to be stating his own position here, the passage does not support the conclusion that he accepted the scholastic sense in which the mind has an aptitude for union with the body.

In sum, for Descartes there is no sense in which the nature of the human mind implies that it should be united to the body; there is no sense in which this is good for the mind. On this issue he sharply departs from the scholastics, and this is crucial. Descartes's comments about the notions of *ens per se* and completeness are quite subtle and intricate and interpreting those comments is no simple task. But it should be very clear that the scholastics gave content to their view that the soul is incomplete and to their conception of the unity of the human being in virtue of a conception of the soul that was radically different from Descartes's. For them, unlike for Descartes, the soul essentially depended on the body to exercise its capacities. Consequently, it is only to be expected that, as I have argued, Descartes's conceptions of the soul's incompleteness and the unity of the human being are very different. His conception of the soul or mind does not allow him to give any substantial content to the idea that without the body it is essentially incomplete, and so the scholastic account of the unity of the human being in terms of incompleteness simply was not available to him.

One final note on the correspondence with Regius. The fact that Descartes refuses in this correspondence to adopt the scholastic account of the union is significant in relation to the issue of his sincerity in these letters. It is tempting to dismiss their content—especially a large part of the letter of January 1642—on the ground that he is merely trying to be diplomatic. But we have now seen that Descartes did not sell out, or at least not nearly as much as one might have thought. He did adopt various expressions from the Aristotelian scholastic tradition, which he only uses when under pressure from opponents. This much would seem to be an accommodation to enemy camps. But upon careful analysis, it turns out that even in this politically charged context he refuses to accept crucial aspects of the usual content of those expressions. This is so despite Descartes's own contention that Regius' dispute with the Aristotelians about the status of the human being as an *ens per se* is merely verbal (AT III 492–493/ CSM III 206; see also AT VII 585). *That* claim of his is, in the end, highly disingenuous.[42]

I have concentrated on Descartes's conception of the mind, but Paul Hoffman defends a sense of the idea that the mind is a substantial form that focuses on the human body. He points to the fact that in letters to Mesland Descartes claims that the human body, as opposed to the piece of matter that constitutes this body, owes its identity to its union with the soul, which informs the body. In the letter of February 9, 1645, Descartes remarks that although the matter in a person's body completely changes over time, we think the person has the same human body "while it remains joined and substantially united to the same soul" and that such bodies retain their numerical identity "because they are informed by the same soul" (AT IV 166–167/ CSM III

242–243). But there are serious problems for the view that this claim gives content to hylomorphism, particularly if it is supposed to offer an account of the unity of the human being.

First, in the letter to Mesland Descartes is not at all concerned with the question of the unity of the human being. He is concerned with the question of how the human body retains its identity over time in spite of continuous turnover in its matter. We saw earlier that his claim that the soul is the form of the body is not enough to show that he regards hylomorphism as the account of the unity of body and soul. Consequently, we must also be cautious on this occasion. Second, certainly most philosophers would accept the view that each of us has the same human body over time. But it is not at all clear how that view distinguishes a hylomorphist from what one might call a pure Cartesian dualist: certainly it is open to a dualist who wants to deny hylomorphism entirely to assert that a person's body retains its identity over time. Furthermore, such a dualist might very well agree that the identity of a person's body is due to its union with the soul. But this admission does not clearly determine the nature of this union. Specifically, I don't see how it should commit a person to a genuine sense of hylomorphism. And given the way Descartes explains to Regius the sense in which the soul is a substantial form, I would say he is just such a nonhylomorphic dualist.[43]

Finally, in the *Passions of the Soul* Descartes goes out of his way to deny that there is an important difference between a body that is united with the soul and one that is not. We must judge, he warns, "that the body of a living man differs from the body of a dead man as much as a watch or other automaton (that is, a machine that has self-motion) when it works and has within itself the corporeal principle of the motions for which it is designed as well as what is required for its action differs from the same watch or other machine when it is broken and its principle of motion no longer acts" (*Passions* I.6).

This statement is very un-Aristotelian indeed.

So it should be clear that Descartes does not propose to offer a hylomorphic explanation of the unity of the human being. But that leaves us with a puzzling question: Why does he call the human soul a substantial form? His doing so is especially striking given that he connects this claim with features of the soul that, from a scholastic point of view, were precisely in tension with its status as a substantial form.

Here some historical background is extremely useful. For in fact

Descartes had strong political reasons for saying that the soul is a substantial form, reasons that go well beyond the local concerns of the trouble at Utrecht. They also explain the fact that he connects that claim with the soul's status as an incorporeal, created, immortal substance—and that he thought it would make sense to do so in the eyes of his contemporaries. For the Church had stated as official doctrine at the Lateran Council of 1513 that the intellectual soul is the form of the human body. In doing so it was reaffirming an earlier statement by the Council of Vienne of 1312.[44] This pronouncement was a response to the fact that various philosophers had denied the possibility of *proving* the immortality of the rational soul, although they generally held that as a matter of *faith* its immortality is a fact. The view that immortality of the soul cannot be proved was part of a revival of Averroes' views in Padua. Averroes' position was that the intellect is one in all human beings, and that this separate intellect is immortal, but not the form of the body. Consequently, on this view immortality could not be established for individual human souls. The response of the Lateran Council was to ordain that one had to hold that the rational soul is the form of the body, that it is immortal and not one in all human beings. So this pronouncement of the Council connected the status of the soul as a form with its immortality. But now one can see why this connection came about, given that the Council was stating this view in opposition to Averroism. For it was Averroes' denial that the intellectual soul is the form of the body that resulted in the denial of individual immortality. The Church wanted the position according to which human beings have individual souls whose immortality can be established. But arguments for the immortality of the soul started from the nature of the intellect, and so it was essential that the intellect was regarded as pertaining to the individual soul, which was the form of the body.

In the Synopsis to the *Meditations* Descartes himself refers to the Lateran Council's demand that philosophers prove the immortality of the human soul (AT VII 3/ CSM II 4). Later in the century Leibniz also refers to this demand.[45] It is not surprising, then, that Descartes would feel compelled to call the human soul a substantial form in response to Voetius' accusations. And we now also have an explanation for his connecting the claim that the soul is a substantial form to its status as immortal. For that connection was part of an important official position of the Church.

5.5 Substance

On the Aristotelian scholastic model of body-soul union the human being is a substance. The conclusion that Descartes did not adopt the Aristotelian model leaves open the possibility, however, that he did regard the human being as a substance on some different model. Indeed, the claim that for him the mind-body composite is a substance is quite common among interpreters and more widespread than the hylomorphic interpretation.[46] I wish to conclude this chapter by briefly addressing this issue.

The first point to note is that Descartes *never* explicitly calls the human being a substance.[47] This fact by itself is perhaps not so significant, but now an observation similar to one made earlier in regard to the term 'substantial form' is in order. For on various occasions, such as in the correspondence with Regius, it would have been very appropriate for Descartes to call the human being a substance—if that was his view. Doing so would have gone some way towards pacifying interlocutors, such as Regius' opponents, who were concerned about his conception of the human being and for whom the human being certainly was a substance. Since Descartes never does so, we have very good reason to think that he did not believe it to be true.

Nevertheless, Descartes does use a variety of expressions that suggest indirectly that he regards the human being as a substance, or at least as a genuine individual in some sense. Some of these are simply too vague to afford any real insight into the sense in which mind and body are united or into the status of the resulting entity. This problem especially affects his claims that the human being is one thing, *unum quid* or *une seule [chose]* (AT VII 81, AT IX 64/ CSM II 56 and *Principles* I.60), and that the human being is a complex subject (AT VIII-B 351/ CSM I 299).[48] More suggestively, Descartes writes that mind and body are united by a real mode of union and a real or substantial union (AT III 493, 508/ CSM III 206, 209; AT IV 166/ CSM III 243; AT VII 219, 228/ CSM II 155, 160; AT VII 585). The expression 'substantial union' in particular suggests the view that the mind-body composite is a substance, and it was used in this sense in scholasticism. But I think that it would be unsafe to conclude that Descartes held this view. In light of the discussion of his use of the term 'substantial form' we need indications from within his own writings about what he means by a particular scholastic term. The explanation of the terms 'real union' and 'substantial union' that Descartes himself provides will have to wait till the next chapter.

A very different problem affects his repeated comparison of the union of the soul and the body with the conception of heaviness as a real quality. Scholars have sometimes taken this comparison to support the view that the soul is the substantial form of the body and that the composite is an *ens per se* and a substance.[49] But this interpretation is seriously problematic. It relies on a failure to appreciate the distinction between real qualities and substantial forms, which was the subject of the previous chapter. For present purposes it is crucial that for the scholastics substantial forms are substances, albeit incomplete ones, and that quality and substance are mutually exclusive categories. In combination with matter, substantial forms constitute complete substances, which are *entia per se*. But if the soul is a quality of body, it would follow that the mind-body composite is an *ens per accidens,* since the combination of substance with accident is a paradigm case of accidental unity. So Descartes's comparison of the union of the soul and the body with heaviness does not constitute support for the view that the soul is the substantial form of the body, or that the human being is a genuine substance and an *ens per se*. On the contrary. And in fact, he simply does not use the analogy to address that issue.[50] Instead he uses it to explain the action of the mind on the body, which, as we shall see, concerns an entirely different aspect of the union of mind and body. This is no minor point because as a result several of the most important texts that have been thought to support a hylomorphic interpretation in fact fail to do so.

Furthermore, as we saw, Descartes writes that mind and body are incomplete substances in relation to the whole human being (AT VII 222/ CSM II 157). This claim might imply that he does regard the entire human being as a substance, a complete one. But we also saw that he explains there that *in so far as mind and body are substances* they have nothing incomplete. They may be called incomplete in a different respect, namely, insofar as they are referred to some other substance with which they compose something one *per se,* the human being. But he does not call the human being a substance, and his not doing so on this occasion has the appearance of studious avoidance.[51]

What Descartes says in this context does imply that he regards the human being as an *unum per se* and thus an *ens per se* (although he does not explicitly say so). The Fourth Replies contains the most important expression of that idea in Descartes's writings, since all the other occasions on which Descartes calls the human being an *ens per se* are found in the context of the dispute at Utrecht, when Descartes is counselling Regius about what to say to keep the peace. So what about this passage in the Fourth Replies?

It is tempting to think that Descartes here uses the term *ens per se* interchangeably with "substance," especially since in the scholastic literature there is a sense in which an *ens per se* just is a substance.[52] Furthermore, Descartes does sometimes explain the notion of substance as something that exists or subsists *per se,* and he does so in this discussion in the Fourth Replies. But in both the scholastic literature and Descartes's writings there are two entirely different uses of the term *ens per se,* and the use of the term where it is simply interchangeable with "substance" is irrelevant to our present concerns. For in that sense an *ens per se* is a being that exists in its own right, and it is contrasted with an *ens per aliud,* a being that exists through another one. Within scholasticism this is the distinction between substance and accident, for Descartes, between substance and mode. It is roughly the distinction between things and properties. But this distinction has nothing to do with the question of unity: that question concerns the contrast between an *ens per se* and an *ens per accidens,* which is an entirely independent distinction. In this sense an *ens per se* is an *unum per se.*

The two distinctions were clearly kept separate by the scholastics. For instance, Suárez explicitly points out the difference in his discussion of the notions of *ens per se* and *ens per accidens:* "I do not speak here of *per se* and *per accidens* by reason of the mode of being *per se* or *in alio,* in which way only a substance is an *ens per se,* other things are said to be accidental; but *per se* and *per accidens* are here taken in relation to unity" (DM IV.III.3).[53] In fact, the difference between the two notions of *ens per se* is present in the very passage in the Fourth Replies where Descartes implies that the human being is an *ens per se.* For it underlies his explanation of the two notions of incomplete substance. He first says it is contradictory to say that a substance is incomplete if that means denying that it exists or subsists *per se.* This claim concerns the first notion of *ens per se,* which is contrasted with an *ens per aliud,* a mode or accident. Then he turns to the second one, and allows that a substance can be incomplete in the sense of composing an *unum per se* with another substance. But in this sense of *ens per se,*

Suárez explains, not just substances, but also accidents can be *entia per se*.[54]

Now one might reply that Descartes's using the term *unum per se* still suggests he regards the human being as a substance. For presumably he would not think that the human being is an accident in this Aristotelian sense of the term. The alternative to its being a substance is, rather, that it be an aggregate. To make matters worse, however, Suárez provides two further applications of the relevant sense of the term *ens per se* where the *entia per se* in question are not substances. First, he writes that there are two kinds of composite beings that are *genuine entia per se,* namely, substances, which consist of matter and form, and supposita, which are composed of an entire nature [*natura integra*] and its subsistence. Suárez uses the idea that a suppositum is an *ens per se* to explain the unity of the human and divine natures in Christ. This unity poses special problems because, unlike in the case of a matter-form composite, both constituents are complete.[55] Second, when he explains the notion of *ens per accidens,* Suárez writes that some such *entia* are also sometimes called *entia per se,* albeit improperly so, namely, "mixed liquids composed of imperfectly altered simple ones, such as diluted wine,[*vinum lymphatum*] and a mixture of honey and vinegar [*oximel*], etc. Although *simpliciter* and absolutely speaking they are *entia per accidens,* it is customary that these are sometimes called *entia per se* by contrast with *entia per meram aggregationem*" (DM IV.III.14). This use of the term *ens per se* is very intriguing in relation to Descartes. For as we shall see in the next chapter, he argues that mind and body are closely united, and, as it were, *intermingled* with one another. Given that he also calls the human being an *ens per se,* it is difficult not to to be struck by the affinity with the use of the term *ens per se* for mixed liquids mentioned by Suárez. And there are other similarities. Descartes claims that the union of mind and body is accidental to each, and it is surely accidental to the elements of the mixed liquids that they are brought together. In addition, for Descartes mind and body are each complete in and of themselves, and so are the components of Suárez' mixed liquids.

Did Descartes have this sense of the term *ens per se* in mind? Since Suárez describes this use of the term *ens per se* as customary, Descartes may well have been familiar with it. Furthermore, if he regarded the human being as an *ens per se* in this sense, that explains why he does not call it a substance. For in that case, strictly speaking, the human being is an *ens per accidens,* and, according to standard scholastic doctrine, substances were not. Nevertheless, I find it unlikely that he had this use of the term *ens per se* in mind. When he uses the term *ens per se* it is almost always in the context of the dispute at Utrecht and in reaction to the use of the term by others, who were concerned with the strict sense of *ens per se.* The one exception is that he implies that the human being is an *unum per se* in the Fourth Replies. On that occasion also he is aiming at the strict use. These considerations can be overcome, but what is more important is that Descartes does attempt to make out some sense in which mind and body are incomplete. If he had Suárez' loose sense of *ens per se* in mind, he would not need to do so. Nevertheless, it is instructive to note that in several ways Descartes's account of the union of mind and body evokes the informal sense of the term *ens per se* discussed by Suárez rather than the strict sense used in scholasticism.

What is most important, however, is that in Suárez' writings we have found two usages of the term *ens per se* that do concern unity but that do not refer to substances. For this means that we cannot assume that Descartes's calling the human being an *ens per se* entails that he regards it as a substance. Moreover, in one respect both these kinds of *entia per se* correspond more closely to Descartes's conception of the human being than the scholastic notion of a hylomorphic substance does, since neither of these types of *entia per se* requires that its constituents are incomplete in and of themselves.

We need an answer to the question what sorts of things can be *entia per se* as opposed to *entia per accidens* for Descartes, an answer which he never provides. He follows scholastic practice in connecting his conception of the human being as an *ens per se* with the incompleteness of mind and body. But we have seen how different his use of the notion of incompleteness is. And his assertion that mind and body are incomplete because they need each other to form a human being does not explain on what grounds he regards the human being as an *unum* and *ens per se,* or what sort of *ens per se* is at issue.[56]

At the end of the next chapter I will briefly return to Descartes's use of the term *ens per se,* as well as the term 'substantial form'. But the fact that he does not call the human being a substance, even when it would have been prudent to do so, strongly suggests that he simply did not think it is one. In fact, I am convinced that he did not, and in my view there are good philosophical reasons why Descartes would not believe that the human being is a substance. Clearly, his conception of mind and body meant that there were serious problems for the unity of the human being, and the idea of a strong kind of unity always has been central to the notion of substance, and it was certainly fundamental to this notion for the scholastics. Descartes himself says little about the issue of unity in relation to the notion of substance. In the Synopsis to the *Meditations,* however, he uses the notion of something he calls a 'pure substance', and claims that "all substances . . . are by their very nature incorruptible" (AT VII 14/ CSM II 10). But natural incorruptibility was generally connected with indivisibility, and so the claim that substances are naturally incorruptible suggests that all 'pure' substances are indivisible and simple, which in fact gives them unity in the strongest sense possible.[57] Furthermore, we have seen in this chapter how the Aristotelian scholastics already struggled to defend the unity of the human being in the face of their commitment to the separability of various of its components. I argued that the differences between their views on the human soul and Descartes's meant he no longer had the means they used in what was already a problematic defense of the unity of the human being. Given the prominence of discussion of the unity of the human being in scholasticism, Descartes must have been aware of this problem. For these reasons I strongly suspect that as Descartes saw it, like it or not, he was not entitled to the view that the mind-body composite is a substance.

Conclusion

Although Descartes does call the human soul a substantial form, we have seen that he does not try to avail himself of this idea as a solution to the problem of the union. When he uses expressions employed in the hylomorphic model, he gives them a different sense in a way that clearly amounts to refusing this model. The conclusion of this chapter is then entirely negative insofar as it addresses the question of the nature of the union of mind and body. But the exploration of the hylomorphic language found in Descartes has allowed us to develop a deeper understanding of the relationship between the Aristotelian scholastic and Cartesian conceptions of the mind or soul. Descartes does not differ from the scholastics in regarding the mind as separable from the body. They agreed with him on that issue. But Descartes and the scholastics were divided by deep disagreements on the nature of the soul. For the scholastics, the human soul is dependent on the body by virtue of its very nature; without the body it is not a complete substance, and it needs the body in order to exercise its functions. In this way they tried to create a logical space for the union of body and soul that falls between this union being genuinely essential and its being entirely accidental to the soul. Descartes did not follow their example in this regard. For him the soul was no longer the principle of life, but of thought, and he relegated most of the traditional functions of the soul to the realm of mechanism. And he also parted company with the Aristotelians in regarding intellectual activity as independent of sensory powers. So for him there is no sense in which the nature of the human mind demands union with the body.

Furthermore, it is worth recalling that I argued in chapter 1.5 that Descartes's principal attribute takes over an important role of the scholastic substantial form. For in a strong sense both these entities determine the nature of a substance. The principal attribute and scholastic substantial form make a substance the kind of substance that it is, which means in part that they determine what kinds of accidents (for the scholastics) or modes (for Descartes) that substance can have. In this sense, extension clearly plays the role of substantial form for matter, thought for mind. In this respect, then, it would not be right to say that the mind is the substantial form of the body. And this is just one way in which Descartes's whole conception of substance reshuffles the conceptual cards.

Finally, it is worth pointing out that from Descartes's own point of view the question whether his use of hylomorphic language has any real content comes at the issue from exactly the wrong direction. For as we saw in chapter 4, he regarded the notion of substantial form as largely derived from our innate idea of the mind, that is, an incorporeal substance. So when he calls the soul a substantial form, we must turn to his own notion of the mind to determine what that means.

CHAPTER SIX

Sensation and the Union of Mind and Body

In the Fourth Objections Arnauld worries that the Real Distinction Argument proves too much: it seems to result, he objects, in the Platonic view that the human being is a soul using a body. Descartes fervently denies this charge and contends that he has provided as strong an argument as any he has ever seen for the view that mind and body are substantially united. He refers to the Sixth Meditation, where he had argued that the mind is closely united to the body on the basis of the nature of sensation. "Nature also teaches me," he had written, "by means of those sensations of pain, hunger, thirst etc., that I am not only present to my body as a pilot is present to a ship, but that I am very closely joined to this body and, as it were, intermingled with it, so that I compose one thing with it." But what about sensation is supposed to show that there is a close union between mind and body, and what do we learn from the nature of sensation about this union? Most importantly for understanding Descartes's dualism, what does he regard as the subject of inherence of sensation: just the mind, or the union or composite of mind and body? These questions will be the subject of this last chapter.[1]

Scholars have offered various interpretations of Descartes's conception of the union of mind and body and its connection with sensation. On one common interpretation the union simply consists in their interaction: the role of the body in sensations is merely that it is the efficient cause of their occurrence, and sensations are just a species of thought and modes of the mind. This interpretation, which I will call 'interactionism', is entirely in line with Descartes's dualism, according to which there are two types of modes, modes of body and modes of mind. According to others Descartes's view of sensation constitutes a departure from this clear-cut form of dualism. They see various Cartesian texts as expressing the view that sensations are modes of both mind and body or modes of something different from mind and body, namely, their union. These scholars have argued that sensations constitute a third type of mode, and that the union results in a new ontological category. They usually attach the claim that sensation corresponds to a third type of substance, different from either the mind or the body. Borrowing a term from one of these interpreters, John Cottingham, I will refer to this kind of interpretation as trialistic. These scholars usually acknowledge, however, that on many occasions Descartes commits himself to the dualistic view that there are two types of modes and that sensations fall under the category of mental modes. Consequently, they tend to regard him as inconsistent on this issue or claim that he changed his mind.

I will propose an interpretation that lies between interactionism and trialism. For like interactionists, I think that Descartes regarded sensations as modes of the mind, consistent with his 'official' dualistic position. But I will argue that he thought they were special kinds of modes of the mind *as united to the body*. I agree with trialists that he held that sensation manifests a stronger sense of the union of mind and body than interactionists allow. On the other hand, I disagree with the trialistic claim that Descartes's conception of sensation implies a departure from his dualism. For Descartes sensations do constitute a new type of mode, which results from the union of body and soul; but they are not a third type of mode *in addition to* modes of thought and modes of extension: rather, they constitute a special subspecies of thought, and they are modes of the mind, not of both mind and body or mind-body union. As various scholars have pointed out, on both trialistic and interactionist interpretations Descartes's position on sensation and its relation to the union of mind and body contains inconsistencies or vacillation. I will argue that on my interpretation we can see Descartes as consistently holding one position. This is not to say that all is well with his position on sensation and the union. In important respects it is rather sketchy, and philosophically it leaves much to be desired.

The chapter is structured as follows. Section 6.1 examines the features of sensation Descartes appeals to in defense of the union of mind and body. Section 6.2 is devoted to the question of the subject of inherence of sensations, which I will refer to as the question of their ontological status. In section 6.3 I discuss passages in Descartes that have been regarded as supporting trialistic interpretations of sensation. In section 6.4 I address aspects of his treatment of sensation that would seem to create problems for my interpretation and support an interactionist interpretation instead. I will conclude by returning to the question whether the union or composite of mind and body is a substance.

6.1 The Union as Source of Sensation

Descartes uses a variety of expressions to describe the union as the source of sensation: for instance, he writes that sensation arises or proceeds from the union, or depends on it (*exoriri, oriri, proficisci, provenir, dépendre,* AT VII 81, 437, AT IX 64, 237/ CSM II 56, 294; AT III 424/ CSM III 190; *Principles* I.48). Sensation shows, he contends, that our mind is closely united to our body. Two features of sensation emerge as due to and as indicative of this union. First, Descartes claims that the union is the explanation of the fact that sensations come to us unexpectedly and are produced by body. Second, he proposes that the qualitative nature of sensation is due to the union. I will discuss these two features in turn.[2]

At *Principles* II.2 Descartes claims that we know that sensation depends on the union because of its unexpected character:

> It can be concluded for the same reason that some body is more closely joined to our mind than all other bodies from the fact that we notice clearly [*perspicue*] that pains and other sensations come to us unexpectedly [*ex improviso*]; the mind is conscious that they do not proceed from itself alone, and that they cannot pertain to it merely by virtue of the fact that it is a thinking thing, but only by virtue of the fact that it is joined to some other, extended thing, which is called the human body.

Although Descartes does not use any straightforward causal language here, elsewhere he connects the unexpected nature of sensation with its being caused by an external entity, which turns out to be the body (AT VII 79/ CSM II 55). So, given that he infers from the unexpected nature of sensation to the union with the body here, it is natural to think that he must be referring to the idea that sensations are caused by body.

This passage does not suggest a strong sort of union for mind and body: Descartes merely infers that the mind is more closely united to one particular body than to all others. This leaves open the possibility that the union merely consists in the fact that my body directly causes or perhaps occasions the occurrence of sensory states of my mind; it does not affect *your* mind in this way.[3] So it is entirely compatible with an interactionist interpretation, and it is hard to see how this account is supposed to support Descartes's claim that there is a real or substantial union between mind and body. My computer is also more closely related to my printer than to others, but why should this amount to a real and substantial union—whatever that may mean? There are other texts, however, where Descartes infers something stronger from mind-body interaction.

Commentators have sometimes contended that Descartes believed that there is no problem at all with such interaction. They note that he is dismissive of Gassendi's objections against the possibility of interaction and especially cite his letter to Clerselier of January 12, 1646, where Descartes seems to dismiss the idea that mind and body being different kinds of substances causes problems for their interaction (AT VII 390, AT IX-A 213/ CSM II 266–267, 275).[4] But just before he makes this claim he does admit that a grasp of mind-body interaction requires an explanation; he comments that such interaction is possible, but that an account of it "presupposes the explanation of the union between soul and body."

This is not the only occasion on which he states this position. A central text for the view that we must turn to the union in order to gain insight into interaction is Descartes's letter to Elizabeth of May 21, 1643.[5] The princess had expressed perplexity about the possibility of the mind acting on the body given that the mind is supposed to be an unextended, incorporeal entity. Descartes responds by saying that we cannot grasp interaction just by thinking of mind and body as thinking and extended substances: we need a different notion, the notion of the union between mind and body, which, he admits, he had so far neglected. He adds:

> First, I consider that there are in us certain primitive notions, which are, as it were, originals on the pattern of which we form all our other cogni-

> tions. And there are only very few such notions; for besides the most general ones, of being, number, duration etc., that apply to whatever we can conceive, we have for the body in particular only the notion of extension, from which follow those of figure and motion; for the soul alone we only have the notion of thought, in which are comprised the perceptions of the understanding and the inclinations of the will; finally, for the mind and body together we have only the notion of their union, on which depends that of the force that the soul has to move the body, and the body to act on the soul, causing its sensations and passions. (AT III 665/ CSM III 218)

So in the letters to Elizabeth and Clerselier Descartes implies that there is more to the union than just the fact of interaction. He thinks that a grasp of interaction requires a grasp of the union and that something about the union affords insight into interaction. And so the union plays a role in explaining mind-body interaction.

But Descartes does not think this is the only role of the union in sensation. Indeed, in his most prominent defense of the close union, in the Sixth Meditation, he appeals to a very different idea:

> Nature also teaches me, by means of those sensations of pain, hunger, thirst etc., that I am not only present to my body as a pilot is present to a ship, but that I am very closely [*arctissime*] joined to it and, as it were, intermingled with it, so that I compose one thing [*unum quid*] with it. For otherwise, when the body is harmed, I, who am nothing other than a thinking thing, would not sense pain as a result, but I would perceive that harm by the pure intellect, as a pilot perceives by sight if something is broken in his ship; and when the body needs food or drink, I would understand this fact explicitly [*expresse*], and I would not have confused sensations of hunger and thirst. For certainly those sensations of thirst, hunger, pain etc., are nothing other than certain confused modes of thinking that arise from the union and, as it were, intermingling of the mind with the body. (AT VII 81/ CSM II 56)

According to Descartes, if he, that is, his mind, were united to the body as a pilot to his ship, his experiences would be different; the mind would perceive what happens in the body by purely intellectual perceptions. He connects this observation with the claim that he is just a thinking thing. But in fact, he points out, he has sensations of hunger, thirst, pain, which arise from the union with the body, and he claims that the union with the body explains the difference between the types of thoughts in question and intellectual perceptions. What we saw before is that he was concerned with the unexpected nature of sensations and that he appealed to the union to explain how their *occurrence* is brought about by states of the body. But the present passage contains no reference to this idea. Instead Descartes is clearly referring to an *intrinsic* difference between pain and a purely intellectual perception of the motion of particles in the body that corresponds to an instance of pain. He is concerned with its qualitative nature and proposes that the union explains this intrinsic feature of sensation.[6] This feature, Descartes contends, indicates the close and intimate nature of the union: he goes so far as to claim that sensation is a manifestation of, as it were, the *intermingling* of mind and body. In the Sixth Meditation he only mentions internal sensations, such as hunger, pain, thirst. But in the Sixth Replies he makes clear that external sensations, that is, sensations of sensible qualities, also arise in this way: he lists "perceptions of pain, pleasure, thirst, hunger, colors, sound, flavor, smell, heat, cold and the like" (AT VII 437/ CSM II 294–295).

Scholarly treatments of Descartes's view of the union of mind and body have paid relatively little attention to the argument from the qualitative nature of sensation, and the distinction between the two roles of the union in explaining sensation has been rather neglected.[7] But this distinction is very important, as we shall see in relation to several issues in this chapter, and I think it is crucial for understanding his position on the action of body on mind, although a full treatment of that issue will have to wait for another occasion. Particularly significant at this point is the fact that the second role of the union, the explanation of the qualitative nature of sensation, is not at all captured by interactionism, which only takes into account the causation of the occurrence of sensations by corporeal states.

Descartes clearly regarded the argument from the qualitative nature of sensation as very important. This is the argument he offers when defending the union in the *Meditations,* and he refers back to it in the Fourth Replies, as well as in the letter to Regius of January 1642. In the Fourth Replies he claims that it proves that mind and body are substantially united and that it is the best argument for this union he has ever seen (AT VII 228/ CSM II 160). In the letter to Regius he first states that no one ever explains the nature [*qualis sit*] of the real and substantial union, and so Regius need not do so either. But then he suggests that Regius explain the union as Descartes himself did in the Sixth Meditation, namely, on the ground that "we perceive the sensations of pain and all others not to be pure thoughts of the mind distinct from the body, but confused perceptions of the mind really united to the body" (AT III 493/ CSM III 206; see also the letter to Hyperaspistes of August 1641, AT III 424/ CSM III 190). In the *Meditations* he had contrasted the union with the relationship between a pilot and a ship, which was a standard Aristotelian analogy for describing a Platonistic conception of the union of body and soul.[8] But now he draws a comparison with an angel united to a body: such an angel would not have such sensations, but only "perceive motions that are caused by external objects, and in this way it would be distinguished from a real human being."

Descartes discusses the issue of the union for both directions of mind-body interaction, but as we shall see in a moment, he describes the union as close only in relation to sensation, not in relation to the action of mind on body. Furthermore, he only compares the union to a mixture when he is specifically concerned with the qualitative nature of sensation, not when he discusses the problem of body causing occurrences of sensation. And again in relation to the qualitative nature of sensation, he specifically contrasts the mind's union with a body, both with the relationship of a pilot to his ship and the relation of an angel to a body.

The mixture analogy must be distinguished from another picture of mind-body interaction in Descartes, which seems closely related, and which is often identified with it. Sometimes he claims that the mind is extended in the sense in which we think of heaviness as extended and that it is whole in the whole body and whole in each of its parts (AT VII 442/ CSM II 298; AT III 667, 694/ CSM III 219, 228; AT V 222–223/ CSM III 358). According to this model, the mind acts on the body everywhere, and this model is in tension with his claim on other occasions that the mind is joined to the body merely at the pineal gland, where it interacts with the body.

It is tempting to identify the mixture analogy with the coextension view, but the point of the two ideas is very different.[9] Descartes introduces the comparison with heaviness to account for the action of the mind on the body in voluntary action, and never for the action of body on mind in sensation. But he uses the mixture analogy only for the latter. This is no trivial distinction. Late twentieth-century philosophers usually assume that the radical difference in nature between mind and body that characterizes Descartes's dualism results in just one problem of mind-body interaction. But in the seventeenth century the question of how a spiritual substance acts on a body was treated quite differently from the question of how a body could act on a spiritual substance. The Aristotelian scholastics, for instance, generally held that bodies cannot exercise efficient causality on minds, because they accepted the principle that the lower can't act on the higher, and they regarded bodies as inferior to spiritual substances.[10] But this problem does not, of course, affect the action of spiritual substances (God, angels, human souls) on bodies. On the other hand, it was common to describe action of a spiritual substance on the physical world by using the idea that the spiritual substance is whole in the whole, whole in all of the parts, in particular in the case of God. In addition, the presence of a spiritual substance where its effects in the physical world occur was sometimes described simply as the presence of its power. Both models can be found in Descartes.[11]

In light of these historical considerations it should not surprise us that Descartes treats sensation and voluntary action, which involve the two directions of interaction, differently. In the *Discourse* the distinction between the two is explicit. When he addresses the union of mind and body, he writes: "it does not suffice that the [rational soul] is lodged in the human body as a pilot in his ship, *unless perhaps in order to move its limbs,* but it must be joined and united to it more closely in order to have, in addition, sensations and appetites like ours, and thus compose a real man" (AT VI 59/ CSM I 141, emphasis mine).[12] So Descartes claims here that sensation requires a closer union with the body than the action of the mind on the body. Now his phrasing here is tentative due to his use of the word "perhaps." But in fact when Descartes defends the *closeness* of the union of mind and body elsewhere, he never refers to the action of the mind on the body in voluntary action, but only to sensation. In light of a further consideration, this is as it should be. For in the letter of April 15, 1649, he writes to More:

> Although I think that no mode of acting belongs univocally to both God and creatures, I think that I find in my mind no idea that represents the way in which God or an angel can move matter that is different from the idea that shows me the way in which I am conscious that I can move my body by means of my thought. And the mind can not be extended at one time or shrunk at another time according to place in the way of a substance, but only in regard to power, which it can apply to greater or smaller bodies. (AT V 347/ CSM III 375)

Earlier in the same letter he explicitly ascribes the same sort of extension to mind, God, and angels: this is an extension of power, not of substance (AT V 342/ CSM II 372–373). Now this description of the action of incorporeal substances on matter is not the same (or at least not clearly the same) as the one he had illustrated earlier with the analogy with heaviness.[13] But what is significant here is that Descartes claims he understands the action of all three types of incorporeal substance on body in the same way. This is significant since he clearly wanted to distinguish the union of the mind with the body from the relation of angels (or God) to bodies they act on. Consequently, given that, in regard to their action on body, he ascribes the same sort of relation with body to all three types of mental substances, he simply cannot use that direction of interaction to defend the special union of the human mind to its body.

In sum, Descartes clearly treats the action of body on mind differently from the action of mind on body. This is very helpful for our purposes, given some obvious problems with the coextension view. We can now set these problems aside because they only affect his treatment of the action of mind on body, and his defense of the close union relies only on sensation. In particular, the coextension view raises the question of the location of interaction. But it is now clear that it does not generate this problem in relation to sensation, and Descartes consistently locates the action of the body on the mind in the brain.[14] Furthermore, he never uses the mixture metaphor to explain the location of interaction in sensation: rather, it is meant to explain the qualitative nature of sensation and its confusion. In fact, in the Sixth Replies and in the *Principles* he speaks of an intimate union of the mind with the *brain!*[15]

But now how should we understand Descartes's defense of the close union of mind and body on the basis of sensation? A number of questions arise regarding both roles of the union sensation. Why does the union explain these two aspects of sensation? In particular, how should we understand the argument for the union from the qualitative nature of sensation that Descartes likes so well? Why does he think the qualitative nature of sensation shows that the mind is closely united to the body, and how does the union result in this difference between sensations and pure thoughts? Finally, if sensations result from the union, are they modes of the mind that result from this union, or, as some commentators have argued, must they be understood as modes of both mind and body, or the union of mind and body?

Let me begin with the argument from the qualitative nature of sensation. When Descartes offers this argument in the Sixth Meditation he is assuming his view that the essence of the mind is the intellect, which we encountered in chapter 2; he writes that if the mind were not "as it were intermingled" with body, it would perceive states of its body by the pure intellect, and so the union explains the presence of a faculty different from the intellect. But that idea already played a role earlier in the Sixth Meditation, in Descartes's attempt to show the existence of body on the basis of the imagination: "I consider that this power of imagination which is in me is not required for my essence, that is, the essence of my mind insofar as it differs from the power of intellection. For even if it were absent from me, I would no doubt remain nevertheless the same as I am now; hence it seems to follow that it depends on something different from me" (AT VII 73/ CSM II 51). Descartes infers that because imagination is not part of his essence, which includes only the intellect, it depends on something else, which, he suggests, is the body. He does not explain why he makes this inference, but we can understand it in terms of his conception of substance. Descartes held that the principal attribute, which constitutes the essence of a substance, determines and explains what properties or faculties a substance has: for they must all be modes of its principal attribute. The argument now makes sense if it relies on the idea that the intellectual essence of the mind can't by itself account for the fact that he has imagination. He does think that imagination *requires* intellect—as becomes clear later in the Sixth Meditation when he writes that imagination as well as sensation include some intellection in their formal concept. But what matters to the argument is that the intellectual nature of the mind is *not enough* to explain its capacity for imagination. Something else is needed as well.[16] Descartes's next step is to propose that the existence of a body to which the mind is united is the explanation. He would understand imagination, he writes, if body existed—which has not yet been established. And so he infers that it is probable that body exists.

I propose that Descartes's reasoning in the argument from sensation should be understood along similar lines. He points out that sensation is different from intellection on the basis of its qualitative nature. He does not now state the view that the intellect constitutes the essence of mind, but that view is clearly present earlier in the same Meditation when he discusses imagination. So he reasons in the same way that sensation, too, must depend on something else. That still leaves us with the question why it should depend on body, and on a special union with body. I don't see any *a priori* argument for that inference, but surely body is the natural candidate. For what else would one appeal to? And it is only commonsensical that sensation involves body in some important sense.

That leaves us with the further question of why Descartes would appeal to a special union with body, but we can make sense of that move as follows. He thinks of body in mechanistic terms, and in the argument from imagination he attempts to show a union with body from images of geometrical figures, such as triangles. But in the argument from sensation he is concerned with sensations of colors, flavors, pain, and the like, which, he thinks, body could not explain simply in virtue of its mechanistic nature. So not just body is needed, but something else. Again, a close union with body would seem to be a natural candidate. And at this point, unlike in his discussion of imagination earlier in the Sixth Meditation, he has already established that body exists. So now no worries about that issue need keep him from concluding that a union with body does indeed explain sensation.

This interpretation is somewhat speculative, but it helps us understand why Descartes thought a close union with body explains the qualitative nature of sensation. And the resulting explanation strikes me as rather interesting and imaginative. The argument derives its force from Descartes's views about the nature of mind and body. Since he thinks the essence of the mind is the intellect, sensation requires explanation in terms of something else, and body is the natural candidate. Since he thinks of body in mechanistic terms, body by itself can't provide this explanation. Whence the appeal to the union.

But we do not yet have an account of *how* the union gives rise to this feature of sensation. One might go on to conclude that, consequently, we do not have an explanation for why Descartes wrote in the Fourth Replies that the argument was the best he had ever seen for the substantial union for mind and body, and that surely he must have more of an answer to this question. But that would be too quick. When writing to Regius Descartes claimed that people always say that mind and body are really or substantially united, but that they fail to explain how, and so, he suggests, Regius need not do so either. Whereas Descartes was confronted with the political need to assert that mind and body are genuinely united, in the end he did not seem to feel a great urge to defend or explain this idea. He thinks it pretty obvious that there is a strong union between mind and body and that very little *could* be said to explain the nature of this union.

The exchange with Elizabeth is useful for insight into Descartes's perspective on this matter. When the princess pressed him on mind-body interaction, he wrote in his first response that answering this question requires addressing their union. In a later letter he displays his sense that the union is pretty obvious: he claims that we experience it daily through our senses, and that "those who never philosophize and who only use their senses do not doubt that the soul moves the body and that the body acts on the soul" (AT III 692/ CSM III 227; see also AT III 694/ CSM III 228 and AT VII 229/ CSM II 160). What does need much work, he believes, is the distinction of mind and body. Furthermore, even after trying to explain the union to the princess, in his last letter to her on this issue, he writes not only that the union is clearly known by the senses, but he also claims that "what belongs to the union of the soul and the body is known only obscurely by the intellect alone or even by the intellect aided by the imagination" (AT III 691–692/ CSM III 227).

Descartes's responses never satisfied the princess, and it is easy to sympathize with her. Indeed, his view about the union is frustrating: a clear, explicit philosophical explanation surely requires a good intellectual grasp of the issue at hand, and it certainly does according to Descartes. But his claim that the union is known clearly only by the senses, and not by the intellect, implies the impossibility of such an explanation. On the other hand, there is nothing incoherent about this claim. After all, it is not obvious that every question raised by philosophers should be susceptible to an answer based on intellectual analysis. It is surely possible that there are certain aspects of reality that can only be sensed, not understood. There certainly is more to be said about this view of Descartes's, but what is important here is that this view makes it unsurprising that he did not come up with a more explicit and more satisfactory account of union and interaction.[17]

6.2 The Ontological Status of Sensation

So Descartes connects sensation with the union of mind and body for two reasons: to explain the causation of occurrences of sensation by states of the body and to account for the qualitative nature of sensation. This second feature he connects with the idea that sensation arises from the union with the body. It is, in particular, this feature and the mixture metaphor that raise the question whether sensations, according to Descartes, inhere in the mind, the composite of the two, or yet something else, the union of mind and body. This question is particularly important for understanding Descartes's dualism, the subject of this book. For it suggests the possibility, as recent commentators have argued, that in his view on sensation Descartes departs from his dualism, that is, from the view that there are two types of modes, modes that presuppose extension and inhere in body and modes that presuppose thought and inhere in the mind. I will, however, propose an interpretation that he does not. And although various aspects of his account of sensation remain unclear, I will argue that his writings do contain a consistent position about its ontological status.

Unfortunately, interpretation of Descartes's view on this question is made considerably more difficult by the fact that he uses the term 'sensation'—*sensus*—in different ways.[18] This variation in use is apparent, for instance, in the Second Meditation. He considers the question whether he senses, and he first denies that he can claim that he does because "this also does not happen without a body, and I have seemed to sense many things in dreams which later I noticed I had not sensed" (AT VII 27/ CSM II 18). But later in the same Meditation he says: "But certainly I seem to sense, hear, be warmed. This cannot be false; this is properly *(proprie)* what is called sensation in me; this so precisely taken *(hoc praecise sic tantum)* is nothing other than to think" (AT VII 29/ CSM II 19). So Descartes is willing to ascribe sensation in a certain sense, 'sensation proper', to himself. He does not make particularly clear, however, what sensation proper is. We get a much better picture from the Sixth Replies, where he gives a detailed analysis of sensation—*sensus*—as consisting of three grades:

> To the first grade pertains only that through which the corporeal organ is immediately affected [*afficitur*] by external objects; and this can be nothing other than the motion of the particles of that organ and the change in

> figure and position resulting from that motion. The second [grade] contains everything that results immediately in the mind from the fact that it is united to the corporeal organ so affected, and such are the perceptions of pain, pleasure, thirst, hunger, colors, sound, flavor, smell, heat, cold, and the like, which result from the union and, as it were, intermixture of mind and body, as explained in Meditation VI. The third grade comprises all those judgements about external objects which we have been used to making since our earliest childhood on the occasion of the motions of the corporeal organ. So, for example, when I see a stick, it must not be thought that some intentional species fly from it to the eye, but only that rays of light reflected by that stick excite certain motions in the optic nerve and through it also in the brain, as I have explained at sufficient length in the Optics. And the first grade of sensation consists in this motion in the brain, which we have in common with the brute animals. From it follows the second grade, which extends only to the perception of color or light reflected by the stick. It arises from the fact that the mind is so intimately joined to the brain that it is affected by the motions which occur in it. And if we want to distinguish it accurately from intellection, nothing else should be referred to sensation. For I judge from this sensation of color by which I am affected, that the stick placed outside me is colored, and I reason similarly about the size, shape and distance of this same stick from the extension of the color, its termination, and the relation of its place to the parts of the brain; although this fact [that I so judge and reason] is ordinarily attributed to sense and I have for this reason referred it here to the third grade of sensing, it is manifest that it only depends on the intellect. (AT VII 436–437/ CSM II 294–295)

As in the Second Meditation, Descartes uses "sensation," *sensus,* in two ways, but it is now clear how the two usages differ. He applies the term to the whole three-grade process, in accordance with common usage, but also just to the second grade. He says that if one wants to distinguish sensation properly from intellection one must only refer to the second grade. This stage is just a sensation of color or light in the mind, which, according to Descartes, can be distinguished from reasoning and judgment about the external object, the third grade of sensation.[19] I take it that in the Second Meditation 'sensation proper' also refers to the second grade of sensation.[20]

Awareness of the variation in Descartes's terminology is essential. Claims about the ontological status of sensation must be accompanied by explanations of the sense in which the term 'sensation' is used. Nevertheless, commentators rarely pay attention to this issue.[21] As a result it is often not clear what items they claim to be modes of the union, or of mind as well as body. But if, for instance, one argues that sensation is a mode of both thought and extension, there is an obvious and significant difference between the claim that the entire three-grade process is a mode of both thought and extension and the claim that the second grade by itself is such a mode.

We are exploring the question how we must understand Descartes's claim that sensation arises from the close union and, as it were, intermingling of mind and body, and now we can see that our question concerns the second grade of sensation. For in the Sixth Replies Descartes singles out this grade as resulting from "the union and, as it were, intermingling of mind and body." But in this passage he presents the second grade of sensation as a mode of the mind: it results from the union of mind and body, but he says that it is *in* the mind *(in mente)*. And so he presents a view of sensation proper here that is perfectly in line with his dualism.[22]

There are numerous texts that support a straightforward dualistic interpretation of Descartes's conception of sensation as a mode of the mind. Although this is the traditional interpretation, it is worth reminding ourselves of these passages in light of the recent support for trialistic interpretations. Immediately after the conclusion of the Real Distinction Argument in the Sixth Meditation Descartes writes: "Moreover I find in me faculties for certain special modes of thinking, namely the faculties of imagining and sensing, without which I can clearly and distinctly understand myself as a whole, but not *vice versa* them without me, that is, without an intelligent substance in which they inhere. For they include some intellection in their formal concept, whence I perceive that they are distinguished from me as modes from a thing" (AT VII 78/ CSM II 54). So here sensations are modes of thought and the mind. At *Principles* I.9 Descartes describes sensations as thoughts and says they are referred to the mind. In article 32 he divides the modes of the mind into two kinds, modes of volition and modes of perception, and classifies sensing as a mode of perception. In addition, at *Principles* I.53 and 63 he gives a clear dualistic analysis of what there is: thinking and extended substances. And he presents sensation as a mode of thinking substance. In article 53 he writes that thought constitutes the nature of the mind and that everything we find in the mind is a mode of thinking. He says that these modes of the mind include imagination, sensation, and volition, which all can only be understood in a thinking thing. At *Principles* I.68 Descartes writes that "pain and color are clearly and distinctly perceived if they are regarded as sensations or thoughts." He holds, furthermore, that a mode cannot be clearly and distinctly understood without its substance and its principal attribute, and so sensations are modes of the mind. If they were modes of the union or of both mind and body, their clear and distinct perception should include the union or both mind and body.[23]

But this clear-cut dualism is not the whole story. To Gibieuf he writes: "I do not see any difficulty in understanding that the faculties of imagination and sensation belong to the soul, because they are species of thought; nevertheless *they only belong to the soul insofar as it is joined to the body,* because they are sorts of thoughts without which one can conceive the soul entirely pure—*toute pure*" (AT III 479/ CSM III 203; emphasis mine). So sensations are impure thoughts and belong to the mind as united to the body. He reiterates this view when arguing, in a letter to Regius that sensation indicates the union with the body: "we perceive that sensations of pain and all other sensations are not pure thoughts of the mind distinct from the body, but confused perceptions of the mind really united [to the body]; for if an angel would be in a human body, it would not sense like us, but only perceive the motions that would be caused by external objects and in this way he would be distinguished from a real human being" (AT III 493/ CSM III 206). In both these passages sensation is presented as a mode of the mind. But it is presented as a special kind of such a mode, which *belongs to the mind by virtue of its union with the body.* And the idea is not that the mind needs the body to cause occurrences of sensation: in this letter to Regius Descartes is clearly referring to the qualitative nature of sensation.

So Descartes holds a dualistic view of the ontology of sensation with a twist, as it were. We saw that in the Sixth Meditation he points to an intrinsic difference between sensations and purely intellectual thoughts, a difference that concerns their qualitative nature and that is due to the mind's union with the body. The qualitative nature of sensation shows that mind and body are closely united, and, as it were, intermingled. Without sensations, he writes to Gibieuf, the mind can be conceived *pure,* and this language of impurity is of a piece with the mixture analogy. In fact, both occur in the passage in the Sixth Meditation.[24] And he describes sensations as modes of the mind as united to the body. If the mind were related as a pilot to a ship, or if it were like an angel, the body would just have modes of extension, such as shape, size, motion, and when it causes states of the mind they would be pure thoughts. But the union with the body affects the mind so that it becomes susceptible to a special kind of thought, sensation.

The mixture analogy is puzzling in various ways. First, the analogy suggests that *the mixture* of mind and body is the subject of sensations, but instead Descartes claims that sensations belong to *the mind,* albeit as united to the body. So the picture is rather that corporeity is, so to speak, mixed into the mind, which has impure states as a result. It is analogous to the way we think of, say, the result of pouring milk into coffee: we don't think of the result as a mixture of coffee and milk, but as coffee with some milk in it, as a result of which the properties of the coffee are altered. This way of thinking is ultimately inaccurate, as *café au lait* really is a mixture of coffee and milk, although an unequal mixture. But I think that what really matters to Descartes is the idea that the union with the body affects the mind so that it becomes susceptible to an additional mode of thought, sensation.

It is important to keep in mind that the idea of mixture is, of course, an analogy. Otherwise, the idea immediately falls victim to the objection raised by Gassendi that the mind is not extended, has no parts, and thus cannot be mixed with anything (AT VII 343–344/ CSM II 238). One may still object that the analogy is useless, on the ground that it is essential to the possibility of mixing that there be parts. But I don't find this objection entirely convincing. It is true that the disanalogy between the purely physical case and the mind-body union means that it is not clear what happens in the latter case. But it does not follow that the analogy is entirely useless, and that what it stands for is impossible.[25] All analogies have their limits. The important idea in this analogy is that the union of mind and body is such that it affects the mind so that it becomes susceptible to a new type of mode of the mind, a subspecies of thought, which the mind in separation does not have. And more important than the analogy is Descartes's description of sensation as a mode of the mind as united to body.

There is, however, something peculiar about the sense in which sensation is a mode of thought in this picture. On one hand, Descartes clearly accepts this idea insofar as he holds that sensation presupposes thought. And the attribute of thought determines what kinds of modes the mind can have, namely, types of thinking only. On the other hand, consider the case of shape: it is a modification of extension in the sense that there is nothing more to it (see AT VII 43/ CSM II 30). But sensation is not a mode of thought in this sense, since it requires the union with the body. But then it may seem that the mind no longer has the same nature, the same principal attribute, once it is united to the body. Or alternatively, perhaps we should see Descartes (whether he intends this or not) as departing from his mode-attribute model in his conception of sensation: whereas thought is the attribute of mind, sensation is not a mode of it quite in the sense in which shape is a mode of extension or pure intellection is a mode of thought.

But I think it makes sense to see the issue in the following way. As a result of the union the mind gains the capacity for an additional type of thought, and its capacity for thought is further diversified by its union with the body. The picture can be developed as follows: Descartes sees the mind as a thinking thing, part of whose capacity for thought can be actualized in separation from the body, but part of which requires its union with the body. So in separation its nature is to be the sort of thing that thinks and whose thoughts can, once united to the body, include sensations. The sense in which the mind is affected by the union is then that the union allows it to actualize this potential for sensation.

Interestingly enough, this view of Descartes's bears a structural similarity to Suárez' position on the subject of inherence of sensation. Suárez rejects Aquinas' view that sensitive powers inhere in the composite of matter and soul—a position akin to the form of trialism according to which sensations are modes of the mind-body composite. Instead, he claims, they inhere in matter, although they "have their subject [*subjectari*] in the composite insofar as they presuppose that it is constituted: for they cannot exist unless first matter is informed by the soul, from which they then arise [*oriantur*]."[26] So for him the subject of inherence for sensation is *informed* matter; matter must be in a certain state in order to be the right kind of subject for sensations, a state that requires union with the soul.

Still, the view that sensations are modes of the mind as united to body seems puzzling and awkward. Some aspects of my understanding of the view will become clearer in the next two sections, but at this point it is useful to dwell on the question why Descartes might have adopted this position.

The question of the ontological status of sensation is important for Descartes's purpose of explaining all physical phenomena mechanistically. He wants to keep sensible qualities out of the physical world and claim that they are mere sensations. But then the problem is the nature of our conscious experience in sensation: it is surely hard to see how having a sensation of red could consist in a configuration of mechanistic qualities.[27] So his commitment to mechanistic explanation gives Descartes a motive for also keeping sensation out of the physical world and confining it to the realm of the incorporeal mind. On the other hand, as we saw in chapter 2, his intellectual inheritance included a conception of the incorporeal mind as the subject of intellectual activity but not sensations, which were regarded as occurring in the body.[28] And Descartes himself thought the essence of the mind is the intellect. So on one hand, he expels sensations from the realm of the body and assigns them to the realm of the mental. But he thinks that their difference from purely intellectual states means that he cannot put them on the same footing, and so he gives them a special status as modes of the mind as united to the body.[29] Philosophically speaking, however, it is easy to make the further move of abandoning altogether the conception of the mind as essentially intellectual and to make all types of thoughts modes of the mind in the same sense. And then we arrive at the way Descartes's conception of the mind is usually interpreted. But in my view Descartes himself did not make that move.

Let me conclude this section with a few historical notes. The idea that an effect of the body on the mind indicates the strong union of mind and body has a precedent in Aristotelian scholasticism. The Coimbra Commentators had written: "if a ship has a defect [*vitium faciat*], the operations the pilot has *qua* human being are unimpaired; but when our body is in trouble, our soul executes its activities with error and imperfection, as we see in people who are drunk or mad. Therefore the soul is not related to the body as a pilot to his ship" (*De anima* 2.1.6.2. p. 97). Like Descartes, the Coimbra Commentators cite the effects in the human soul produced by events in the body as a refutation of the view that the soul is to the body as a pilot is to his ship. The effects they cite are different, however, from the ones Descartes focuses on. He draws attention to the qualitative nature of sensation, but the Coimbra Commentators point to the interference in human activity due to mishaps in the body.

On the other hand, Descartes's mixture analogy has an antecedent in the description of the union of the soul with the body in Plato's *Phaedo*. Plato writes that in this life the soul is "interspersed with a corporeal element," and he claims that the union with the body pollutes the soul and makes it impure. So Plato also uses a metaphor that depicts the soul as containing a corporeal element, admixture, in this life. It is especially interesting to note that, like Descartes, Plato presented the mixture analogy as resulting in special goings on *in the soul,* but not in the body. And Plato too saw the union as a source of confusion in the soul, although the nature of the confusion is not the same.[30] The fact that the mixture analogy can already be found in Plato might explain Descartes's appeal to it, but I don't know whether Descartes would have been familiar with its Platonic use. But it is ironic that in refuting the Aristotelian analogy for the Platonistic view of the union of body and soul—the pilot and his ship—Descartes should appeal to a metaphor for this union used by Plato himself.[31]

6.3 Against Trialism

Some commentators have detected in Descartes's writings a view of sensation according to which they constitute a third type of mode, in addition to modes of thought and modes of extension. Sensations, some have argued, are not just modes of the mind, but modes of both mind and body, the composite. Or, on a different interpretation, they are modes of something different from either, the mind-body union.[32] In ascribing such positions to Descartes, these commentators see him as deviating from his 'official' dualistic position in favor of a 'trialistic' one. Proponents of these interpretations do not address the question how his position on sensation relates to his interest in defending a mechanistic conception of body. One might think that trialism is incompatible with such a conception, but I don't think it is. For Descartes's interest lies in keeping certain types of qualities or states out of the physical world. He could accomplish this goal by assigning sensations either to the mind or to yet another subject, the composite or union of mind and body. Either alternative is compatible with regarding body itself as just the subject of mechanistic properties.

Trialistic interpretations have been supported on the basis of, in particular, *Principles* I.48 and Descartes's letters to Elizabeth, which are central to many interpretations of his views on sensation and the union of mind and body. This is especially the case for the letter of

May 21, 1643. I will discuss both this letter and *Principles* I.48 at length. Proponents of this type of interpretation usually hold that a trialistic view of sensation can be found in Descartes's writings *in addition to* the clear-cut dualism according to which there are just two types of substances, mind and body, with each one type of mode. They argue that Descartes changed his mind or was inconsistent on the issue. Thus John Cottingham writes that Descartes's trialism "does not obviously square with his official dualistic doctrines." Daniel Garber and Tad Schmaltz propose that the letter to Elizabeth indicates that Descartes changed his mind from a dualistic view. Passages in the *Comments on a Certain Broadsheet* prompt Schmaltz to add that Descartes later returned to his dualism. Furthermore, Garber and Schmaltz think that both views can be found in the *Principles,* and so there is vacillation within that work—which, they surmise, may be due to parts of the work having been written at different times.[33]

I will argue, however, that the texts do not really support the claim that Descartes sometimes deviated from his 'official' view that there are two types of modes, modes of thought and modes of extension. In addition, I will contend that the version of trialism that comes closest to having good textual support implies more serious inconsistencies within Descartes than have so far been recognized, as well as clearly unacceptable philosophical consequences. I will first discuss the letter to Elizabeth of May 21, 1643, which I will examine in particular detail on account of its importance in recent scholarship. Then I will turn to *Principles* I.48.

As we saw above, in this letter Descartes introduces the notion of the union of mind and body as a third primitive notion, in addition to extension and thought, and he claims that this notion is necessary for a grasp of mind-body interaction. His treatment of this third primitive notion has been taken to mean that sensations are modes of this *union* of mind and body instead of modes of thought and of the mind. Some interpreters, such as Laporte and Gouhier, have come very close to claiming that Descartes regards the union as a third principal attribute, in addition to thought and extension. Schmaltz commits himself explicitly to this idea.[34] This view would indeed be quite different from Descartes's dualism.

On the face of it, this letter does indeed lend itself very well to this interpretation. Descartes presents the union as a third primitive notion, on a par with extension and thought, and he writes that "being primitive, each of them can only be understood through itself," and that the notion of mind-body interaction depends on the notion of the union. These statements are certainly reminiscent of his conception of principal attributes and modes, according to which each substance has "one principal property which constitutes its nature and essence, and to which all the other ones are referred" (*Principles* I.53). The other properties are modes, which cannot be understood without these attributes, which themselves, however, are not understood through each other or through yet other properties. Indeed, if in this letter Descartes is expressing the view that sensations are a third type of mode, he is doing so by claiming that they are modes of a third principal attribute. For this reason I will focus on this particular trialistic interpretation. I will argue that it leads to very serious philosophical and textual problems and propose that the letter should be read quite differently.

Let me begin with the philosophical problems. The conclusion one hopes to reach by way of the union being a principal attribute is that this attribute corresponds to a substance that is the entire human being, an entity that includes both mind and body.[35] But the result is just the opposite. It is worth quoting the crucial passage again:

> we have for the body in particular only the notion of extension, from which follow those of figure and motion; for the soul alone we only have the notion of thought, in which are comprised the perceptions of the understanding and the inclinations of the will; finally, for the mind and body together we have only the notion of their union, on which depends the notion of the force that the soul has to move the body, and of the body to act on the soul, causing its sensations and passions. (AT III 665/ CSM III 218)

If Descartes is talking about principal attributes here, he presents the union as a principal attribute distinct and independent from thought and extension. In the sense in which this is true for principal attributes, the union cannot be understood through either, that is, it does not presuppose thought and extension in the specific sense relevant to the distinction between principal attributes. But then Descartes is not stating the view that the composite of mind and body is a single substance with one attribute: on the contrary, he would be stating the view that the human being has three such attributes, each with its own kinds of modes. He insists that we should keep the three primitive notions and what pertains to them apart, and if he is talking about principal attributes, that would involve keeping the three types of modes apart and assigning each to its proper principal attribute. But if Descartes were trying to unify the human being by way of a single principal attribute, the union, he should suggest just the opposite. That is, he should suggest that all modes of a human being, including the modes of thought and extension, be assigned to the union.

Furthermore, by way of the reasoning of the Real Distinction Argument, it would follow that the substance of which the union is the principal attribute is really distinct from mind as well as from body and can exist apart from both. For as we saw in chapter 1, Descartes's argument for dualism relies on the idea that we can understand mind and body apart because our notions of thought and extension are entirely independent from one another, and the sense in which this is so means that each represents a principal attribute. We can conceive of something as having thought but not extension and *vice versa.* So if the union is independent from thought and extension in this sense, and thus a principal attribute, there is a third substance, distinct and separable from mind and body. But this result is completely unacceptable. Needless to say, Descartes thinks that the union of mind and body cannot exist without either of these substances and that sensations—which are supposed to be modes of this union—require both mind and body. This is surely an extremely serious problem, and it warrants concerted effort to offer a different reading of the letter, which I will do in a moment.

The second problem with this trialistic reading of the letter is textual. Descartes warns in this letter that one should keep the three primitive notions apart. If he is talking about attributes and modes, he is saying that one should be careful to ascribe the right modes to the right attribute. But in that case some of his other comments in this letter clearly violate this warning, since in this very letter he sometimes seems to ascribe interaction to the mind and sometimes to the union. And on several occasions in this letter Descartes presents the notion of the union as a notion *of the soul or something in the soul.* Thus he introduces his remarks about primitive notions by saying: "there are two things in the human soul, on which depends all the knowledge that we can have of its nature. One of these is that it thinks, the other that being united to the body it can act on it and be acted upon by it" (AT III 664–665/ CSM III 217–218). Descartes speaks here of two things *in the soul:* the fact that it thinks and the fact that, being united to the body, it interacts with it. Now these remarks could perhaps be read differently. But the problem comes up again later, and this time in a clearer form. The next paragraph is the one where Descartes lists the three primitive notions and claims that our notion of mind-body interaction depends on the notion of the union. At this point he warns that it is important for us to keep the primitive notions apart and that we must be careful to attribute them to the right objects. Next he turns to what is supposed to be an application of this warning to the issue Elizabeth had raised: the question how one should understand the action of mind on body. He first points to the risks of trying to understand this kind of interaction on the model of interaction between bodies. Then he turns to the notion of the union of mind and body and explains how we have misused this notion. And now we find a disturbing example of confusion of two principal attributes—if the letter should be understood to concern such attributes:

> Thus I believe that we have in the past confused the notion of the force with which the soul acts in the body with the force with which one body acts in another one. And that we have attributed both not to *the soul,* for we did not know it yet, but to the various qualities of bodies, such as heaviness, heat, and others, about which we imagined that they are real, that is, that they have an existence distinct from that of the body, and consequently that they are substances—although we called them qualities. And in order to conceive of them we have sometimes used notions that are in us for knowing the body, sometimes those which are there *for knowing the soul,* according to whether what we attributed to them was material or immaterial. For example, when supposing that heaviness is a real quality of which we only know that it has the force to move the body in which it is towards the center of the earth, we have no trouble conceiving how it moves this body nor how it is joined to it: and we do not think that this happens by some real contact between two surfaces, for we experience in ourselves that we have a particular notion for conceiving it. I believe that we used this notion badly in applying it to heaviness which is nothing really distinct from body, as I hope to show in my Physics, but that it has been given us for conceiving the way in which the soul moves the body. (AT III 667–668/ CSM III 219; emphasis mine)

Descartes is here talking about what earlier in this letter he called the notion of the *union* of soul and body, which is supposed to allow us to grasp their interaction. But now he says that we misapplied this notion by using it for various qualities of bodies rather than for *the soul,* as we should have done. But if he meant to distinguish between three principal attributes and types of modes when talking about the primitive notions for body, soul, and their union, he makes the same type of error he warns against right in this very letter.

Now I think Descartes is simply not concerned in this letter with the question what modes belong to what attribute or substance. But suppose he is concerned with this question, and consider the fact that he ascribes what belongs to the union also to the mind. Then, if anything, this letter supports my view that modes of the union are a special subset of modes of thought due to the union, rather than supporting the view that they belong to a third principal attribute instead of thought.

Furthermore, in light of other texts it should not be surprising that Descartes here proposes that the notion of heaviness is derived from the notion of the soul or mind rather than the union. For we find the same idea in the Sixth Replies and in the letter to Arnauld of July 29, 1648 (AT VII 441–442/ CSM II 297–298 and AT V 222–223/ CSM III 358). On both of these occasions he claims that the notion of heaviness is a confusion and that part of it originates in our notion of the *soul*—he does not mention the notion of the *union* of soul and body. The mentalistic elements he lists on these occasions he also mentions to Elizabeth, including the conception of heaviness as a substance and of its way of moving a body. In the Sixth Replies Descartes also mentions that the confused notion of heaviness contains the idea of knowledge. This is a further item borrowed from our idea of the mind, but not from the idea of the union of the mind with the body. So on this occasion we find a mixture of items that come from both the notion of the union and the notion of the mind as a thinking thing.

But now how should we understand Descartes's warning that the notions of thought, extension, and the union of mind and body are primitive and that we should keep them apart? The first thing to note is that the letter is not addressing the question of the ontological status of sensation; it is concerned with interaction and it is in view of this issue that Descartes turns to the union. His claim that the union of mind and body is a primitive notion routinely raises eyebrows among his interpreters. After all, it is puzzling how the notion of the union of two things can only be understood through itself and could fail to depend on the notions of the two things in question. But I think that more has been read into these remarks about primitive notions than is necessary. For consider the point Descartes is trying to make. He wishes to make clear that the way in which the mind acts on the body is unique, and he is especially concerned to argue that we cannot understand it on the model of interaction between bodies. Analogous claims apply presumably to the action of the body on the mind. But this point does not require that the notion of the union would contain *no reference at all* to mind and body. It is true that Descartes holds that the notions of thought and extension are separate in this very strong sense. But in this letter he is concerned with a more modest goal of criticizing the view that completely *reduces* the notion of the union to the notions of mind or body alone. And he especially wishes to reject the reduction of mind-body interaction to body-body interaction.[36]

Furthermore, in light of the fact that in analyses of the analogy with heaviness Descartes sometimes speaks of the notion of the mind, sometimes of the notion of the union, we should view his claim that the action of mind on body pertains to the union as really a more nuanced version of the view that it pertains to the mind. He writes to Elizabeth that there are two things to note in the soul, the fact that it thinks and the fact that it is united to body. He admits to her that he has not said enough on the issue of the union because he was more concerned with their distinction (AT III 664–665/ CSM III 217–218). But then he specifically addresses the union because he thinks this is necessary to clarify interaction. But both when Descartes writes about heaviness to Arnauld and in the Sixth Replies he simply does not distinguish between the two notions of the soul, the one for the soul alone, the other for its union to the body. This is not surprising, as on those occasions he is not concerned to explain the union and the difference between the two aspects of the mind: instead he is focused on the difference between mind and body. As his comments to Elizabeth make clear, this difference was usually his concern, and he regarded it as more important than explaining the union. But when writing to the princess he is concerned precisely with the differences between the union of mind to the body, as opposed to the mind as just a thinking thing. So it is clear why in that letter he does draw the distinction between what belongs to the soul alone and what belongs to the soul as united to the body.

Also there is a clear reason why later in this same letter Descartes describes the action of the mind on the body as a notion of the mind. Early in the letter he wishes to explain that there are different notions for the mind by itself and for its union with the body. But once he has made this point and turns to the details of the union, he is primarily concerned to distinguish the notion of the action of the mind on the body from interaction between bodies. Thus again he is focused on distinguishing what pertains to the mind from what pertains to body.

We can now see why Descartes's discussion of heaviness in this letter does not immediately violate his own warning that one should distinguish the primitive notion of the mind from the primitive notion of its union with the body. For his position that we must distinguish between the three primitive notions should be understood as follows. In view of establishing the real distinction we must distinguish between the notions of the mind as thinking, the body as extended, and for this purpose we must focus on the notion of the mind as thinking. But for understanding the interaction between mind and body we pay attention to another notion of the mind, namely, the notion of its union with the body. We must distinguish the notion of the union from the notion of the mind as thinking, as Descartes himself points out in this letter, because the latter notion helps us recognize the real distinction, the former obstructs such recognition (AT III 665/ CSM III 218). But once the real distinction has been established, the notion of the union does afford knowledge of what features belong to the soul by virtue of this union, features that we must not attribute to body.

So the distinction between the notions of thought and extension on one hand, and between the notions of thought and the union on the other hand are not of the same kind. The former corresponds to a difference between principal attributes and mutually exclusive sets of modes. But the point of the latter is more modest, and it is just that one notion allows us to know one thing, the other another. Focus on the wrong notion for the wrong purposes obstructs knowledge of the real distinction and of interaction, respectively.

The other main text that has been a source of inspiration for trialists is *Principles* I.48. The first part of this passage sounds quite dualistic:

> I do not, however, recognize more than two highest types of things: first, intellectual or thinking things, that is, those pertaining to the mind or thinking substance; second, material things, or those which pertain to extended substance, that is, body. Perception, volition, and all the modes of perceiving and willing are referred to thinking substance; magnitude, or its extension in length, width and depth, shape, motion, place, the divisibility of parts and the like are referred to extended substance.

Immediately afterwards, however, Descartes adds:

> But we also experience certain other things in us, which must be referred [*referri*] neither to the mind alone, nor to the body alone, and which, as will be shown below in its proper place, arise from [*proficiscuntur*] the close and intimate union of our mind with the body; namely the appetites of hunger and thirst etc; similarly, the emotions or passions of the soul, which do not consist in [*consistunt*] thought alone, such as the emotion of anger, joy, sadness, love, etc; and furthermore all sensations, such as the sensations of pain, pleasure, light and colors, sounds, smells, flavors, heat, hardness and the other tactile qualities.

It is important to examine closely what Descartes says in this passage. He says that the third category of items must not be *referred* to the mind alone, that it *arises from* the union of the mind with the body, and that the emotions do not *consist in* thought alone. The French is slightly different: it says they must not be *attributed to* [*attribuées à*] the soul alone, but to the union between body and soul, and that the emotions do not *depend on* [*dépendent de*] thought alone.[37] Some of these expressions might stand for the relationship between modes and principal attributes: Descartes uses 'refer' to discuss this relationship at *Principles* I.53. So he could be presenting sensations here as modes that inhere in the union or composite of mind and body rather than just in the mind.

It is possible to read article 48 in this way. But the passage definitely does not require this reading and thus it fails to provide genuine support for a trialistic interpretation. One problem is that it is not obvious exactly how one should interpret Descartes's use of the crucial expressions in this article ('refer to', 'attribute to', 'consist in', 'depend on'). For instance, at *Principles* II.3 he says that the perceptions of the senses are *referred to* the conjunction of mind and body, but there he is clearly not at all interested in the ontological status of sensations. Instead his point is that the information they convey concerns the conjunction of mind and body rather than the nature of body. At *Principles* I.53 Descartes does clearly use the term 'refer' to talk about the relationship between modes and principal attributes, but now he says that sensations must be referred to thought. And at article 9 he writes that they must be referred to the mind. So there is no passage where he both clearly uses the term 'refer' for the mode-attribute relation and claims that sensation should be referred to the union.

When in article 48 Descartes writes that sensations must be referred (in the Latin) or attributed (in the French) not to the mind alone or the body alone, but to the union of the mind with the body, he adds that this claim "will be established below"—*ut infra suo loco ostendetur.* So this view is supposed to be defended later in the *Principles,* although Descartes does not specify where exactly. But in the rest of the work he never argues that sensations are modes of the union; instead he always presents sensations as modes of the mind. In a footnote Adam and Tannery propose that Descartes is talking about *Principles* IV.189–191, which concern the causal interaction that gives rise to sensations. But the role of the body described there consists *only* in causing occurrences of sensation in the mind.[38]

Finally, I have pointed out before that interpretation of Descartes's view of sensation is complicated by the fact that he uses the term in different ways, namely, either for the full three-grade process of sensation or for just the second grade of sensation. I have proposed that the second grade of sensation is a mode of the mind, and now there are two ways of reading *Principles* I.48 that are compatible with my interpretation as opposed to a trialistic one. First, Descartes may be using the term 'sensation' here in its broad sense. In that case what he has in mind is that the complex process of sensation includes not just thought, but also mechanical processes in the body (and similarly for the other items he lists—appetites, passions). Alternatively, he may have in mind his view that sensations are due to body in the sense that the mind must be joined to the body in order to have sensations. Either interpretation fits very well with the fact that elsewhere in the *Principles* Descartes describes sensations (by which I take it he then means the second grade of sensations) as modes of the mind or modes of the mind as joined to the body. They also fit the fact that when he specifically addresses the role of the body late in part IV he merely refers to its role as the efficient cause of sensations. So the passage poses no problems for my own interpretation.

I think one must conclude that the passage is simply not clear enough about the ontology of sensations and similar types of states to lend support to any particular interpretation. *A fortiori,* the passage does not provide support for the view that sensations are modes of the union or composite of mind and body rather than modes of the mind. In fact, I don't think that article 48 is meant to provide a clear statement of Descartes's ontology. He is giving a list of "everything that falls under our perception," and he is at this point simply laying out the items that need to be analyzed. The exposition of his ontology really only begins with article 51, where he states his conception of substance.

In sum, Descartes's writings do not support a trialistic interpretation of his conception of sensation. Such interpretations derive their appeal in part from the fact that they seem to depict Descartes's conception of sensations as philosophically attractive, a point I will turn to in a moment. But they do so at a price, because they generally ascribe inconsistency or changes of heart to Descartes on the ontological status of sensations. I have argued that these inconsistencies would exist even *within* the letter to Elizabeth that is so prominent in these interpretations, and what is more, right next to Descartes's own warning against precisely the relevant confusions. In addition, the letter most plausibly puts forth the version of trialism that recognizes a third principal attribute, but this has the unacceptable implication that mind, body, and the union are three different substances, each of which can exist without the other.

My view that Descartes regards sensations as modes of the mind as united to the body avoids these problems, while preserving the trialistic insight that he does not regard sensations as straightforward modes of the mind. But now one may well wonder whether the position I ascribe to Descartes is really different from some sort of trialism. One might wish to argue that the view that sensation is a mode of the mind as united to body in the end reduces to the view that sensation is a mode of both mind and body. Perhaps one would do so on the ground that on my view sensation is possible only when the mind is united to a body, and so its occurrence depends on and presupposes body. But not just any dependence on body establishes that sensation is a mode of it. I am not proposing that for Descartes sensation presupposes body as its subject of inherence; and this is the sort of dependence relevant to the notion of a mode, as I discussed in chapter 1.1 and will again discuss in section 6.4. Nor does my interpretation reduce to the form of trialism I have focused on, the view that sensation would have to be a mode of a third principal attribute that is different from both thought and extension. For as I see it Descartes thinks that sensation does presuppose thought, and so in this sense sensation pertains to thought, and not to some attribute entirely different from thought. If anything, as I mentioned in section 6.2, my interpretation raises the possibility that the mind has a different principal attribute when united to the body than when it is separated from it. But that is not the same as there being a third principal attribute in a human being distinct from and in addition to thought and extension.

Finally, it is worth pausing over the philosophical appeal of trialism. This appeal derives from the fact that the classification of sensations as modes of the mind is found philosophically objectionable because it underestimates the role of the physical in sensation.[39] On a trialistic view Descartes presumably takes into account the importance of the body for sensation. Now my interpretation achieves the same effect by presenting Cartesian sensations as modes of the mind as united to the body. But I must confess that, from a philosophical point of view, each interpretation does so only superficially and not in a genuinely satisfactory way. For neither really addresses the reasons why the view that sensations are modes of an incorporeal mind is often found problematic. Dissatisfaction with this view can come from two sources. First, it can be dissatisfaction with the idea that sensations would be states of an incorporeal entity. Now this problem is simply not going to go away, since it would be foolish to deny that Descartes believed that the mind is an incorporeal substance. And in some form or other he clearly did hold that sensation pertains to such a substance: a pure body just won't have sensory states on his view.

The other source of dissatisfaction lies in the idea that sensations are inherently states of an embodied being because it is part of their essence to pertain to a being that has physical states, such as physical sensory stimuli and modes of behavior. Ideas of this kind underlie behaviorist criticisms of Cartesian dualism, and they figure in Aristotelianism, where only beings with the capacity for locomotion were thought to have sensation.[40] Now Descartes did not countenance any important connection with modes of behavior, but he was of course clearly aware of the role of the bodily organs in the production of sensation. He did not, however, seem to consider this role essential to sensation, at least not to what he called "sensation proper," and so in this regard his position is indeed vulnerable to the type of criticism at issue.[41] On the other hand, philosophically speaking, the view that conscious states belong to an incorporeal entity would seem to be quite compatible with the idea that whether a conscious state is or is not a sensation depends on its relations to bodily causation and behavior.[42] That is to say, one could hold that sensations are essentially related to bodily states, but that in human beings (for instance) the entities that are so related are themselves incorporeal states.

Furthermore, whereas Descartes did regard embodiment as necessary for sensation, I have argued that he bases his view that sensations are modes of the mind as united to body on the qualitative nature of sensation. And this idea has nothing to do with the consideration that there are essential connections with bodily states like sensory stimuli or types of behavior.

Perhaps trialism or my own interpretation speaks to the general sense that it would be wrong to classify sensations as purely incorporeal events. But neither yields a sense of dependence on body that satisfies the lines of objection at hand. To some extent this is due to the fact that Descartes was writing in the seventeenth century rather than the twentieth century. I think his conception of sensation was somewhat awkward. But as I explained in the previous section, it reflects his position as initiator of the modern conception of the mind even if he himself does not make the full transition to what we usually consider to be the Cartesian view of the mental.

6.4 The Union and Interaction

At the opposite end of the spectrum from trialism we find interactionism: the view that the union of mind and body merely consists in their interaction, and that sensation is simply a mode of the mind.[43] On this view the role of the body is confined to causing occurrences of sensation. And there would seem to be no obstacle to the mind having sensory states even when not united to a body: God could bring them about. I will now turn to those aspects of Descartes's position that seem to suggest this view. They constitute a source for objections to my account as well as to other interpretations that see a stronger conception of mind-body union in Descartes, such as trialistic ones.[44] But it is important to note that interactionism is also in tension with those aspects of Descartes's treatment of sensation that seem to commit him to a stronger conception of the union and to the view that we cannot have sensation without body. As in the case of trialism, interactionism makes Descartes come out inconsistent. I will argue, however, that the passages at issue do not require an interactionist interpretation and that they are compatible with the view that sensation is not possible without body. On the view I propose the apparent tensions can be resolved.

The most important issue in this section is the relationship between the ontological status of sensations and the question whether they can occur without the mind being united to the body. But I will begin with an apparent source of support for interactionism that does not focus on this issue. This source lies in Descartes's explanation of the correlations between brain states and sensations that he provides in the Sixth Meditation. He writes that "any of those motions that happen in that part of the brain that immediately affects the mind brings about in it only one particular sensation," and he explains that the particular correlations are set up by God, who picks ones that are maximally beneficial to us (AT VII 87–88/ CSM II 60–61; see also *Treatise on Man,* AT XI 143/ CSM I 102). Margaret Wilson, who has been particularly sensitive to the tensions in Descartes's view of sensation, has called this position the Natural Institution theory.[45] She thinks that on this theory the union simply consists in interaction, and that it is inconsistent with Descartes's claim that the close union of mind and body is supposed to explain something about sensation. For the Natural Institution theory, she contends, seems to imply that we do not have sensations "*because of* a state of affairs designated as the close or intimate union or intermingling of mind with body. Rather, what we call the close union or intermingling of this mind with this body is nothing but the arbitrarily established disposition of this mind to experience certain types of sensations on the occasion of certain changes in this body, and to refer these sensations to (parts of) this body."[46] Wilson's discussion raises an important issue. For indeed the fact that Descartes often claims that the union *explains* the nature of our sensation counts strongly against the view that the union simply consists in interaction. She concludes that the presence of the Natural Institution theory shows that there are two different accounts in Descartes.

But in fact the Natural Institution theory is quite compatible with Descartes's claim that the union explains something about sensation. To see this it is useful to remind ourselves of the distinction between the two different roles for the union in relation to sensation: (1) its role in explaining the action of body on mind in the causation of occurrences of sensation by brain states, and (2) its role in explaining the qualitative nature of sensations in virtue of the idea that they are modes of the mind as united to the body. Descartes thinks that the union explains that my brain can act on my mind, and that it explains sensation as a type of mode. But either of these explanations still leaves us with the question why a particular kind of state of the body causes an occurrence of a particular kind of sensation. How is it that certain motions in the brain cause pain rather than a sensation of red, or pain as if in the foot rather than pain as if in the head? The connection seems arbitrary. Given a mechanistic conception of body, the question of its origin arises even if one accepts the first role of the union, which is supposed to explain that body can act on mind. And as concerns its second role, the question arises regardless of one's view of the ontological status of sensations. But this point merits a little more discussion.

The idea that sensations are modes of the mind as united with the body does not at all remove the seeming arbitrariness of the particular causal correlations. It is no less puzzling why a certain motion should cause a pain if the pain is a mental state a mind can have only because it is united with the body, than if the pain is a purely mental state the mind could have even in separation (say, caused by God). Furthermore, the Natural Institution theory is meant to address the question where these correlations come from. God had choices about what connections to establish between states of the body and states of the mind. The special union of mind and body is relevant to his choices because it means that they were not limited to purely intellectual states, but include sensations. For when the mind is not united, and, as it were, intermingled with the body, it is not in a state in which it can have these kinds of modes. (Descartes might well add that God created these choices himself, since he made it the case that human minds are united to bodies in the way peculiar to human beings. God could possibly have connected minds to bodies merely in the way in which angels are connected to bodies.)[47]

Consequently, the Natural Institution theory does not imply that the mind can have sensations without body and that their union merely consists in interaction. So Descartes's adherence to this theory does not support interactionism, and the theory is not in conflict with his claim that the close union of mind and body explains the qualitative nature of sensation.

But the most prominent and pervasive source of apparent support for interactionism lies in the observation that Descartes seems to commit himself to the possibility of sensations without body. Such a commitment would be inconsistent with the argument for the union from the qualitative nature of sensation since that argument implies that sensation is not possible without body: it presents the very nature of sensations of pain, heat, color, and not just their occurrence, as due to the union.[48] As will become clear in a moment, the distinction between the two roles of the union in regard to sensation is quite important for the issue at hand. I will consider three ways in which Descartes seems to imply that we can sense without a body.

(1) One source of the idea that sensation can occur without body is Descartes's argument for the existence of body in the Sixth Meditation. There he contemplates the possibility that God or angels produce sensations. He rejects this possibility on the ground that God would turn out to be a deceiver, but otherwise he seems to regard it as coherent. This attitude would seem to suggest that he thinks we can have sensations without body.

Now the first thing to note is that in the *Meditations* Descartes sometimes considers positions that he himself ultimately regards as incoherent (such as the possibility of a deceiving God). And he discusses the possibility that God causes our sensations, which he rejects, before he has argued that sensation shows the close union of mind and body. So the fact that Descartes considers this scenario does not necessarily mean that he thinks it is really possible. For it could be his view that, given the connection between sensation and the union, God could not in fact cause sensations, and that this possibility only seems to make sense before we recognize this connection. But in addition, I don't think that the possibility that God causes our sensations is incompatible with Descartes's view that sensation requires the close union with the body. Again, the role of the union with the body is to explain both that the body can act on the mind and that the mind is in the right state to have mental states qualitatively characteristic of sensation. The possibility that sensations are caused by God or angels, who are all thinking substances, concerns only the first of these two roles. But if God causes our sensations, that role for the union is simply no longer necessary. If bodies don't act on minds, then there is no need to appeal to a special union to explain such action, and so this scenario does not affect the idea that mind-body interaction requires a special union. The possibility that God causes our sensations does not affect the second role of the union either. Descartes could hold, for instance, that God causes our sensations on the ground that bodies have no efficient causal power—a view sometimes ascribed to him.[49] But that is compatible with the idea that the mind must be intimately united with a body in order for it to be in the right state to have sensations in terms of their qualitative nature.

(2) Another source of support for the view that sensation is possible without body is Descartes's claim that we can be certain that we sense—or at least that we seem to sense—while doubting that there are bodies. The most prominent place that he makes this claim is the Second Meditation: "I am the same who senses, or who notices corporeal things as if through the senses: that is, I see light, I hear sound, I feel heat. These things are false, for I am asleep. But certainly I seem to see, hear, become warm. This cannot be false; this is properly what is called sensation in me; and this precisely so taken is nothing other than thinking" (AT VII 29/ CSM II 19). In this passage Descartes identifies seeming to sense with sensing proper. And the thought experiment of the Second Meditation seems to propose that it is conceivable that we have sensations proper while there are no bodies. This epistemological point is usually understood to imply that sensation in the strict sense, that is, the second grade of sensation, is possible without body existing at all.[50]

In order to solve the resulting problem, we must return to the question what the thought experiment of the Second Meditation is meant to establish. This thought experiment certainly implies the possibility of sensation in the absence of body—if Descartes thinks that the mere conceivability of sensation without body is sufficient to establish its possibility. It is common to think that he does accept this line of thought and that it underlies his principal argument for dualism, the Real Distinction Argument. But matters are more complicated, and there are two reasons why this argument does not commit Descartes to the possibility of sensation without body. First, as I argued in chapter 2, the Real Distinction Argument relies on a conception of the mind that includes its capacity for pure thought, purely intellectual activity, but not for sensation. That is to say, it relies only on the conceivability of pure thought without body to establish the distinction of the mind from the body, and so the Real Distinction Argument itself does not commit Descartes to the possibility of sensation without body.

But one might object that the line of reasoning of that argument, in combination with the implication of the Second Meditation, suggests that it is conceivable that we sense without body. This objection leads to the second reason why the Real Distinction Argument does not imply that we can sense without body. As we saw in chapter 1, the argument relies on the notions of a complete thing and a principal attribute. Descartes thinks that mind and body are really distinct and can exist without one another because we can conceive of each as complete by virtue of a different property, its principal attribute. So not just any conceivability will do. Sensation, however, is not a principal attribute, but a mode. Thus the reasoning of the Real Distinction Argument does not imply that we can conceive of a thing as complete by virtue of thinking of it as something that senses. This response may well leave the objector dissatisfied. For, she may argue, doesn't the Second Meditation indirectly imply that sensation is possible without body? After all, Descartes seems to think one can conceive of oneself as a complete thing that senses and has the attribute of thought while presuming that body does not exist, and so it should follow that one can sense without body. Some of the force of this objection will be addressed in a moment when I turn to questions that arise from the theory of distinctions. But where the Second Meditation is concerned we must take into account the following considerations.

In the first place, it is important to consider the content of the doubts about the existence of body. When Descartes argues that we can be certain that we imagine and seem to sense, these doubts focus on the existence of bodies as objects of our thought. Elsewhere in the Meditation they also include the question whether "I have a face, hands, arms and this whole machine of limbs such as I discern in a corpse, and which I call 'body'," and whether "I am some thin air infused in these limbs, a wind, fire, vapor, breath." He also writes that body is conceived of as "whatever is apt to be terminated by some shape, circumscribed by some place, fills some space so that it excludes any other body," that is, as extended. But the consideration of body in this Meditation (or in analogous passages) does not include the idea fundamental to his view that sensations are modes of the mind as united to the body, that is, the idea that as a result of the union the incorporeal entity itself is in a state such that it now can be the subject of inherence for sensations. When Descartes writes in the Second Meditation that he cannot doubt that he senses, he simply has not addressed the role of body he introduces later in the Sixth Meditation. So in the Second Meditation he considers various ways in which our thinking, including our sensing and imagining, might be dependent on body, none of which seem to obtain, thus leaving us with the impression that sensation does not depend on body at all. But then later, in the Sixth Meditation, he develops a view on which sensation does depend on body, although in a way previously not envisaged.

Secondly, at this point it is important to distinguish properly between different types of dependence. In chapter 1 I argued that the thought experiment of the Second Meditation makes the following contribution to the Real Distinction Argument: The conceivability of my thinking while doubting the existence of body shows that thought is not a mode of body. Similarly, the conceivability of my sensing while doubting the existence of body is meant to prepare the way for the position that sensation is a mode of mind rather than body. But—and this is very important—sensation being a mode of mind is compatible with sensation requiring the existence of (and union with) a body for reasons other than body being the subject of inherence of sensation. Or so I will argue in response to the next objection.

(3) The third and final source of the idea that Descartes must hold that we can sense without body lies in his theory of distinctions. On my view sensations are modes of *just* the mind, but they are not *simply* modes of the mind, and they require the existence of body. One might object that since the mind can exist without the body existing, given that mind and body are really distinct substances, it follows that the mind can have sensations without body existing. This result implies that sensation is simply a mode of the mind, and it is incompatible with sensation being a mode of mind as united to body.

This objection requires additional premises, however, which are not contained in the theory of distinctions. For the objection holds only if Descartes adheres to the view that if anything is a mode of a particular substance, then that mode can occur without any other substances existing. But his theory of distinctions does not entail this position. It does commit Descartes to the view that different *substances* can exist without one another, but it does not follow that the *modes* of one substance can exist without any other substances existing.[51] One might think there is still a problem because at *Principles* I.61 Descartes writes that a real distinction also obtains between a mode of one substance and another substance (or from the mode of another substance), because "those modes are not clearly understood without the really distinct substances of which they are modes." The substances at issue could surely exist without one another. But again Descartes does not say anything, and nothing follows, about the possibility of a mode existing without another substance or without a mode of another substance.

A really persistent objector might argue that Descartes's notion of *modal* distinction implies that if sensation is not possible without body, then it is not a mode of just the mind. According to Descartes

> The modal distinction is twofold: one is between a mode properly speaking and the substance of which it is a mode; the other between two modes of the same substance. The first is known *(cognoscitur)* from the fact that we can clearly perceive a substance without the mode which we say differs from it, but we cannot, *vice versa,* understand that mode without it. Thus shape and motion are modally distinct from the corporeal substance in which they inhere *(insunt);* and affirmation and memory from the mind. (*Principles* I.61)

Descartes holds the epistemological view that we cannot clearly and distinctly understand a mode without the substance to which it belongs, as well as the ontological view that if a mode inheres in a substance it cannot exist without that substance. It will be easier to discuss what is at stake at the ontological level.

My view is ruled out if Descartes also holds the reverse: that is, if he holds that if a mode cannot exist without a certain substance the mode inheres in that substance. For on that view the idea that sensation requires the existence of body implies that it is not just a mode of mind. But again, he never commits himself to that claim.

The importance of this observation should not be underestimated: The view that Descartes does hold this claim misses the point of his distinction between modes and substances. For, as I argued in chapter 1.1, the fundamental idea in this distinction is that a mode *inheres in* its substance, it is a property of the substance, and it is not a complete thing without it. The relation of inherence entails that a mode cannot exist without its substance, and it *explains* why it cannot so exist. So the dependence of a mode on the substance that it inheres in is due to a particular factor, namely, the relation of inherence. Similarly, our inability to conceive of a mode without its substance is a result of the fact that we must conceive of it as inhering in that substance.

In fact, we have already seen this point in relation to the Argument for the Real Distinction. For this argument relies on the idea that we can conceive of a mind *as a complete thing* while not regarding it as corporeal in any way, and that idea leads to dualism by way of the theory of distinctions. But the fact that we can conceive of mind in this way merely rules out a particular kind of dependence: It rules out that thought inheres in body. Descartes thought that sensations inhere in the mind, and not in the body, but it simply does not follow that one can sense without having a body, since this view does not rule out other forms of dependence on body.[52] In sum, it is crucial to keep in mind that real and modal distinctions are concerned with a particular kind of dependence, which does belong to modes but not to substances. The theory does not address other forms of dependence, and so Descartes's conception of the relation between a mode and its substance allows for the possibility that sensation is not a mode of body, although it is dependent on body in some other sense and cannot occur without it.[53] For Descartes sensations have a dependence on body because the union of mind and body makes it the case that the mind can be a subject of sensations.

It is tempting to think that the impossibility of one item occurring without another (while the latter is not so dependent on the former) implies that the first is a mode of the second. No doubt Descartes's formulation of the various kinds of distinctions encourages the view that separability is the whole story. But it is important to realize that he often focuses on separability because of the importance of the separability of the soul in view of its immortality, and because of his opposition to qualities that are separable from their subject of inherence. The focus on separability, I believe, often derives from this last preoccupation.

Conclusion

Descartes defends the close union of mind and body on the basis of two aspects of sensation: its occurrence as a result of the action of body on mind and its qualitative nature. Interactionism focuses on the first feature and claims that the union merely consists in interaction, that is, in the fact that occurrences of mental states are caused by physical states (and *vice versa*). This interpretation is in tension with Descartes's claim that the union *explains* interaction, and it ignores the role of the union in regard to the qualitative nature of sensation. Indeed, there is much more to Descartes's view of the union than interactionists allow. Nevertheless, I have argued, he was not a trialist. He did not countenance a third principal attribute to which sensations pertain instead of to thought, nor did he think that sensations proper were modes of both mind and body. Instead he held that the mind-body composite is characterized by the fact that one of its parts, the mind, has modes, a subspecies of thought, that in isolation it does not have. So Descartes's conception of the union does not compromise his dualism in the sense envisaged by the trialistic literature. He regarded sensations as a special subspecies of thought because sensations inhere in the mind as united to the body. Consequently, he maintains his view that there are just two types of modes that correspond to two principal attributes and two types of substances.

This much clarity can be gained about his view of sensation. Unfortunately, a number of issues remain unclear. Descartes does not really explain *how* mind and body are united, nor how this union gives rise to sensations, either with respect to their special qualitative nature or with respect to the idea that the union allows for mind-body interaction. We saw that this is not surprising given his own observations about how much can be said about mind-body union, but it means that his account of sensation is rather sketchy.

One important question we have not yet addressed in this chapter is whether Descartes's defense of the union on the basis of sensation explains how we should understand the status of the resulting entity, the mind-body composite. In what sense is this entity one thing—*unum quid, une seule chose*—as Descartes sometimes writes? One possible answer is this: It is a substance. The idea that a substance has a strong kind of unity was always central to this notion, and it was fundamental for the scholastics. Trialists have sometimes claimed that on their interpretation the entire human being is a substance. If the human being has one single attribute, the union of mind and body, one could see how this might be so, since the human being then has one single, unified nature. But we saw that the text that counts most in favor of this interpretation, the letter to Elizabeth of May 21, 1643, does not support that version of things. On a different form of trialism, the human being is a substance because sensations are modes of both mind and body, and so the human being is a subject of modes.[54] But on that view it is not clear how mind and body are *unified* to form a substance.

In chapter 5 we saw how Descartes could not and did not take recourse to the means the scholastics used in what was already a problematic defense of the unity of the human being. I discussed his use of various expressions that seem to imply the scholastic position, and I argued that his use of none of these warrants the inference that he saw the human being as a substance. One such expression worth revisiting briefly is the phrase 'substantial union'. In section 6.1 we saw that he defends the substantial union of mind and body on the basis of sensation (AT VII 228/ CSM II 160 and AT III 493/ CSM III 206). So we should look to this defense for the content of the phrase 'substantial union'. But insofar as I can see nothing about this defense entails that the resulting composite is a substance.

I pointed out in chapter 5 that Descartes himself never calls the mind-body composite a substance, even though there are several occasions on which his doing so would have been a most appropriate means of placating his opponents. For this reason one should at the very least be skeptical towards the view that he regarded the human being as a substance, and I myself am convinced that he did not. This conviction also derives from the fact that I don't see in Descartes an answer to the question how mind and body are unified so that together they constitute a substance. The present chapter has brought no solutions, nor do I see how he could answer this question. His defense of the union on the basis of sensation does make clear that for him mind and body were *united,* connected in a special, close way—even if various aspects of this union remain obscure. It is clear that Descartes thought this union explains interaction and the possibility of sensation, a special type of thought. But it does not show that he regarded the resulting entity as *unified* in so strong a sense as to constitute a genuine unity and a substance.

It is frustrating that Descartes does not give more of an account of the status of the mind-body composite, and that he does not commit himself to a clear, strong claim about its unity. This is a serious problem, as we certainly tend to experience ourselves as unified entities with both corporeal and mental aspects. But Descartes's reticence makes sense philosophically, since his radical distinction between mind and body makes it very difficult to see how they are united to constitute a genuinely unified entity. I find it very likely that Descartes himself concluded he could not regard the mind-body composite as a substance for lack of the proper sense of unity. In my view that was precisely the right conclusion to draw.

Postscript

In this book I have approached Descartes's dualism and his defense of it not just by examining his own writings, but also by asking how this position was different from Aristotelian scholasticism, the most important part of his intellectual background. When we think of his dualism what stands out is the idea that the mind or soul is an incorporeal thing that can exist without the body. But what is striking in relation to the Aristotelian scholastics is quite different, since they already accepted the incorporeity and separability of the soul. From their point of view what is remarkable is Descartes's view on the question what belongs to mind and soul and what belongs to body: He redrew the boundary between the mental and the physical. Various of his arguments and positions look different or become more intelligible in light of this perspective.

But another important theme in the book is this. Interpretations of a number of elements central to Descartes's thought tend to focus on questions of separability, and there is no doubt that such questions mattered to him. But on several occasions I have argued that one must go beyond separability and look at further and deeper questions about the nature of the entities in question. I have done so for his notions of substance, essence, mode, the real distinction and his argument for it, as well as his conception of sensation. The observation that separability does not get to the heart of the matter is not true just of Descartes, but also of the scholastics. I argued so in particular in chapter 5 in regard to the conception of the soul or mind as the form of the body, and it also applies to their conception of essence, as is illustrated by their notion of necessary accidents. Indeed, this is a place where a fundamental trait of Descartes's thought unites rather than separates him from the scholastics. Besides, this point about separability is not limited to Descartes and the scholastics. Elsewhere I have defended it in relation to Leibniz' view of the union of body and soul.[1] And this line of thought is not, in my view, merely of historical interest. Contemporary philosophers tend to focus on separability and other modal questions, and I think that in doing so they frequently miss out on fundamental issues.[2]

This observation bears on the following question: Given the rather different image of his dualism and his defense of it that emerges from this book, what are the implications, if any, for contemporary interest in Descartes? This is an interesting and important question, which I have not been able to address much in this book. In my own view, on some issues at least (for instance, the Real Distinction Argument, the elimination of sensible qualities), Descartes's thought becomes more interesting philosophically and less obviously reliant on philosophical mistakes (even if one is not convinced to agree with him). On the other hand, some readers will perhaps conclude that parts of Descartes's thought are less relevant to their concerns because he turns out to be more different from them than expected. It is important to keep in mind, however, that we often learn the most from differences between our own outlook and the views of a historical figure. If Descartes were just like us, there would be much less reason to study him. And whether or not we like dualism, his concerns with the mind-body problem are deeply linked with twentieth-century questions about this problem and its relationship to the scope of science. Perhaps we can learn something from how one of the first and most prominent promotors of modern science addressed questions that still preoccupy us.

But in order to learn from Descartes we first need an interpretation of his thought, and such an interpretation benefits from considering his historical background. In this book I hope I have contributed to a better understanding of Descartes's thought and its relation to Aristotelian scholasticism.

Notes

Preface

1. When I use the terms 'Aristotelians' or 'scholastics' and cognates, I always intend to refer to scholastic Aristotelians.
2. Descartes refers to Aquinas on various occasions (for instance, AT II 630/ CSM III 142; AT III 274/ CSM III 166; AT III 359/ CSM III 179). Descartes reports that he remembers the Coimbra Commentators in a letter to Mersenne of September 30, 1640 (AT III 185/ CSM III 154). He mentions Eustachius several times (AT III 185, 232, 233, 259, 470/ CSM III 154, 156, 157, 161). Suárez is mentioned in the Fourth Replies (AT VII 235).

1. The Real Distinction Argument

1. For instance, while expressing certainty that dualism is false, Sidney Shoemaker has written that the argument appeals to a "tiny dualist faction" in his soul. See Shoemaker 1983, p. 235.
2. What I call the Real Distinction Argument is not Descartes's only argument for dualism. Also in the *Meditations* he argues that mind and body are distinct on the ground that the mind is indivisible, while body is divisible (AT VII 85–86/ CSM II 59). In the *Discourse* and other places he lists various human capacities in favor of the idea that the human being is not just a body (AT VI 55–60/ CSM I 139–141).
3. Whereas Descartes says here that sensation and imagination are modes of his mind, it has been argued that he held (at least some of the time) that they really belong to the union or composite of mind and body, rather than just the mind. I do not think that that position is necessarily incompatible with Des-

cartes's aim to defend a purely mechanistic conception of body. I discuss this position, which I do not accept, in chapter 6.3.

4. Clear appreciation for both these points can be found in Weinberg 1977, p. 72. It should be mentioned, however, that the idea that the soul or mind is different in nature from the body and not extended is important for immortality as well as for a mechanistic conception of body. For corporeal, extended things tend to go out of existence by decomposition. The crucial point is that separability is *not* directly relevant to a defense of a mechanistic conception of body.

   Daniel Garber points out an interesting problem for the argument's success in defending Descartes's view of the scope of mechanistic explanation (Garber 1992, pp. 92–93, 111). There are important questions, relating to the Real Distinction Argument, about the kinds of modes Descartes assigned to mind and body, respectively. I say little about this issue in the present chapter, but it will be addressed elsewhere in this book. See in particular chapters 2 and 3.

   Incidentally, it is interesting to note the difference on this issue between Descartes and Locke. The latter was also committed to the mechanistic philosophy, and, most notably, also confined sensible qualities to the mind. But Locke did not seem to connect his mechanistic commitments to substance dualism. In particular, he did not think that one can rule out the possibility of thinking matter by means of philosophical argument (*Essay* IV.III.6). In regard to the defense of substance dualism, it is crucial that Locke did not share Descartes's conception of substance, according to which a substance has one nature that determines what types of qualities it has. This is a complicated issue, however. For discussion see Wilson 1979 and Ayers 1981. As I shall argue, this conception of substance is fundamental to the Real Distinction Argument.
5. Suárez discusses these issues at length at DM VII. He provides the characterization of real distinction as the distinction of one thing from another at DM VII.I.1 and he uses it throughout the disputation. See also Eustachius, SP IV, p. 80.
6. In the Fourth Replies Descartes comments on the employment of the term in the *Meditations* and says that he had used it to stand for complete things, which are substances. He points out that he did not call the faculties of imagination and sensation *res,* but distinguished them accurately from *rebus sive substantiis*—things or substances (AT VII 224/ CSM II 158). For this use of the term *res* see also the letter to Hyperaspistes of August 1641, AT III 435/ CSM III 197. On other occasions Descartes uses the term more loosely. A clear example is *Principles* II.55, where Descartes calls both substances and their modes *res*. See also my discussion of incomplete things in chapter 5.4.
7. See Garber 1992, pp. 85, 89; Hoffman 1986, p. 343 n; Wilson 1978a, pp. 190, 207. Hoffman writes that it is sufficient for real distinction of mind and body that they can exist apart. In principle one might think separability is sufficient for *establishing* real distinction without being *constitutive* of real

distinction. But Hoffman thinks that real distinction simply consists in separability. Descartes, on the other hand, thinks that separability is a sufficient indication, a sign, of real distinction, because he thinks that only two (or more) substances, entities existing in their own right, can be separated from one another.

8. If Descartes does not think that real distinction consists in separability, the question arises why he provides the definition in the Geometrical Exposition in terms of separability. He must have been moved to do so in view of its use in the argument for the real distinction of mind and body a little later in that text. Also it is noteworthy that Descartes's precise formulation—"two substances *are said to be* really distinct when each of them can exist without the other" (emphasis added)—does not clearly commit him to the idea that real distinction *consists in* separability.
9. DM VII.II.9–27.
10. *Principles* I.51. Strictly speaking, of course, this definition only applies to God, since all created substances depend on Him, as Descartes immediately makes clear in this article of the *Principles.* He concludes that the term 'substance' does not apply univocally to both God and creatures. In article 52 he specifies that created substances "need only God's concourse in order to exist." The French edition says instead that in order for us to recognize created minds and bodies as substances it is sufficient "that we perceive that they can exist without the help of anything created." I will generally omit this type of qualification. Jean-Luc Marion offers a detailed comparison of Descartes and Suárez in their treatments of this issue in Marion 1991, pp. 110–139. He points out the interaction between Aristotelian and Christian views about dependence in regard to this issue. See also ch. 6 n. 53.
11. Cf. Garber 1992, pp. 65, 85, 89.
12. See Curley 1969, pp. 4–11, for the view that this way of distinguishing substances and modes was common at the time. Louis Loeb sees Descartes's characterization of substance as a subject of inherence and as independent as two different, although related strands in his conception of substance. See Loeb 1981, pp. 78–100.

    In the Fourth Replies Descartes also gives a weaker characterization of substance in terms of the *ability* to exist *per se:* "this is the very notion of substance, that it can exist *per se,* that is, without the help of any other substance." On the same page, however, he gives a stronger description of substances as *res per se subsistentes*—not merely as things that *can* exist *per se* (AT VII 226/ CSM II 159). It is important to note that existence *per se* is compatible with being joined to another substance in some way other than by inhering in it, and that it should be distinguished from existing without or apart from other substances. Thus the mind exists *per se,* without the *help* of any other substance, in particular without inhering in another substance. But in this life it does not exist without the body existing, or in separation from it, because it is united to the body.

Paul Hoffman has argued that for Descartes the soul is the form of the body in a sense found in Scotus and Ockham. In his defense of this position he relies on the view that for Descartes a substance is something that *can* exist apart, but that also can exist in, inhere in, something else (Hoffman 1986, pp. 352–355). The mind does so when it is joined to the body. So Hoffman disagrees with my interpretation of Descartes's notion of substance, according to which it does not (and could not) exist in or through something else. But in fact his view that for Descartes the soul is the substantial form of the body (which I criticize in ch. 5) does not require that a substance can inhere in something else. The reason is that, for the Aristotelian scholastics, substantial forms are very different from accidents. Substantial forms fall under the category of substance (although they are incomplete ones), they are not accidents. For the scholastics the relationship an accident bears to its substance is different from the relationship of a substantial form to what it is united with. This difference is manifested by the fact that they often say that accidents inhere in, exist through, or are in substances: but substantial forms, such as the human soul, *inform* the body (Cf. Eustachius, SP I, p. 97, IV, pp. 45, 46, and Aquinas in Gilson 1979, pp. 275–277). The precise terminology is not essential here, what is important is the difference between the relationships. Consequently, the view that the soul is the substantial form of the body does not require that it can inhere in the body. Nor does it require that the soul can be a quality of the body. On the contrary; qualities and substantial forms are mutually exclusive types of entities for the scholastics. And indeed for Descartes something that is a substance cannot be a quality. There is a passage in the Sixth Replies in which he does seem to allow for this possibility. I discuss this passage in chapter 4.4.1. For general discussion of the distinction between substantial forms and qualities see chapter 4 and chapters 5.1 and 5.5.

13. SP I, p. 97. For several more references see Gilson 1979, pp. 275–277.
14. Strictly speaking, this is not quite accurate, given that Descartes believes God continuously creates the world. Thus really the existence of a substance continuously comes from God. One might say then that God gives a substance its existence directly—its own existence. A mode does not receive existence directly from God but exists by virtue of inhering in a substance: it participates in the existence of the substance.
15. I return to this issue in chapter 6.4.
16. This is a bit of a simplification. For Descartes allows for a third category of properties, such as duration, existence, number, that belong to any substance (*Principles* I.48; for discussion of this issue see Garber 1992, pp. 66–68).

    Descartes often describes the relationship between modes and their principal attribute using the term 'presupposition'. He says that the modes of body presuppose extension (*Principles* I.53), and in the Sixth Meditation he argues that the active faculty of producing ideas is not in me because it does not presuppose intellection (AT VII 79/ CSM II 55). These remarks would seem to imply that the modes of the mind *presuppose* thought. But it is striking that he never says so explicitly, and the question arises whether he thought that the term 'presuppose' captures the relationship between thought and its modes less well than the relationship between extension and its modes. It certainly seems that there is a difference between the two cases. Nevertheless, I will use this term to refer to the relationship between an attribute and its modes for both the mental and the physical.

There are two aspects to this relationship, an epistemic and a metaphysical one. It is not clear to which of these the term 'presuppose' is meant to refer. I will use it to refer to the metaphysical aspect.

17. This view can be found in Locke, for instance, in *Essay* bk. II, ch. XXII. For a comparison with Descartes see McCann 1986. For a different interpretation of Locke's conception of substance see Ayers 1977.
18. There was debate among the scholastics about the question whether a substance can have more than one substantial form. I briefly discuss this debate in chapter 5.1.
19. It is also relevant that Descartes writes that the principal attribute and the substance are merely distinct by reason. This view by itself is not clearly sufficient, however, to conclude that he identified them. For at *Principles* I.62 he also writes that the distinction between a substance and its duration is a distinction of reason. But surely he does not regard a substance and its duration simply as the same thing considered in different ways, not at least, in the same sense in which he does of a substance and its principal attribute. The distinction of reason is too blunt an instrument to bring out the nature of the relationship between substance and principal attribute. It is all right insofar as the separability between substance and its attributes is concerned: neither the principal attribute nor the other ones can be taken from it. But as I have pointed out, there is more to the relationship between a substance and its principal attribute.

On the other hand, one might believe that the distinction of reason between a substance and its principal attribute indicates that Descartes does not identify the two, for it indicates that there is some distinction between them. In a letter to an unknown correspondent of 1645 or 1646 Descartes claims that a distinction of reason is always founded in a distinction in reality (AT IV 349–350/ CSM III 280–281). One might think that this means that there is a distinction in reality, though not a *real* distinction, between the principal attribute and the substance, and that this suggests that there is a subject of inherence over and above the principal attribute.

This letter does not support this conclusion, however. The question at issue in this letter is the nature of the distinction between essence and existence. The distinction in reality results there, Descartes claims, from the fact that there is a distinction in reality between the *thought* of the essence of the thing and the *thought* of its existence. In addition, there is a distinction in reality between something as it exists in the intellect and as it exists outside the intellect. But in the thing as it exists outside thought, there is no distinction between its essence and its existence. Thus, similarly, for the subject and the attribute there would not be a distinction in the thing as it exists outside thought.

20. For a discussion of the question whether the substance is identical with its principal attribute see Laporte 1988, pp. 185–190, and Alquié 1957. The latter is a presentation by Fernand Alquié, followed by discussion that includes as its other main protagonist Martial Gueroult. See also Marion, 1986, pp. 161–180. Marion argues that there is an asymmetry between mind and body in regard to the relationship between principal attribute and substance. Thus on pp. 169–170 he writes that extension inheres in a subject as in something else, but thought does not.
21. Cf. Suárez, DM XV.I.7, 8, 13, X.64; DA I.I.9, 11; Coimbra Commentators, *Physics* 1.9.9.2, pp. 179–180; *Principles* I.53; and AT VIII-2 349/ CSM I 298. See also Garber 1987, p. 574, Garber 1986, pp. 65–70, and chapter 4.3.
22. Aquinas, SCG II.68, p. 204.
23. He speaks of *real* extension to distinguish the feature that characterizes body from the sense in which he is willing to say that mind is extended. See also AT III 420–421, 694–695; AT V 269–270, 341–342/ CSM III 198, 228, 361, 372; and AT VII 442/ CSM II 298.
24. But it is important to note that in the letter to Mesland he describes exclusion in a different way:

    There is a great difference between abstraction and exclusion. If I said only that the idea that I have of my soul does not represent it to me as dependent on body, and as identified with it, that would only be an abstraction, from which I could only form a negative argument, that would be unsound. But I say that this idea represents it to me as a substance that can exist even if everything that belongs to body is excluded from it, from which I form a positive argument, and conclude that it can exist without the body. (AT IV 120/ CSM III 236)

    Unlike in the letter to Clerselier, exclusion does not here amount to the claim that mind does not have corporeal characteristics, rather it specifies that the mind can exist without such characteristics.
25. For discussion of its ambiguity see Curley 1978, p. 196, and Kenny 1968, pp. 86ff.
26. For this view see Wagner 1983.
27. See Shoemaker 1983.
28. Wilson 1978 pp. 191–197.
29. There is a complication in that Descartes also uses the term 'thought' to refer to the modes of the mind. He distinguishes carefully between these two uses of the term, however. See *Principles* I.63 and 64, and the letter to Arnauld of July 29, 1648, AT V 221/ CSM III 357.
30. There are two aspects to the notion of a principal attribute: (a) it does not presuppose another property; (b) it is presupposed by other properties. The

argument as I present it relies on (a), and Descartes's discussions of the argument focus on this aspect of the notion. But in the Third Replies he presents the case for dualism by emphasizing (b) (AT VII 176/ CSM II 124).

31. One might think that in light of the letter to Gibieuf Descartes should be saying that he already knows at this point that he is not a body. But that is not so. The letter to Gibieuf explains how one can find out whether the *idea* of a thinking substance depends on the idea of extension, and thus whether the idea of a thinking thing is an idea of a complete thing. It does not say that one can find out whether any thinking thing actually has the property of extension by means of the procedure described. This is important, for it is consistent to hold that the completeness of some entity, that is, its status as a substance, might be guaranteed by thought and not require extension, while the entity is, nevertheless, extended. Failing to see this distinction would amount to failing to distinguish between having a complete idea of something (which is the same as having an idea of it as complete) and having an adequate idea of it, which requires knowing everything about it. Descartes makes this distinction in the Fourth Replies (AT VII 220–221/ CSM II 155–156).

32. It is often thought that God plays a much larger part, such as by bridging a problematic gap between two types of possibility by virtue of his omnipotence (See Curley 1978, pp. 198–200, Wagner 1983). One reason that has moved interpreters to adopt this position is that, in relation to the argument, Descartes refers to God's power rather than his veracity. But this is not a convincing reason. For Descartes clearly thought that limits on God's power would create problems for the reliability of our perceptions (cf. *Meditations,* AT VII 21/ CSM II 14). Besides, in the Geometrical Exposition he writes: "It must be noted that I have here used the divine power as a means, not because some extraordinary capacity [*vi*] is necessary for separating the mind from the body, but because I did not have anything else I could use since in what precedes I had only dealt with God" (AT VII 170/ CSM II 120). So Descartes himself claims that the special features of God's power are not relevant to separability: our conceptions guarantee the separability of mind and body. And the only way for him to state this separability is, for accidental reasons, in terms of God's power.

    For this issue see also Rodis-Lewis 1971, pp. 338–339; Gueroult 1953 II, pp. 62–64/ 1984 II, pp. 48–49. Both argue that it is important that Descartes tries to establish the real distinction in the face of the union of mind and body. In a different context Gueroult argues that God's veracity follows entirely from his omnipotence because deception is an imperfection for Descartes (Gueroult 1953 I, pp. 42–49/ 1984 I, pp. 21–26).

33. We saw above that although Descartes does not mention extension explicitly here, it is covered in this passage.

    The roles of certainty about thought and doubt about body in the Second Meditation are not limited to what I am describing here. Descartes also uses doubt to include various operations, in particular, sensation and imagination, in the category of the mental. In chapter 2 I argue that the Real Distinction Argument does not rely on claims about sensation and imagination, but only about intellect, to establish the incorporeity of the mind. The inclusion of sensation and imagination in the mental is an additional claim, over and above the real distinction of mind from body, a claim which the thought experiment of the Second Meditation also serves to establish.

34. Really what Descartes should be saying here is that his notion of himself does not depend on his *notion* (or idea) of body, rather than body. But this must be what he means. It is what he needs, and in addition, it is more plausibly what he is entitled to. What he has said in this paragraph provides support for the idea that his notion of a thinking thing does not entail corporeity, but it does not address the question whether this notion could exist without body existing (although Descartes thinks that this also is true).
35. Sometimes Descartes seems to commit himself to the idea that the argument relies on the stronger claim that he clearly and distinctly perceives that extension does not belong to the essence of the mind. See especially AT VII 8, 219/ CSM II 7, 154. He is entitled to such a perception when the implications of the weaker claim (that he does not perceive that extension belongs to the mind) are combined with further views he held and that the Real Distinction Argument relies on. The weaker claim supports the idea that he perceives that thought is not a mode of body but a principal attribute. Given Descartes's view that the essence of a substance consists in its principal attribute, and that a substance has only one such attribute, he can derive the clear and distinct perception that extension does not belong to the essence of mind. So the occurrence of that stronger claim can be explained by these further aspects of Descartes's views. But the contribution of the thought experiment by itself is just the weaker one.
36. There is an ambiguity in the claim of exclusion. Descartes might mean that we can exclude extension from our conception of the mind, or that we can form a conception of the mind as something from which extension is excluded. This ambiguity, however, makes no difference to his purposes. Descartes would wish to make both claims, given that the point is that one is not forced to think of a mind as extended. What *is* really different is the claim that we perceive that extension is excluded from the mind.
37. For its shortcomings see Wilson 1978a, p. 190, and Williams 1978, pp. 111–112.
38. There are places where it does look as if Descartes uses the Argument from Doubt for the real distinction, in particular in the *Search for Truth* (AT X 518/ CSM II 412), *Discourse* (AT VI 32–33/ CSM I 127), and at *Principles* I.8. Wilson thinks that it is not necessary to attribute the argument to Descartes in the latter two places. Furthermore, since the *Search* is a questionable source it does not force one to attribute the argument to Descartes (Wilson 1978a, pp. 242–243). I think that the passage in the *Discourse* is the most troubling

and that it is very hard not to see Descartes as using the argument in that passage—if read in isolation. But elsewhere he claims that in the *Discourse* he is summarizing arguments that really require more extensive treatment (letter of March or May 1637 to an unknown correspondent, possibly Silhon, AT I 353/ CSM III 55). The Real Distinction Argument receives such treatment in the *Meditations* and other texts, where the role of the skeptical doubts is clearly much more subtle.

39. I know of only two places where Descartes seems to allow for the possibility of one mode presupposing another mode, which then in turn presupposes a principal attribute. In Meditation III he seems to describe the modes of body as ordered in a hierarchy of presupposition (AT VII 43/ CSM II 30). In a letter (probably to Mersenne for Hobbes) he says "there is no problem or absurdity in saying that an accident is the subject of another accident, as one says that quantity is the subject of other accidents" (AT III 355/ CSM III 178). Descartes is interested here in the relationship between movement and its determination.
40. When writing to Gibieuf Descartes claims that if there were such a connection, and we had no idea of it, God would be a deceiver (AT III 478/ CSM III 203).
41. See Kripke 1972. This problem certainly arises for the widely accepted view that the basic idea is simply that Descartes argues that it is conceivable for mind to exist without body and thus possible. See Shoemaker 1983, pp. 245–246. For more on that interpretation, see section 6 in this chapter.
42. In a sense, neither of these two points about body rely on peculiarities of the notion of a principal attribute. The first one could be stated by saying that the essence or nature of body is extension. The importance of the second point lies in the idea that something can be a corporeal, nonthinking substance. But the notion of a principal attribute is important for the premise now under discussion ("extension is the principal attribute of body") in view of the way in which this premise gets used in the argument. For it is combined with the claim that a substance has just one principal attribute, to reach the conclusion that mind and body are really distinct.
43. This passage was pointed out to me by Jeremy Hyman.
44. The quote from the *Comments* suggests that Descartes might have yet another qualification in mind, namely, that the Attribute Premise applies only to attributes that (a) constitute the natures of things *and* (b) neither of which is contained in the concept of the other. Clearly that condition applies to thought and extension. But I don't think this is supposed to be an additional qualification. There are no examples in Descartes of attributes that constitute the natures of things without satisfying this condition. Indeed, I suspect that he did not really mean to suggest that there are such attributes, and that the clause is there just because he wanted to mention this characteristic of attributes that constitute the natures of substances. Alternatively, he may be using

the term 'attribute' broadly enough to include modes, which do include other attributes in their concepts, in particular, the principal attributes they belong to.

45. It is worth noting that Descartes's statements of the argument in major texts, such as the *Discourse, Meditations,* and *Principles,* tend to be quite elliptical and omit not just the role of the notion of a principal attribute. When responding to questions and objections he came up with various elaborations that have contributed significantly to our understanding of the argument and Descartes's confidence in it. For instance, whereas in his statements in these major texts he does not appeal to the notion of a complete thing, in the Replies and in correspondence Descartes is quite explicit about the importance of this notion for the argument. For the *Discourse* and the *Meditations* the explanation could be that the role of the notion of a complete thing was really an elaboration Descartes developed later. But that explanation does not apply to the *Principles.*
46. For a defense of something akin to this premise, see Schiffer 1976, pp. 36–37.
47. The comparison with substantial forms is based on the notion of substantial form as used by Suárez and Aquinas, who were both committed to the view that a substance only has one such form. But many scholastics held that a substance can have several substantial forms (see ch. 5.1). This idea might seem to be incompatible with the line of thought I am proposing. Indeed, the 'unitarians' argued that the unity of essence requires that there be just one substantial form in a substance (see Zavalloni 1951, p. 476). On the other hand, the 'pluralists' saw the forms present in one substance as presupposing one another in a hierarchy. For instance, in a human being there could be several substantial forms, which together determine the full nature of a rational animal—a living creature that among its manifestations of life includes rational activity. This is very different from Descartes's view of extension and thought, which are entirely independent of one another.
48. *Essay* II.XXIII.32, IV.III.6. For relevant discussion see the references in n. 4.
49. See also ch. 2 n. 6.
50. Wilson 1978a, pp. 197–198.
51. Wilson 1978a, pp. 190, 206–207.
52. Cf. Wilson 1978a, pp. 193–198, especially 193–194.
53. Versions of this interpretation can be found in Wagner 1983, Hooker 1978. Bernard Williams' interpretation is different in important respects, but he also holds that the argument relies on *de re* modal claims (Williams 1978, pp. 115–116). Hooker's interpretation is adopted in Van Cleve 1983. Shoemaker 1983 uses the interpretation offered in Malcolm 1977. The term "Essentialist Premise" is taken from Shoemaker's article. Van Cleve and Shoemaker are concerned with philosophical rather than scholarly issues. Curley writes that Descartes relies on God's omnipotence. But he finds this approach philosophically unsatisfactory and considers the possibility that the necessity of identity, and in particular, Kripke's notion of a rigid designator, might be

the solution to the type of problem the premise is meant to solve (Curley 1978, pp. 200–206). Margaret Wilson does not interpret the argument as relying on *de re* modal claims. But she thinks the real distinction simply consists in separability of mind and body. As a result, she does not need to make the step from what is possible to what is actual, for which the Essentialist Premise is introduced.

54. Stephen Wagner pays more attention than others to the question of textual evidence for the Essentialist Premise. He claims that there is no question that Descartes held it. But he thinks that Descartes failed to supply it explicitly, or argue for it, and suspects confusion on Descartes's part on the distinction between the Essentialist Premise, which is a *de re* claim, and the *de dicto* claim that necessarily bodies are extended (Wagner 1983, p. 505).
55. One might drop the premise that what is conceivable is possible. The question then arises how else one could establish that it is possible that one exists and thinks without being extended. Sidney Shoemaker has argued that there is no way of doing so without begging the question. That is to say, he argues that in order to establish that one can exist without being extended, one has to determine first that one is not extended. But that is the intended *conclusion* of the argument (Shoemaker 1983, pp. 247–248). For a different version of the same criticism see Van Cleve 1983, p. 41.
56. Shoemaker 1983, pp. 248–249.
57. Nevertheless, there are clear reasons why separability of mind and body is bound to emerge in Descartes's statements of the argument. After all, he is interested in separability in view of the issue of the after-life and in the rejection of separable accidents.
58. For more discussion of the chronology, see Garber 1992, pp. 23–26.
59. For discussion of related ideas in contemporary terms, see the reference to Schiffer in n. 46, and also Van Cleve 1983.

2. *Scholasticism, Mechanism, and the Incorporeity of the Mind*

1. See also AT VII 385, 387/ CSM II 264, 265, and letter to Mersenne, October 16, 1639, AT II 598/ CSM III 140.
2. Wilson 1978a, pp. 177–185.
3. Wilson 1978a, p. 180.
4. Wilson 1978a, pp. 181–185.
5. Wilson might well agree with my view about Descartes's point in the passages in question. In addition to pointing out his nonparallelism, she also characterizes pure understanding as independent of physical processes (Wilson 1978a, p. 181). Her claim that Descartes did not accept parallelism for intellection is not intended to be a claim about his point in these passages, but about the difference between Descartes's dualism and modern 'Cartesian' dualism. For my purposes the distinction between nonparallelism and independence is important, however.

6. There is, however, the following difference between Descartes and the Aristotelian scholastics. I will focus on Aquinas, but the views in question were widely accepted by the Aristotelian scholastics, including Eustachius, Suárez, and the Coimbra Commentators. On one hand, Aquinas thought that the intellect is independent of the body in the sense that the soul alone is the subject of inherence of the operation of intellection. The Independence Thesis is meant to refer to this sense of independence. On the other hand, he held that human intellection does require a body in a different sense, because it requires the activity of the imagination—which he regarded as a corporeal faculty, an activity of an organ. He held that the imagination is needed for two reasons. First, he thought that intellectual ideas—intelligible species, as they were called—are derived from sense experience through the imagination (cf. ST 1.84.6, 85.1). Second, he believed that human beings cannot understand without also forming images; intellectual activity is always accompanied by imagination (ST I.84.7, 86.1). The distinction between these two roles of imagination is particularly clear in Aquinas at ST I.85.1 ad 5. See also Coimbra Commentators *De anima* 2.1.4.2, p. 98; Eustachius, SP III, p. 417; Suárez, DA IV.VII.3. I return to this issue in chapter 5.2.

   Descartes did not think that intellection depends on imagination in either of these ways. Thus he thought that intellection is independent from the body in a stronger sense than the scholastics did. One might think that this stronger sense of independence plays a role in the Real Distinction Argument, but I don't think that this is the case. See n. 40 below.
7. See also Coimbra Commentators, *De anima separata* disp. III, art. I, p. 545; Suárez, DA VI.III.3; Eustachius, SP III, pp. 286–287. Unlike these scholastics, Ockham held that the sensitive soul is the subject of sensation. See *Reportatio* IV, qu. 9, OTH VII, p. 162. But for him the sensitive soul is really distinct from the intellectual soul. Aquinas also mentions the will here. Much of what I will say about the intellect is also true of the will, but the discussions, both in scholasticism and in Descartes, focus on the intellect.
8. For other places where Descartes discusses the differences between animals and human beings, see especially the letter to Plempius for Fromondus of October 3, 1637 (AT I 413–415/ CSM III 61–63); to the Marquess of Newcastle, November 23, 1646 (AT IV 574–576/ CSM III 303–304); and to More, February 5, 1649 (AT V 275–279/ CSM III 365–366). See also Gilson's very useful notes on the *Discourse* in Gilson 1976, pp. 420–438.
9. In the Fourth Replies he writes that there is no reason to think animals have souls (cf. AT VII 229–231/ CSM II 161–162).
10. Cf. Ryle 1967, pp. 346–347.
11. For this reaction, see the letter by Fromondus to Plempius of September 13, 1637 (AT I 403).
12. See Gilson 1976, especially pp. 425–429 and 435–436. He writes that a friend of Descartes's, Silhon, discussed the problem posed by the difficulty of

distinguishing animals and humans at length, and envisioned the immortality of animal souls in order to defend immortality for human souls.

13. Again, Arnauld shared this view of the matter (AT VII 204–205/ CSM II 144). He writes that Descartes's view about animals is a solution to the problem of the difference between animal souls and human souls. In his words the problem is that "according to the principles of commonly accepted philosophy [the immortality of the human soul] by no means follows [from the distinction of mind and body], since people ordinarily take it that the souls of brute animals are distinct from their bodies, but nevertheless perish with them."
14. This position was held by Aquinas, Suárez, Eustachius, and the Coimbra Commentators. But according to another scholastic view, there are several really distinct souls in a human being, a nutritive soul, a sensitive one, and an intellectual one. I briefly discuss this view in chapter 5.1. Descartes thinks he can dismiss that view pretty quickly by claiming that it is heretical. (See two letters to Regius of May 1641, at AT III 369, 371/ CSM III 181, 182). And again, souls other than the rational one he eliminates in favor of mechanistic explanations.
15. See also Eustachius, SP III, pp. 413–414; Coimbra Commentators, *De anima* 2.1.1.6 and 2.1.2.2; and *De anima separata* disp. I, art. 3. Suárez stated the argument slightly differently. He wrote that the soul is spiritual on the basis of the spirituality of some of its operations (DA I.IX).

    Medieval Aristotelians attributed the idea that intellection is not an operation of the body to Aristotle. Relevant texts are *De anima* III, 4, 429a, 18–28 and 5, 430a, 10–25.
16. Cf. Suárez, DA I.X; Eustachius SP II, pp. 413–441; Coimbra Commentators, *De anima separata* disp. I, art. 3. Aquinas argues that the soul is incorruptible (ST I.75.6).
17. See, for instance, ST I.76.1 and SCG II.68. The question is central to Aquinas 1968a. See also chapter 5.1.
18. For a discussion of Averroes' treatment of this issue see the introduction by Beatrice Zedler to her translation of Aquinas 1968a. As she points out, there was yet a third position, adopted by Avicenna, according to which only the agent intellect is separate.
19. This representation of Descartes's conception of the human soul as intellectual may seem inaccurate in light of the fact that he did assign to the mind sensation, imagination, and other mental states that involve the body. Several points need to be made here. First, in the argument in the *Discourse* that we are discussing, Descartes clearly insists on the intellectual or rational nature of the human soul. The idea that the human soul is also the subject of sensation and the like is entirely absent. Second, on Descartes's view, the inclusion of sensation and other similar types of mental states causes no problems for distinguishing human souls from animal souls, since he held that animals only have the mechanistic part of sensation, and not the conscious states that he

assigns to the mind. Finally, sensation and similar states do not, on his view, belong to the *essence* of the mind. This is in fact an important point for the Real Distinction Argument, and I shall return to it later in this chapter. It will also be relevant in chapters 5 and 6.

20. As I pointed out in n. 6, the scholastics thought that even the intellect depends on the body,.in the sense that it requires activity by the imagination. But Descartes rejected that view.
21. In the Sixth Meditation, he writes that he can understand himself clearly and distinctly as a whole (*totum*) without sensation and imagination (AT VII 78/ CSM II 54). Again, in the Replies to Gassendi he says that the whole (*tota*) nature of the mind consists in the fact that it thinks (AT VII 358/ CSM II 248).
22. Wilson thinks that the passage in the *Discourse* shows that Descartes reflected seriously on the possibility of a mechanistic account of human behavior (Wilson 1978a, pp. 184–185). Jeanne Russier claims that Descartes's appeal to the human capacities discussed there was actually not an unusual move in defense of the spirituality of the human soul (Russier 1958, p. 48). She refers to Silhon and Boucher. I have been unable to lay hands on either of the works she cites. Russier's claim, if correct, raises questions about how seriously we can assume Descartes considered the possibility of mechanistic explanations for all human behavior.
23. Wilson also thinks that intellection, but not sensation and imagination, is involved in the Real Distinction Argument (Wilson 1978a, pp. 180–181, 201, 220). But she does not state a clear view of where Descartes's conception of the intellect figures in the argument. Thus she raises the question whether the Real Distinction Argument *supports* Descartes's conception of the intellect and suggests that it does not (Wilson 1978a, p. 181). She also does so in Wilson 1978b, p. 201. On the other hand, in that paper she seems to consider the possibility that the Real Distinction Argument *relies on* the immateriality of intellectual activity (pp. 206–207).

    For another scholar who notes the difference between sensation and intellection in relation to the Real Distinction Argument, see Beyssade 1976, p. 21.
24. The beginning of the discussion of the mind in the Second Meditation reflects this attitude. Descartes there introduces the idea that he thinks, after eliminating other properties of himself on the ground that they require a body. But he seems to assume, or seems to think it is clear, that thought does not require a body. For he concludes without argument that he thinks. ('Thought' should be taken there in the sense of intellectual activity, as I will argue in a moment.) He does not even mention the possibility that thought requires a body, whereas he does discuss this possibility for sensation and imagination later on in the Second Meditation. This difference in treatment reflects the difference between these various faculties in scholasticism, where sensation and imagination were not regarded as belonging to the mind. As a result Descartes

needs to go through more trouble to include them among the modes of the mind. (AT VII 26–27/ CSM II 18).

25. An exchange between Gassendi and Descartes is interesting in this context. Gassendi had written that in order to show that the mind is different from the body Descartes had to come up with an operation that the mind performs independently of the body (AT VII 269/ CSM II 188). As we saw before, Descartes replied that he had shown that the mind does have such an operation, namely, pure intellection (AT VII 358/ CSM II 248). This reply supports the view that Descartes thought the operation of intellection shows the real distinction.

    On the other hand, another aspect of this reply might be thought to cause a problem for my view that the Independence Thesis plays a role in the Real Distinction Argument. For Descartes seems to present the independence of the intellect from the body as support for the incorporeity of the mind *in addition to* the Real Distinction Argument. In a letter of 1638 Descartes gave yet a different picture of the relationship between the two ideas: there he claimed that the possibility of the mind thinking without the body is a *consequence* of the real distinction, which he there derives from the Real Distinction Argument (AT II 38/ CSM III 99).

    So Descartes expresses different views of the relationship between the Independence Thesis on one hand, and the real distinction as well as the Real Distinction Argument on the other hand. He may have been unclear about these issues. The comments in question are very brief, however, and he may have had particular points in mind that would turn out to be compatible with one another as well as with my account of the role of the Independence Thesis in the Real Distinction Argument.

26. On the other hand, even today some philosophers find it intuitively strange to hold that thought is motion or some other physical process. My point is that given Descartes's purposes and historical context, dismissing the possibility that thought is a physical process was more feasible than it is today.
27. Letter to Mersenne, January 28, 1641 (AT III 297–298/ CSM III 173).
28. These two characterizations of the mind correspond to the two important modifications Descartes makes in the conception of the soul: first, the restriction of the soul to the mind; second, the assignment of a part or aspect of sensation, imagination, and other functions to the mind. I discuss this second idea below.
29. For the scholastics the distinction between the corporeal and the incorporeal or the material and the immaterial is not always an all-or-nothing matter. For a brief discussion see chapter 4.4.2. For discussion of one relevant issue in Aquinas, see Hoffman 1990a. But the scholastics generally regarded the mind, unlike other parts of the human being, as entirely incorporeal and free of materiality.
30. These are all instances of what Descartes calls internal sensations. In the passage just quoted from the Sixth Replies he also describes external sensa-

tions, such as of colors, flavors, and the like, as arising from the union of mind and body.

31. See, for instance, a letter to Mersenne of July 1641, AT III 395/ CSM III 186. For the view that the attribute of thought should be identified with intellection see also Gueroult 1953 I, pp. 62–67, 76–82/ 1984 I, pp. 35–38, 44–48, and McRae 1972, pp. 55–70.
32. It is clear that Descartes thinks the same relevant differences obtain between sensation and intellection as between imagination and intellection. See for instance, AT II 598/ CSM III 140; AT VII 73/ CSM II 51; and the Conversation with Burman, AT V 162/ CSM III 344–345.
33. Descartes's view is not that we can only think about non-corporeal entities by means of the pure intellect; we can make the mistake of trying to imagine God. But rather his view is that we can only have genuine knowledge, clear and distinction perceptions, of these entities by means of the pure intellect.

    It is tempting to think Descartes identifies pure intellection with clear and distinction perceptions. But in the Fifth Meditation he speaks of distinctly *imagining* quantity (AT VII 63/ CSM II 44), and he held that a perception cannot be distinct without also being clear (see *Principles* I.46). So it is not the case that clarity and distinctness can be found only in pure intellection. Nor do I see any reason for thinking that for Descartes pure intellection is *always* clear and distinct. It is true that he often characterizes the senses as the source of all sorts of confusion and obscurity. But to my knowledge he never claims that avoiding that source of error and using just the pure intellect is sufficient to guarantee that we have only clear and distinct perceptions.
34. For discussion of other faculties, see McRae 1972, pp. 64–66.
35. See also *Principles* I.9. Incidentally, these definitions do not *identify* thought with consciousness. Rather they identify thought as that *of which we are immediately conscious*. For this point see also McRae 1972, pp. 55–57.
36. Gueroult 1953 I, p. 78/ 1984 I, p. 45.
37. McRae and Gueroult both offer philosophical arguments that connect consciousness and intellection. But in my view neither succeeds in establishing that Descartes accepted the connections they propose (McRae 1972, p. 66, and Gueroult 1953 I, p. 76–81/ 1984 I pp. 44–47).
38. The aspect of imagination, and sensation, in virtue of which ideas appear extended is not the only role of the body in these activities. When Descartes defends the union of mind and body on the basis of sensation, he emphasizes a different point, namely, its confused qualitative nature. There is good reason, however, to think that the appearance of extension is particularly important to the role of the Independence Thesis in the Real Distinction Argument. For Descartes brings up the Independence Thesis on various occasions precisely when he contrasts intellection with imagination in relation to the extended appearance of images. Furthermore, this appearance of extension specifically suggests dependence on the principal attribute of body, extension. Consequently, it is particularly important for the Real Distinction Argument that intellection does not involve seemingly extended images.

39. Two views should be distinguished. (1) The imagistic content of imagination constitutes an obstacle to *establishing* the incorporeity of the mind on the basis of consideration of imagination. This view concerns the question whether imagination can be used to establish the real distinction. (2) The imagistic content of imagination, a faculty of the mind, shows a dependence on the body, once the incorporeity of the mind is established. Only the first view is important to the Real Distinction Argument. The second one would seem to be in tension with Descartes's position that in sensation, on the occasion of events in the body, ideas occur in the mind in accordance with correlations established by God. Nevertheless, his claim to Gassendi that imagination requires an image that is a real body suggests Descartes accepted it. See chapter 6 for discussion.
40. We are now in a position to answer the question raised in n. 6. This question was whether the Real Distinction Argument relies on Descartes's view that intellection is independent from imagination. The answer to this question is negative for the following reason. The independence of the intellect from the body comes into the argument via the idea that thought does not presuppose extension, in the sense that it does not require an extended substance as a subject of inherence. But this idea is compatible with the view that intellection requires imagination in the ways in which Aquinas and others thought it does. That is, it is compatible with the view that intellectual activity must be preceded and accompanied by activity of the imagination. For a different view, see Carriero 1986.
41. Or at least, this is the case for worries that are relevant to the Real Distinction Argument. The mind-body problem also plays a part in twentieth-century contemplation of the question whether machines can do what we can do, and there the question concerns human intellectual capacities. But when we consider that question, our concerns are related to the argument of the Fifth Part of the *Discourse* rather than the Real Distinction Argument.

3. Sensible Qualities

1. For Descartes's use of the term 'sensible qualities'—*qualitates sensiles* or *qualitates sensibiles*—see *Principles* IV.198 and AT V 268–269/ CSM III 361. But mostly he simply lists a number of such qualities without using any specific term.
2. Descartes also rejected the scholastic notion of prime matter, but that issue is not directly relevant to his aim of defending a mechanistic conception of body. I briefly addressed this notion in chapter 1.5. Furthermore, he was also in debate with the atomists, whose conception of the physical world is different from his in important respects. But that debate is not directly relevant to his dualism. For a discussion, see Garber 1992, ch. 5. Nevertheless, disagreements with the atomists will be important in section 3.4.
3. For detailed analysis of the First Meditation in light of this purpose, see Rozemond 1996.

4. See, for instance, Burtt 1954, pp. 107, 118. As scholars have pointed out, however, Descartes did not offer or even try to come up with much in terms of quantified laws, and he derives the principal laws of motion from the notion of God (Dijksterhuis 1961, p. 414). Furthermore, confining the physical world to mechanistic qualities implies that the qualities of bodies can be described in quantitative terms, but it does not guarantee that the laws of nature can be expressed mathematically. For it does not follow that changes in these qualities obey mathematical regularities (see Hatfield 1990, p. 114, and also n. 19).

   Nevertheless, Descartes may have expected that a purely mechanistic conception of the physical world would eventually lead to mathematical treatment of all natural phenomena. Already before the scientific revolution, the Aristotelian scholastics recognized a set of disciplines that are a mixture of physics and mathematics, such as optics, mechanics, and astronomy, and that study the physical world in mathematical terms. Perhaps Descartes assumed that if mechanics could be extended to all physical phenomena, its mathematical methods could also be extended in this way (see Weisheipl 1985, pp. 265–268).
5. Anneliese Maier proposes this view for early modern mechanistic philosophers. She writes: "What [the mechanistic theories] want is not measurement of qualities—at least not at once, and it is also not always the case that this ideal stands in the background—what they want is an interpretation, a determination of essences [*Wesensbestimmung*], an answer to the question *quale*—of what kind?—and not to the question *quantum*—how much?" (Maier 1968, p. 25).
6. For this view see, for instance, Popkin 1979, ch. 9, and Rodis-Lewis 1992, p. 54.
7. The view that the physical world has sensible qualities is not the only deceptive effect of the senses according to Descartes. In the Third Meditation, for instance, he points out that our sensory idea of the sun is misleading, and he thought reliance on the senses is to blame for the mistaken belief that when we don't sense anything in a space, it is empty (AT VII 39, 83/ CSM II 27, 57).
8. See also the *Discourse on Method,* AT VI 37/ CSM I 129, where he explicitly identifies the phrase as referring to the scholastic position. In the Sixth Replies he describes another aspect of the scholastic view, the idea that when we understand we always use our imagination as well (see ch. 2.1 n.6 and ch. 5.2). On that occasion, he identifies this way of understanding as one that dates back to his childhood (AT VII 441/ CSM II 297).
9. For discussion of the discrepancy between the species theory and Descartes's representation of it, see Schmaltz 1996. For an illuminating discussion of relevant features of scholastic theories of qualities and sense perception, see Maier 1968, pp. 16–26. Not all Aristotelians believed in the species theory. Most famously, Ockham rejected it (cf. Maier 1968, p. 20.) As Maier points out, however, unlike the mechanists, Ockham did not banish sensible qualities from the physical world.

10. Maier 1968, p. 19. She points out that the question how perception of mechanistic qualities is caused was controversial. I also discuss Aristotelian scholastic conceptions of sensible qualities in section 3.2.
11. Descartes mentions a different problem at *Principles* IV.198. See section 3.4.
12. Like Descartes, other corpuscularians and atomists have also insisted on the explanatory virtues of the mechanistic model. Cf. Lucretius 1975 II, 758–794 and Locke, *Essay* II.VIII.
13. Garber 1992, pp. 84–85.
14. In the Sixth Meditation he does say that "I have never judged that anything cannot be brought about by him [God], unless because it was contradictory [*repugnaret*] for me to perceive it distinctly" (AT VII 71/ CSM II 50). But there is an important difference between a failure to perceive something clearly and distinctly and a case where it is *contradictory* to have a particular perception (by which Descartes means, I take it, that we would perceive something that is contradictory).
15. Garber raises this objection to the use of the present strategy against the scholastic notions of real quality and substantial form (Garber 1992, p. 107).
16. For discussion of this issue see also Hatfield 1985, p. 156. Hatfield writes that for Descartes the *a priori* demonstration of his first principles was "the only means of disposing of other explanatory principles, such as substantial forms, once and for all." Hatfield does not specify how he thinks this strategy works.
17. See, for instance, Hatfield 1986.
18. According to Hatfield, Descartes's claim that his physics is nothing but geometry is ambiguous because it is not clear whether it is a claim about methodology or content (Hatfield 1990, p. 113). Dijksterhuis points to the scarcity of mathematical details in Descartes's physics and claims that its mathematical character lies in its methodological nature, namely, the "axiomatic structure of the whole system, in the establishment of indubitable foundations and the deduction of the phenomena" (Dijksterhuis 1961, p. 414).

    Garber proposes that in the Fifth Meditation Descartes claims that ideas of mechanistic qualities are clear and distinct on the ground that we can use these ideas to perform proofs. He then argues that Descartes presents mechanistic qualities as *real* on the basis of this possibility of proofs (Garber 1992, p. 81). I believe that this focus on proofs is on the right track, but I pursue it in a different way. In my view, the crucial feature of proofs for Descartes is the fact that they allow one to know things with certainty.

    Incidentally, it is important to see what the proofs in question are about: they are about the properties of bodies as they fall under geometry, such as triangles, and so they allow one to establish many facts about the mechanistic qualities of bodies. Consequently, there is a clear sense in which we know what we ascribe to the world when we attribute mechanistic qualities to it. But these proofs do not describe the motion of bodies, and they do not establish mathematical laws of nature.
19. See Burtt 1954, p. 118, and Buroker 1991.
20. Margaret Wilson does briefly note this issue (Wilson 1978a, p. 109). Inciden-

tally, I will not attempt to analyze the notion of material falsity, which has received considerable attention from interpreters. My discussion is not meant to offer a full analysis of this difficult passage. As I see it Descartes's argument against sensible qualities does rely on the charge that ideas of them are confused and obscure, but not on the (closely related) claim that they are materially false. But the notion of material falsity is important for his epistemology, in particular, for the question whether ideas of these qualities are inherently deceptive. For discussion, besides Wilson, see, for instance, Gueroult 1953 I, pp. 302–308; II, pp. 164–165/ 1984 I, pp. 216–220; II, p. 131; Nelson 1996; Hoffman forthcoming.

21. In what follows I am heavily indebted to work by Anneliese Maier, as well as to Partington 1961 and Kargon 1966.
22. Existence in reality is not, however, what Descartes means by the term '*real* quality'. Frequently when he uses this term, he focuses on the scholastic conception of certain types of qualities as *res* in the technical sense of that term (see, for instance, AT VII 434/ CSM II 293). I don't see any trace of that issue, however, in the Third Meditation, and Descartes is clearly concerned with the question whether hot and cold exist in the physical world at all. He does use the term '*res*' in this passage, but in a nontechnical sense. For he says that *all* ideas are *tanquam rerum,* but ideas of modes are not of *res* in the technical sense. I discuss the issue of qualities as *res* in the technical sense in chapter 4. For a different view of this passage, see Menn 1995, pp. 199–201.
23. Kargon 1966, pp. 51–52, 59.
24. Boyle thought so. See Partington 1961, p. 509.
25. Kargon 1966, pp. 51–52. He writes that for Bacon "heat is an expansive motion, and in an upward direction. Cold is also a motion, but contractive and downward."
26. Gassendi 1964, p. 394.
27. Gassendi 1964, p. 401.
28. Partington 1961, p. 11.
29. Partington 1961, p. 415.
30. In reporting Gassendi's views I have referred to a work that was published only in 1658, after Descartes died. It is quite possible, however, that his views were known well before then.
31. He mentions Telesio in a list of philosophers while making the observation that philosophers hold many different views. His point there is quite general, and he is not concerned with the question of the nature of qualities. But it is interesting that there is an analogy with the remarks in the Third Meditation. For I am arguing that these remarks are inspired precisely by there being a lack of agreement concerning the nature of cold.
32. Terms such as 'cold' were also used for whatever it is out there that causes my sensations of cold and the like, which is compatible with a mechanistic account. But in the Third Meditation Descartes is clearly using these terms to refer to the qualities as we experience them, and the existence of such qualities

in the physical world is at issue. For he is considering ideas of mechanistic and sensible qualities in order to determine what kinds of entities we can infer exist from an examination of the objective reality of these ideas. He draws different conclusions about each.

33. Similarly, in *The World* Descartes describes the qualities he rejects as things "in the nature of which one can say there is something that is not evidently known to everyone" (AT XI 33/ CSM I 91).
34. Buchdahl gives a hint of such a problem. In the *Rules* Descartes says "whatever power (*vis*) you may suppose color to be, you will not deny that it is extended and consequently has shape." He suggests that we can take account of the differences between colors by means of shape (AT X 413/ CSM I 40–41). Buchdahl writes about this passage: "seeing that science finds difficulty in coping with such things as colour, Descartes suggests, let us abstract from every feature except shape" (Buchdahl 1969, p. 89). I see no evidence in the text that Descartes had in mind scientific difficulties in dealing with color, but Buchdahl's comment is intriguing. For another problem, see the reference to Maier in the next note.
35. Maier 1982, pp. 136–138.
36. Cf. Maier 1968, pp. 17–18, and Maier 1982, pp. 130–132. She writes that among the qualities derived from *primae qualitates* there was the following further distinction: the elements do have other *tactile* qualities in addition to hot, cold, dry, and wet, but smell, taste, and color only belong to mixed bodies. Sound, she claims, was treated as an exception, as it was thought to be produced by motion (Maier 1982, pp. 135–136).
37. For instance, Gassendi's introduction of his discussion of hot and cold reflects their special importance (Gassendi 1964, p. 394), which may also have something to do with the fact that in *The World* Descartes starts his mechanistic account of the world by explaining phenomena thought to be produced by heat.
38. For discussion of the role of childhood in our belief in sensible qualities (as well as other 'prejudices'), see Garber 1992, pp. 100–103, Garber 1986, pp. 81–116, and Gilson 1984, pp. 168–173.
39. For the view that the exclusion of sensible qualities is *expressed* by the claim that the essence of body is extension, see Garber 1992, pp. 63 and 64. The idea that Descartes uses this view of the essence of body for the exclusion of sensible qualities can also be found in Garber 1992, pp. 85–89, 134, as well as in Hatfield 1990, p. 114; Williams 1978, p. 236; Cottingham 1986, pp. 136–137; and is implicit in Gueroult 1953 II, pp. 12–14/ 1984 II, pp. 7–8.
40. Garber 1992, p. 134. For his discussion of Descartes's conception of substance, see pp. 63–70. He writes that given the intimate connection between the principal attribute and the modes of a substance, the claim that the essence of body is extension does not merely mean "that all bodies have extension and necessarily so, as his scholastic contemporaries might have meant such a claim; he is saying something stronger, that everything that can really

be attributed to body as such must be some way or another of being an extended thing" (p. 69). Whereas I agree with this statement of Descartes's conception of body, I don't think the view of the scholastics Garber presents here is right. Essence, for the scholastics, was not the modal notion he seems to attribute to them on this occasion. In fact, Garber himself argues in this very section that the scholastics allowed for necessary accidents, properties that are inseparable but yet not part of the essence of a substance (Garber 1992, pp. 68–69, and also 79–80).

41. Garber 1992, p. 86.
42. One may be tempted to read the passage in the Sixth Meditation as saying that sensible qualities can *only* be found as sensations in the mind, on the ground that there is a certain analogy between this passage and *Principles* I.66 and 68, where Descartes does make that claim. In those texts his point is that sensible qualities can only be clearly and distinctly perceived if merely regarded as sensations in the mind. But he simply does not make that stronger claim in the passage in the Sixth Meditation, and he leaves the discussion of sensible qualities for later in that Meditation.
43. Recently scholars have argued that sensation and imagination were not, for Descartes, modes of the mind, but modes of the mind-body composite. I discuss this issue in chapter 6. This view need not be incompatible with the mechanistic conception of body: as long as sensation and imagination are not modes of body as such, whether they be modes of the mind, or of the composite or the union of mind and body, a complete mechanistic account of body is safe. By contrast, the scholastic view is one on which sensation and imagination are definitely located within the physical world.
44. Similar comments apply to the Third Replies, where Descartes concludes mind and body are distinct by way of the claim that "acts of thought have nothing in common with corporeal acts, and thought, which is their common concept, is entirely different in kind from extension, which is the common concept of corporeal acts" (AT VII 176/ CSM II 124; for more on this argument, see chs. 1.3 and 2.2). Again, however, Descartes does not mention sensible qualities. He could be confining sensible qualities to the mind here, if he relied on the assumption that the combination of lists of 'acts' is exhaustive. But this passage, like the one in the Sixth Meditation, is simply not meant to address the issue of sensible qualities. It is concerned to establish that mind and body are different substances.
45. Williams considers the objection that one might regard color as a mode of extension (Williams 1978, p. 236). Part of his reply is that Descartes assumes that body can only have quantifiable modes of extension. But he supplies no textual evidence, and in section 3.2 I have argued that Descartes does not rely on the impossibility of quantifying sensible qualities to exclude them from body.

    Did Descartes abstain from arguing that sensible qualities don't belong to body because of the sorts of problems that beset this argument for qualities like color? I don't know, and can only speculate about this question. But the view that this reason plays a role is made plausible by a comment in the *Rules* that we saw above. Descartes writes, speaking about the state of the body that we call color: "whatever power (*vis*) you may suppose color to be, you will not deny that it is extended and consequently has shape" (AT X 413/ CSM I 40–41).

46. Bernard Williams adopts this interpretation (Williams 1978, p. 236), and Alison Simmons (Simmons 1994, pp. 190–197).
47. It is true that sensible qualities could be excluded from body on the basis of the following combination of claims: (1) they are not modes of body, and (2) the notion of a real quality is incoherent. But again, Descartes never argues this way. Whereas he often offers (2), he never uses (1) against sensible qualities.
48. *Essay* bk. II.VIII.9. Locke also observes that when one puts, for instance, some blood under a microscope, its color disappears (*Essay* II.XXIII.11). For discussion of Locke's treatment of secondary qualities, see Curley 1972 and Alexander 1974.
49. Galileo 1957, p. 274. Galileo's list of mechanistic qualities is different from Descartes.
50. Lucretius 1975/ 1995 II, 740–748.
51. Lucretius 1975/ 1995 II, 749–756. Recent commentators have contended that Locke's arguments have the form that the changes in secondary qualities are more easily explained on a corpuscularian theory than on an Aristotelian one (cf. the references in n. 49). Lucretius relies on this idea as well (Lucretius 1975/ 1995 II, 757–816). In fact, there is considerable overlap between the arguments against sensible qualities in Lucretius and those in Locke. Incidentally, I do not wish to claim that my presentation of the Arguments from Change and Elimination does justice to their details in Locke, Lucretius, and Galileo.
52. See, for instance, Burtt 1954, p. 117, and Buchdahl 1969, p. 90. Margaret Wilson argues that the wax passage does not establish the distinction between mechanistic and sensible qualities, but she does think that "some related points are made" (Wilson 1978a, pp. 77, 88). It is my view that the wax passage has *nothing* to do with the issue of sensible qualities, other than by way of the very generic point that the senses do not tell us what the nature of body is.
53. See, for instance, Burtt 1954, p. 117, and Marion 1991, p. 100. Whereas Wilson's interpretation of the term is broader, she emphasizes change with respect to motion (Wilson 1978a, p. 88).
54. This point is recognized by Williams 1978, pp. 213–224, and Garber 1992, p. 78, and Garber 1986, pp. 99–100.
55. See Garber 1992, pp. 77–80; Kenny 1968, p. 207; Wilson 1978a, pp. 82–88; Alquié III, p. 150; and Beyssade 1976, p. 13. See also Buchdahl, who seems to focus on article 11, but erroneously identifies it as article 2 (Buchdahl 1969, p. 95).
56. Garber 1992, p. 80.

57. The argument about hardness seems puzzling at first sight. Descartes claims that we can think of bodies being such that they always recede when our hands approach them so that we never have the sensation of hardness. That may strike one as a rather unconvincing thought experiment, but Alquié has a helpful comment. He suggests that Descartes must be thinking of gases, which behave in this manner (Alquié III, p. 149). As we shall see, this is an important point for Descartes: for one might think there is nothing where in fact there is air or some other gas.
58. Cf. n. 41.
59. The Argument from Change seems to make a brief appearance in this article. For Descartes writes: "we reject cold and hot and all other qualities either because they are not considered as in the stone, or because when they change, we do not therefore think that the stone has lost the nature of body." But he should not be using the Argument from Change here: for it simply does not follow from the fact that the temperature of a stone can change, that having *some* temperature does not necessarily belong to it. But that is the conclusion he needs here.

    It is puzzling, furthermore, because it seems implausible that Descartes considers the possibility of a stone not being either hot or cold. In a letter to More he also envisions the possibility of a body that has neither of these qualities (February 5, 1649, AT V 268/ CSM III 360), and perhaps that letter provides the explanation for this idea. For Descartes also argues there that there are bodies that we cannot sense because they are too small. Perhaps what he had in mind at *Principles* II.11 is simply that bodies may fail to cause sensations of heat or cold in us.
60. For discussion of this argument see Garber 1992, pp. 127–136.
61. Although I will not take the time to discuss this issue, Descartes's view that there is no empty space is also important in his discussion of rarefaction. Consequently, the idea that bodies need not be sensed is important for that issue as well. Thus in his discussion of rarefaction at *Principles* II.7 he brings up the point that "there is no compelling reason to believe that all the bodies which exist must affect our senses."
62. Wilson 1978a, p. 85.
63. In their commentary on the *Principles,* Vincent Carraud and Frédéric de Buzon write that the atomists, but not the scholastics, defined matter in terms of sensible properties, in particular, hardness and weight. They refer to Lucretius. They do not seem to recognize, however, that Descartes is indeed addressing the atomists rather than the scholastics in article 4 of part II. (Carraud and de Buzon 1994, pp. 45–49).

4. Real Qualities and Substantial Forms

1. Gilson's classical treatment of real qualities and substantial forms (in Gilson 1984) clearly displays awareness of the difference between them in scholastic

thought, but he repeatedly confuses them in his discussion of Descartes. He runs the two notions together at p. 149, where he wrongly calls gravity a substantial form—something Descartes never does. He discusses the difference at p. 159 n. At p. 161 n. he claims that for Aquinas there was no distinction, whereas there was one for the Coimbra Commentators. (See also Gilson 1976, p. 384.) Garber claims that Descartes does not take the distinction into account, and for this reason he does not either in his analysis of Descartes's arguments against these notions (Garber 1992, p. 333 nn. 6, 9). He cites the case of heaviness, a real quality, as an instance of a substantial form (Garber 1992, p. 97). Marjorie Grene says Descartes "hardly" draws the distinction; her discussion does not reflect it at all. See Grene 1986, p. 311, and also Grene 1991, p. 16. Curley does not distinguish them (Curley 1978, pp. 4–5). Paul Hoffman respects the distinction in a useful discussion of real qualities and substantial forms in his dissertation (Hoffman 1982, ch.2). But his thought-provoking defense of Descartes's hylomorphism ignores crucial aspects of the distinction (Hoffman 1986, pp. 350–355).

2. On the other hand, in an earlier exchange with Mersenne and Morin he seems to impress his correspondents with his grasp of scholastic thought (see letter to Morin of July 13, 1638, AT II 196–219/ CSM III 106–111, and a letter from Mersenne of August 1, 1638, AT II 287). The content of this exchange does not establish that Descartes's knowledge of scholasticism is very detailed. (For a discussion of this exchange see Ariew 1992, pp. 70–72.) But a basic understanding of the notions of substantial forms and real qualities is fundamental to even a rather superficial grasp of scholastic thought.
3. Cf. Aquinas, ST I.76.4; Aquinas 1965, ch. 1; Coimbra Commentators, *Physics* 1.9.9.2, p. 179; Suárez, DM XXXII.I.4.
4. For more on the question of proper accidents, see Garber 1992, pp. 68–69.
5. John D. Kronen argues that Suárez emphasizes arguments for substantial forms that rely on this role. Kronen regards this as a difference from the traditional position, which focuses on the argument from substantial change (Kronen 1991, pp. 335–360). This view is interesting in light of the fact that Descartes never refers to the role of substantial forms in accounting for substantial change.

   Substantial forms account for the unity of a substance in two ways: the combination of matter and form is the right one for a substance to be a genuine unity (see ch. 5.1). In addition, the substantial form unifies the accidents of a substance, which is at issue here. For a discussion of the general importance of this second idea in scholasticism, see Zavalloni 1951, p. 476. Zavalloni presents this role of the substantial form as an aspect of the view that a substance can have only one such form. Many scholastics disagreed, but the view is adopted by Suárez and the Coimbra Commentators as well as Aquinas. For the use of this role of substantial form as an argument against a plurality of substantial forms, see Suárez, DM XV.X.64.
6. DM XV.I.8.

7. Garber identifies form with proper accidents (Garber 1992, p. 68). It is true that these are accidents that necessarily belong to a particular type of substance. They change only when these substances are generated and corrupted. But still the process of substantial change is *constituted* by a turnover in substantial forms. Suárez argues that some accidents are so inseparable from certain subjects that their loss implies a complete transformation of their subjects. But he uses this consideration to argue for the presence of a form that is substantial, not accidental (DM XV.I.13).

   Garber does not claim to identify *substantial* form with proper accidents because he has in mind the scholastic notion of metaphysical form, which is different from physical form. The latter is the substantial form. But this distinction does not affect my point. For the metaphysical form differs from the physical form in a substance that is a composite of matter and form only in that it includes matter as well. Thus in the case of the human being, the soul is the physical, substantial form, while 'humanity', which includes materiality, is the metaphysical form. The metaphysical form does not consist in accidents either: it is identical with the essence, and accidents, whether they be necessary or not, are external to essence. See Suárez, DM XV.XI.3, 4, and Gilson 1979, p. 276.
8. Cf. M. M. Adams 1987, p. 633, and the references in n. 3.
9. I have found no scholastics using the term in the way Descartes does. For uses of the term 'real accident' that seem to be different, but at least related, see Suárez, DM XXXII.I.22–23. In his *Lexicon philosophicum* Goclenius explains a use of the term 'real quality' that has nothing to do with Descartes's: "Among the qualities of natural bodies some are material or corporeal, such as redness in the face; others are spiritual, such as the species of a colored thing. The scholastics also call the former 'real', the latter 'intentional'" (p. 912). This explanation of the term 'real' is different from Descartes's, however. For Goclenius' distinction divides qualities in bodies from their intentional species. It does not address the question whether a quality is a *res* or not, which is the issue that interests Descartes when he talks about real qualities. For a different angle on the comparison of Descartes and Goclenius, see Garber 1992, p. 333 n. 6. See also Gilson 1984, p. 170.
10. For a discussion of Suárez on this issue see Gracia 1982, pp. 231–232, and Menn forthcoming.
11. DM VII.I.19.
12. See also ch. 1.1 for the use of the term *res* in the scholastics and in Descartes.
13. For discussion see M. M. Adams 1987, pp. 277–285, and Menn forthcoming.
14. Suárez, DM XLII.II.1; Eustachius, SP I, p. 118; M. M. Adams 1987, p. 280; Aristotle, *Categories* 8.
15. M. M. Adams 1987, p. 280; Ockham, OPH I, pp. 182–183.
16. DM VII.I.19, XXXIX.I.17.
17. Eustachius' position seems to be different. He held that all qualities are real entities, *verae entitates,* as opposed to mere modes of being, *modi essendi.* He

does not use the term *res* in this context. See SP I, pp. 117–118. Whereas he denies that qualities are modes, it is not entirely clear whether he thinks they are *res*. See also his discussion of distinctions, SP IV, pp. 79–82.

18. M. M. Adams 1987, p. 278. The problem of the Eucharist, briefly, was this. In transubstantiation, the Catholic interpretation of the Eucharist, the body and blood of Christ take the place of the bread and wine. The problem is then to explain the fact that the transformed entities continue to display the sensible qualities of bread and wine. One interpretation required that the real qualities of the bread and wine remain without inhering in a substance. According to another view of transubstantiation, the accident of quantity remains, and the qualities we perceive inhere in it as their subject. See Aquinas, ST III.77.2. For the two views see Menn forthcoming.
19. DM XXXVII.II.2, 3.
20. See Eustachius, SP IV, p. 45. Suárez' discussion is very complicated, DM XXXVII.II.
21. Cf. Jolley 1992, pp. 397–399. For discussion of the issue of the Eucharist in Descartes, see Armogathe 1977; Gouhier 1924, pp. 248–258; Rodis-Lewis 1950, pp. 68–74. The question how to explain that the wine and bread don't change their appearance was not the only issue about the Eucharist that seemed newly problematic, given Descartes's views. See the letter to Mesland of February 9, 1645 (AT IV 162–170/ CSM III 241–244).
22. Ockham, *Quodlibeta* VII, qu. 2, OTH IX, pp. 707–708; *Summa Logicae* I.55, OPH I, p. 180. Menn claims that Suárez offers the same reasoning (Menn 1995). He does not, however, provide a text where Suárez states this idea, and I have not found one. For discussion see also M. M. Adams 1987, pp. 277–285. She explains that other scholastics had claimed that *all* qualities are *res* because all change is due to a *res* coming into being or ceasing to be (p. 280).
23. In a letter to Mersenne Descartes seems to suggest that there is a question about whether motion is a *res* or a mode. He writes: "I do not attribute more reality to motion nor to these other varieties of substance that are called qualities, than the philosophers usually attribute to shape, which they do not call a real quality, but only a mode" (April 26, 1643, AT III 648/ CSM III 216).
24. See Maier 1968, pp. 17–19.
25. In a discussion of qualities in the Sixth Replies, Descartes seems to give a tripartite division of qualities that is similar to Locke's in the *Essay* and that separates heaviness from sensible qualities. The text is not entirely clear, however (AT VII 440/ CSM II 297 and Locke, *Essay* II.VIII.10). Locke does not mention heaviness. What is similar is that both identify the third group of qualities by their power to affect a body other than the one in which it inheres. The distinction between the second and third groups reflects the scholastic distinction between qualities that only affect the senses and ones that produce other types of change as well. See chapter 3.1. Incidentally, it is hard to see how heaviness causes a distinct sensation. I know of no intrinsic

difference between the sensation caused by a book resting on my hand and the pressure it exercises when I lay my hand against it while it stands upright on my shelf.

26. This explanation of belief in real qualities is rather different from Descartes's account of the source of our belief in sensible qualities at *Principles* I.71. On that account we believe bodies have such qualities due to a thoughtless assimilation to mechanistic qualities that occurs in childhood. In the Sixth Replies the idea is that the belief is based on a view about the explanation of sense perception. Alan Nelson sees the source in our childhood as just a different form of bad theorizing from the kind done in philosophy or science (Nelson 1996).
27. For a discussion of this dispute in the context of the seventeenth-century Netherlands, see Verbeek 1988, 1992a, and 1992b. For the pronouncement by the Lateran Council, see Denzinger 1991, pp. 482–483, art. 1440–1441, and p. 390, art. 901.
28. There are also some differences with respect to the time at which the different arguments appear. See Garber 1992, pp. 103–111.
29. Garber sees it this way (Garber 1992, pp. 108–111).
30. On the other hand, in the *Meditations* he claims that he never rules out that God can do something unless "it is contradictory that I perceive it distinctly" (AT VII 71/ CSM II 50). This may seem inconsistent with the passage just quoted from the Fourth Replies. But there is clearly a difference between merely not being able to perceive something (clearly and distinctly), which is what he refers to in this passage, and a perception being contradictory, or it being contradictory that one have a certain perception—which is at stake in the passage from the Sixth Meditation. The latter applies to real qualities. Nevertheless, his remark to Arnauld seems insincere, given that he argues elsewhere that the notion of real quality is contradictory.
31. Descartes offers this strategic kind of reason for his silence about real qualities and substantial forms on various occasions. But in a letter of June 1645, probably to Huygens, he writes that he has abstained from refuting the arguments of the Schools because of his respect for several Jesuits (AT IV 225/ CSM III 252).
32. In the letter to Arnauld of July 29, 1648, the only sense in which Descartes mentions that heaviness is regarded as corporeal is in that it is ascribed to body (AT V 223/ CSM III 358).
33. For more on the analogy with heaviness and mind-body union and interaction, see ch. 6, especially sections 6.1 and 6.3.
34. See, for instance, Aquinas, ST I.76.8, and Aquinas 1968b, qu. 10 ad 4. In addition, the notion of being whole in the whole and whole in the parts was used to account for God's presence in the world, to provide an explanation of God's acting in different locations without himself being extended in the ordinary sense. (See Grant 1981, pp. 223–228, 350 n. 127). This use of the notion is closer to Descartes's, but still different. For further comments on

Descartes's use of this notion, see ch. 6.1 and 6.3, but I intend to provide a full discussion on some future occasion.

One might argue that here is a place where Descartes does confuse substantial forms and real qualities, since for the scholastics the human soul is such a form, and they regarded it as united to the body, whole in the whole and whole in the parts. But the mismatch between the scholastic and Cartesian use of this special sense of extension is so radical that it makes little sense to look at the relationship in this way.

35. In the Third Replies he relates the issue to the degree of reality of the accidents in question (AT VII 185/ CSM II 130).
36. Daisie Radner writes that Descartes's choice of an analogy with clothes is a bad one because "clothes cannot be called qualities of the man" (Radner 1971, pp. 164–165). She adds that he admits in the Sixth Replies that not clothes, but only being clothed can be a quality. But I don't think we need ascribe any mistake to Descartes on this issue. Hoffman cites this passage as support for the idea that a substance can be a quality, although he qualifies this claim in a footnote (Hoffman 1986, p. 351).
37. For this view of the relationship of clothes to a clothed person, see also Suárez, DM LII.I.2.

    Descartes also uses the notion of heaviness as a real quality to explain the union of mind and body. This might make it seem as if the mind is both a quality and a substance for him after all. But when offering this explanation in a letter to Elizabeth, he writes that he does not worry about the problems with thinking of this quality as real because the princess already conceives of the mind as a substance distinct from body (AT III 694/ CSM III 228).
38. For discussion of this accident in scholasticism, see M. M. Adams 1987, ch. 6. According to a common account of transubstantiation, the accident of quantity of the bread and wine continues without its substance, and without subject of inherence, and it serves as subject for the other remaining accidents. Cf. n. 18.
39. See Aquinas, ST I.76.1; SCG II.68; Coimbra Commentators, *Physics* 1.9.10.1.
40. In addition, Aquinas recognized degrees of different forms of incorporeity in relation to sense perception. For discussion see Hoffman 1990a.
41. See, for instance, Garber 1992, pp. 97–98.
42. The argument is theological in a modern sense, because it concerns religious issues. On the other hand, the scholastics often used the term 'theology' in a different sense, where it is identical with metaphysics. Thus Aquinas writes that it is the science that deals with anything that can exist without matter. This science concerns "substance, quality, being, potency, and one and many, and the like." It is called theology because "its principal object is God" (Aquinas 1955, qu. V, art. 1). But the term 'theology' may no longer have been used in Aquinas' sense at the time of Descartes. For a discussion see Courtine 1990, pp. 61–74, 195–201, 485.

43. He does speak in this passage in the *Discourse* of souls of animals, but it is clear that he thinks animals are merely conglomerates of particles with mechanistic qualities. The same applies to his occasional talk of entities other than human beings having substantial forms. In the passage quoted from the letter to Regius he suggests that he only rejects substantial forms as conceived as substances. He says "we see daily, however, that many of those forms which are called substantial begin to exist from nothing." In a letter to Morin he writes that the substantial form of the sun "is a philosophical being unknown to me in so far as it differs from the qualities that can be found in matter" (AT II 367/ CSM III 122). Such claims clearly amount to a rejection of substantial forms in the entities in question, since substantial forms are supposed to be distinct from any qualities a substance has.
44. *De anima* I.II.III, p. 77.
45. See also Aquinas, SCG II.86–87; Eustachius, SP III, p. 28; Coimbra Commentators, *De anima* 1.2.3, pp. 77–78.
46. The scholastics also commonly distinguished, among spiritual forms, between informing and assisting or separate forms. Angels are assisting ones: they do not inform any body. Only human souls are informing spiritual forms: they are both independent of matter and inform it. (See Suárez, DM XV, introduction, and section 10.)
47. See chapter 5.1.
48. See Suárez, DM XV.II.9.
49. Others have followed his lead on this issue. Hoenen 1967, p. 362 n., and Miles 1983, p. 27 n.
50. For a discussion of this aspect of Descartes's method, see Galison 1984.
51. John Cottingham emphasizes this argument in his discussion of sensible qualities. See Cottingham 1986, pp. 135–143. The argument may seem inconsistent with Descartes's admission, in the same article, that mechanistic qualities can produce sensations. After all, on his view there is clearly a great dissimilarity in that case as well. Since Descartes makes this admission in the same article, he must think there is no inconsistency here. One reason why he might hold that view is that there is a distinction between the case where the thing in which the effect is produced is of the same kind as the agent, and the case where they are dissimilar. Given the difference between mind and body, that idea would remove the inconsistency.
52. For discussion and further references regarding Descartes's views of the causal efficacy of bodies, see Garber 1992, pp. 299–305, Garber 1987, and Hatfield 1979.
53. See M. M. Adams 1987, p. 282, where she discusses Ockham's view on the question whether qualities of the mind are *res*. In the letter to de Launay Descartes does complain that the scholastics ascribe "various things to the soul that only belong to body" (AT III 420/ CSM III 188). But he does not give any examples. He might have in mind his view that the scholastics tried to explain many things by an appeal to souls, which he explained in mechanistic terms.

54. See chapter 1.5 for Descartes's rejection of prime matter. The scholastics distinguished quantity and extension although they thought the two were intimately connected. Descartes thought it was a mistake to distinguish the two and often identified them.

5. *Hylomorphism and the Unity of the Human Being*

1. Gilson 1984, p. 247. See also Gilson 1976, pp. 431–432, and Gouhier 1987, p. 358. Laporte writes that for Descartes the soul is not merely the form of the body: because for Descartes, unlike on the Aristotelian-scholastic model, the soul is not merely distinct from the body by abstraction (Laporte 1988, pp. 227–8).
2. Rodis-Lewis 1950, pp. 76–81, and Hoffman 1986, pp. 339–369. Marjorie Grene follows Hoffman in Grene 1986 and Grene 1991. Garber cites Descartes's claims that the soul is the form of the body among statements that he regards as expressing Descartes's conception of the union of body and soul (Garber 1992, p. 89). See also R. M. Adams 1994, p. 293 n.
3. Cf. M. M. Adams 1987, p. 633; Suárez, DM IV.III.1, 3, 13; Eustachius, SP IV, pp. 20–21, 92. Suárez discusses the distinction between *ens per se* and *ens per accidens* at length, and I will primarily refer to him. Eustachius' discussion, as is usual with him, is very brief. Suárez comments on the difficulty of defining the notions in question. He points out that Aristotle, the source of the distinction, does not define unity *per se* and *per accidens,* but merely provides examples (DM IV.III.1).
4. DM IV.III.2–3.
5. See Aristotle, *De anima* 413a3–9, 413b24–26, 429a18–29, 430a18–25. Some aspects of Aristotle's view, however, seem to imply the inseparability of the intellect.
6. Cf. Aquinas, ST I.75.2; SCG II.49–51; Aquinas 1968b, qu. 1. See chapter 2.1 for more on this argument and its relation to Descartes's argument for dualism. Suárez also bases the incorporeity of the rational soul on freedom of the human will (DA I.IX.35).
7. *Quodlibeta* 1.10, OTH IX, p. 64.
8. M. M. Adams 1987, pp. 639–647; Eustachius, SP III, pp. 21–22; Suárez, DM XIII.V.
9. ST I.76.1 ad 5. Scholastics who awarded some sort of actuality to matter responded by saying that a substance can contain several partial acts of existence. Cf. Ockham, *Quodlibeta* II.10, OTH IX, p. 161, and Suárez, DM IV.III.4.
10. For this assessment see also M. M. Adams, p. 669, and Zavalloni 1951, pp. 496, 500.
11. Ockham, *Summula Philosophiae naturalis* I.10, OPH VI, p. 182; Suárez, DM XIII.V.8–11; Eustachius, SP III, pp. 21–22. Suárez ascribes the distinction between types of actuality to Scotus. The case of the Coimbra Commentators is more complicated. They rejected the view that matter has any actuality, and

thus they are in verbal agreement with Aquinas on this issue. On the other hand, they did claim that matter has an existence of its own, and so in fact they reject Aquinas' view and agree with the one found in Eustachius, Suárez et al. (Coimbra Commentators, *Physics* 1.9.3.1, pp. 156–157.) For a discussion of composite substances in Aquinas, Scotus, and Ockham, see M. M. Adams 1987, ch. 15. She discusses the status of prime matter at pp. 639–647.

12. ST III.75.6, I.66.1. Suárez writes that the motivation for the view that matter cannot be conserved separately is the view, which he rejects, that matter has no existence of its own (DM XV.IX.2).
13. Eustachius, SP III. pp. 25, 34, IV, pp. 80–81. Eustachius adds a qualification to separability as a criterion for real distinction: he says it is sufficient if it is separability by virtue of different existences. For Suárez see DM XV.IX. Suárez discusses the connection between separability and real distinction in DM VII.II.9–27. For Descartes real distinction comes with mutual separability. This was true for Suárez and Eustachius as well, but, as M. M. Adams discusses, not for the scholastics generally. The question whether matter and form can each exist separately does not seem to be quite so clear in Ockham and Scotus (see M. M. Adams 1987, pp. 17–18, 644–646). Zavalloni seems to hold a different interpretation of Scotus (Zavalloni 1951, pp. 305–306). Matter and form were, however, widely regarded as really distinct. For the notion of real distinction see also chapter 1.1.
14. Aquinas, ST I.76.3, 4, and Coimbra Commentators, *De anima* 2.1.4.1, p. 84, 2.1.6.2, p. 96. Suárez devotes a lengthy discussion to this issue. See DM XV.X. He states his unitarianism in XV.X.61. Eustachius held yet a different view, according to which a single substance as a whole does not have several substantial forms. But a substance with heterogeneous parts does have several partial forms, for flesh, bones, and so on (SP III, pp. 267–276). For extensive discussion of the debate between the pluralists and unitarians, see Zavalloni 1951 and also M. M. Adams 1987, ch. 15. I borrow the terms 'pluralists' and 'unitarians' from Adams.
15. There is a difference, however, in that Descartes ascribes a mental component of sensation, imagination, and the like to the mind. For Ockham those operations do not belong to the intellectual soul, but to the sensitive soul. For sensation see *Reportatio* IV, qu. 9, OTH VII, p. 162.
16. Marilyn Adams has suggested to me in conversation that Ockham *assumed* that the soul is the form of the body.
17. Zavalloni 1951, pp. 312–315, and M. M. Adams 1987, p. 665.
18. In this respect I disagree with Hoffman. On his view Descartes's account of the unity of the human being fares no worse than that of scholastics who thought a substance can contain more than one component with actuality (cf. Hoffman 1986, pp. 363–364). But Hoffman does not distinguish between the threat to unity posed by the actuality of matter and the threat posed by a plurality of substantial forms and he does not specifically discuss the latter.
19. For this idea in Aristotle, see *Metaphysics* 8.6, 9.6. See also Coimbra Com-

mentators, *Physics* 1.9.3.1, pp. 156–157; Suárez, DM IV.III.4; Eustachius, SP IV, pp. 20–21.

20. See also Ockham, *Quodlibeta* II.10, OTH IX, p. 161; Suárez, DM XXXIII.I.5–6; Eustachius, SP III, p. 416.
21. Coimbra Commentators, *Physics* 1.9.11.4, p. 187. See also their *De anima separata,* disp. II, art. 1, pp. 532–536. For Aquinas' use of the phrase, see ST I.89.1. The Coimbra Commentators also write that matter 'desires'—*appetit*—form, which means that it has an inclination for receiving form (Coimbra Commentators, *Physics* 1.9.5.1, p. 160). For Suárez, see DM XXXIII.I.11; for Eustachius, SP III, pp. 466.

    Sometimes the scholastics described the union as a good for the composite, or the human being, instead of as a good for the soul itself. In this case, that good was also sometimes cited as a source for the soul's union with the body or its appetite for the union. See Eustachius, SP III, p. 466, and Coimbra Commentators, *De anima* 2.1.6.3, p. 100. Nevertheless, these scholastics also clearly held that the union is good for the soul in that it allows the soul to exercise its functions, as the Coimbra Commentators point out at once.
22. See SCG II.68; ST I.76.1; Aquinas 1968b, I.
23. DA I.IX.16.
24. Eustachius, SP III, pp. 34 and 446. Coimbra Commentators, *De anima* 2.1.6.3, p. 99. See also Suárez, DM IV.III.8, and the references in n. 22 above.
25. Goclenius expresses a very interesting opinion on this issue: "I have said above that when the soul has left the body, it is called 'soul' homonymously. Why? Because properly speaking, the soul is what animates the body. But the soul that migrates from the body no longer animates it, nor can it exercise any actions of the organs, but only its own proper ones, for which it does not need the help of the body" (Goclenius 1613, p. 104).
26. Along the same line Eustachius writes that if the soul is not an informing soul, that is, a substantial form of the body on the hylomorphic model, but a *forma assistens,* on the Platonic model, then "it would follow that the operations proper to the soul would not depend in any way on the body, as the operations proper to demons in an assumed body, as intellection and moving something in place etc. depend in no way on the assumed body itself. But it is absurd to admit this in the case of the rational soul. For although some of its operations are above [*supra*] sense and body, they can not, however, happen in this life without the help of the senses and the body; for we experience that we do not understand or reason without phantasms" (SP III, p. 417).
27. The scholastics did think that when the soul is separated from the body it can exercise its intellect, but it does so in a different way. They also sometimes argued that intellectual activity without help of the body is superior *tout court.* But they contended that this mode of intellection is not the one *natural* to the human soul, and they regarded this observation as important. Cf. Aquinas, ST I.89.1; Coimbra Commentators, *De anima* 2.1.b.3, p. 100, Eustachius, SP III, pp. 440–441. Aquinas held that understanding without help of

the body is superior *tout court,* but not the best for human beings. Suárez, however, thought that the human soul understands better in separation, although he did regard understanding in union with the body as the mode of understanding natural to the soul. DA VI.VIII–X.

28. Hoffman 1986, pp. 350–351.
29. DA I, introduction, p. 467.
30. Gilson makes a similar point. In Thomistic scholasticism, he writes, the soul is a substantial form "because it is not a substance in the full sense of the term, but one of the integral parts of this substance that is a man. . . . According to Descartes, on the other hand, *the soul is the substantial form of the body precisely because it is a real substance*" (Gilson 1976, p. 432).
31. Descartes also speaks of the soul *informing* the body when writing to Mesland, as well as on other occasions. But he seems to use that term interchangeably with the soul being united to the body. One can then adopt either one of two different interpretations of his use of this term: (1) his claim that mind and body are united means that the mind *informs* the body; (2) the claim that the mind informs the body means no more than that it is united to the body. In light of the absence of a robust sense of hylomorphism, I think we should adopt the latter interpretation.
32. For this use of the distinction in scholasticism, see Aquinas 1968b, I ad 1. In the First Replies, where Descartes first uses the terminology, he uses it in precisely this sense. But there he does not speak of incomplete substances, but incomplete *beings.* The examples he gives are modes: shape, motion. Complete beings are substances: body, mind. But for our purposes the use of the distinction within the category of substance is most important.
33. DM IV.III.13.
34. Hoffman thinks that Descartes gets himself in trouble by allowing something to be both an *ens per se* and an *ens per accidens* (Hoffman 1986, pp. 368–369). But we can now see what the solution to this problem is. Descartes's view is simply that both expressions apply because the union is not essential to mind and body, but it is essential to the composite human being. It is true, however, that Descartes's language is not always very clear on this issue.

    This interpretation can also be used to explain Descartes's otherwise rather puzzling illustration of the union of mind and body by means of the relation between mice and the material they are made of. He explains this analogy by saying that "what is an *ens per se* can come to be *per accidens,* thus mice, are generated or come to be *per accidens* from dirt" (AT III 460/ CSM III 200). His point is that it is accidental to the dirt that it comes to constitute mice; nevertheless, the mice themselves are not accidental beings: their parts are essential to them.

    According to Verbeek, what is crucial here is a distinction between *fieri per accidens* and *esse per accidens* (Verbeek 1992a, pp. 278–279). It is true that Descartes speaks in terms of this distinction in the letter to Regius of December 1641 (AT III 460–461/ CSM III 200). But I think the distinction between what is essential to the whole as opposed to the parts is more fundamental in this passage.

35. Gilson argues that Descartes maintains the Thomistic position only *in verbis,* because unlike Aquinas Descartes claims that soul and body are complete (Gilson 1976, pp. 431–432). But since Descartes claims that soul and body are *both* complete and incomplete, matters are a bit more complicated. In addition, Gilson ignores the fact that Descartes would say that even on Aquinas' conception the soul is complete in a sense, because it can exist without the body. Gilson does not acknowledge the fact that Aquinas tries to have it both ways by wanting the soul to be a substantial form but also capable of existing apart. But his conclusion is basically right: The substance of Aquinas' view that mind and body are incomplete is lost in Descartes.
36. For scholastic examples of the rejection of the Platonic view of the human being, see Aquinas, ST I.76.1, SCG II.57, and Coimbra Commentators, *De anima* 2.1.6.2. Verbeek discusses the importance of the idea that the human being includes the body in religious disputes that were relevant to the Regius affair (Verbeek 1988, pp. 42–44, and Verbeek 1992a, p. 282).
37. It is worth nothing that here, unlike later in correspondence with Elizabeth, Descartes gives no sign of seeing difficulty in grasping both the union and the distinction of mind and body.
38. Such a position has affinity with the one held by Locke (*Essay* II.XXVII).
39. In addition to the view that the human being consists in the mind, and the view that it consists in the mind-body composite, there is the view that the human being consists in just the body. Averroes, I take it, held a version of this view. He held that the ensouled body is the human being. The intellect is a separate, incorporeal entity that is not part of the human being.
40. For the importance of this idea to the Real Distinction Argument, see chapter 2. I have not found the scholastics, when discussing the union of mind and body, making explicit claims about relevant functions being essential to the soul. But for them the soul is the principle of life, and the functions at issue are various expressions of life.
41. See also the letter to Arnauld of July 29, 1648 (AT V 223/ CSM III 358). In this letter he writes that the mind "is apt to be united to the body," but he provides no explanation or clues for how we should understand this claim.
42. Although, the claim is true in regard to the very specific point that prompts Descartes to make it. For he is concerned with Regius' calling the human being an *ens per accidens*. Descartes writes that the reason for this label was that mind and body are really distinct, but he rightly points out that the scholastics don't use the term *per accidens* in this way. For them real distinction between items was not sufficient for calling something an *ens per accidens*. Matter and form were generally regarded as really distinct, but together they were thought to constitute an *ens per se*.
43. In addition, questions arise about the idea that Descartes is committing himself to a robust form of hylomorphism as result of a remark he makes earlier

in this same letter: "we can say that the Loire is the same river as ten years ago, although it is no longer the same water, and although perhaps also there is no longer the same earth that surrounds this water" (AT IV 165/ CSM III 242). Like the human body, the river Loire continues to be the same in spite of the turnover in matter. The question arises how, according to Descartes, the identity conditions of the human body differ from those of the river Loire, since obviously the identity of the Loire is not determined by a substantial form. But Descartes offers no such account.

In correspondence, Hoffman has pointed out that the remark about the Loire comes in a discussion of the identity conditions of a *surface* that remains the same although the underlying bodies change. Hoffman infers that Descartes seems to think of the Loire as something like a surface. The identity of the human body, on the other hand, is not a matter of the identity of a surface, but of a body. It is true that the remark about the Loire comes when Descartes discusses the identity of surfaces. But it seems very surprising that Descartes should think of the Loire as a surface. It seems more plausible that he thought of the Loire's identity as depending on the identity of its surface. The individuation and identity of bodies in Descartes is a thorny issue, however, which I do not wish to go into at this point.

44. Denzinger 1991, pp. 482–483, art. 1440–1441, and p. 390, art. 901. The issues that provoked these statements from the Lateran Council are discussed in detail in Gilson 1983. Pomponazzi was a central figure among those whose views provoked the pronouncement of the Council. See also Kessler 1988, pp. 500–507. According to Kessler, Pomponazzi actually abandoned Averroes' position for a more materialist one.

    Incidentally, Verbeek argues that to a significant degree Regius' views on the human being predate his exposure to Descartes, and that they were due more to the influence of Italian Renaissance Aristotelianism than to Descartes (Verbeek 1988, p. 43).

45. Letter to Arnauld of November 28/December 8, 1686(Leibniz 1965, vol. IV, p. 75). For the English, see Ariew and Garber 1989, p. 78.

46. For the view that Descartes regards the human being as a substance, see Hoffman 1990b, p. 318, and especially Hoffman 1986, p. 346; Laporte 1988, p. 183; Broughton and Mattern 1971, p. 27; Rodis-Lewis 1971, pp. 353, 543; Richardson 1982, p. 35; Schmaltz 1992, pp. 288–289; Gueroult 1953 II, p. 147/ 1984 II, p. 117; Gilson 1976, p. 432, etc. Richardson says that Descartes regards the person as a substance *in a sense,* because he thinks that for Descartes the mind-body composite is a subject of modes. Cottingham denies that Descartes thinks there is a substance corresponding to sensation and different from mind and body (Cottingham 1985, p. 229). Gouhier makes some very thoughtful comments about the issue. He says that nothing in the definition of substance prevents the existence of a third created substance, but that hesitation on this issue is understandable (Gouhier 1987, p. 363 n). Such hesitation is displayed in Alquié 1991, p. 308, and Mesnard

1957. On the other hand, Gouhier does claim that the notion of the union corresponds to a *res,* since it cannot be understood through something else (Gouhier 1987, p. 330). But then it would follow that it corresponds to a substance, since in this sense of *res* Descartes thinks all *res* are substances. Schmaltz takes Descartes's remarks about primitive notions in a letter to the Princess Elizabeth to mean that he thought there is a third substance. I discuss those remarks in chapter 6.3.

47. I owe this observation to Jeremy Hyman.
48. The French of the *Meditations* is less definite than the Latin *unum quid*: it says that "I compose *as it were one whole* with it [the body]—*je compose comme un seul tout avec lui*" (AT IX 64, emphasis mine). In the letter to Elizabeth, June 28, 1643, Descartes speaks approvingly of considering the mind-body composite as one thing—*comme une seule chose* (AT III 692/ CSM III 227). The expression *unum quid* was sometimes used by the scholastics to address the question whether soul and body constitute a genuine unity, an *ens per se.* See Eustachius, SP III, p. 416, and Coimbra Commentators, *Physics* 1.9.11.1, pp. 182–188. I don't think the expression *unum quid* was a technical term, however. I discuss the term *ens per se* below.
49. See Hoffman 1986, pp. 350–355; Grene 1986, p. 311; and Grene 1991, p. 16. For instance, Hoffman cites the Sixth Replies, where Descartes writes that the mind can be regarded as a quality (AT VII 441–442/ CSM II 297–298). For a discussion of that aspect of this passage see chapter 4.4.1.
50. One might think that the analogy with heaviness is incompatible with Descartes's view that the human being is an *ens per se.* But it is important to see that he thinks the notion of heaviness includes the idea that it is both a quality and a substance, and that we should drop the idea that this is a notion of a quality. The notion is useful once we do that.
51. For similar observations see Alquié II, pp. 902 and 914.
52. See, for instance, Hoffman 1986, p. 346; Rodis-Lewis 1971, p. 355; Laporte 1988, p. 227.
53. See also Gilson 1979, p. 275.
54. DM IV.III.3, 7, 12.
55. For more discussion of all these notions in Suárez, see Olivo 1993. Olivo argues that for Descartes the human being is an *ens per se* in the sense of Suárez suppositum.
56. Paul Hoffman has suggested in correspondence that Descartes simply took it for granted that the human being is an *ens per se.* On the face of it this suggestion is plausible, and it is in line with Descartes's relative neglect of the union of mind and body. But the dispute at Utrecht should have forced him to reflect on the fact that on his account of mind and body the status of the human being as an *unum per se* cannot be taken for granted. Furthermore, the fact that discussions of the union of body and soul were common in scholastic writings should also have made him sensitive to the difficulties at hand. At any rate, it still leaves us without an answer to the question what

makes a human being an *ens per se,* and in what sense it is one. And even if Descartes did simply assume that the human being is a *ens per se,* it does not follow that he thought it was a substance.

57. It is important to note that the fact that Descartes regards bodies as infinitely divisible is not an obstacle to the unity of corporeal substance in the same way that the heterogeneity of mind and body is. For Suárez, an *ens per se*—and a substance is one of those—is unified in the sense that it has *one essence* (cf. DM IV.III.13). Eustachius also connects the status of the human being as an *ens per se* with the idea that it has one essence (SP III, p. 416). The idea that mind and body together constitute something with one essence is really fundamental to the scholastic reliance on incompleteness. This sense of unity is compatible with divisibility as it pertains to bodies. Thus for the scholastics the elements as well as mixed bodies like gold, for instance, are substances, but obviously these are divisible into parts.

    Similarly, for Descartes body is a substance and simple in regard to essence, although divisible into parts in another sense. The same is not true for the human being, which contains two parts with different, and independent essences. See Descartes's discussion of the distinction between unity of nature and unity of composition, Sixth Replies (AT VII 424/ CSM II 285–286).

6. *Sensation and the Union of Mind and Body*

1. In my discussion I only explicitly address the question of sensation. But the same issues arise for imagination and the passions of the soul, which also rely on the union of mind and body. Descartes himself, however, rarely discusses the issues in question for mental states other than sensation. I follow his example.
2. Besides sources referred to in later notes, for discussion of Descartes's remarks about sensation as the key to his conception of the union, see also Gueroult 1953 II, pp. 123–127/ 1984 II, pp. 97–100, and Gilson 1976, pp. 430–435.
3. There are complicated questions about whether Descartes really thought that body acts on mind in sensation. Such questions arise in particular because in this passage and elsewhere he seems to avoid straightforward causal talk, and in various places he writes that sensations occur *on the occasion of* events in the body. Various commentators have argued that Descartes's views don't allow for any genuine causal activity on the part of bodies. Garber has argued that over the course of the period that elapses from the *Meditations* to the French edition of the *Principles* Descartes drops language that commits him to the possibility of action of the body on the mind (Garber 1992, pp. 72–75; see also Garber 1993, pp. 9–26). Clearly, if Descartes held that bodies have no causal efficacy or that they cannot act on bodies, his argument from sensation based on their being caused by body is in trouble. I cannot do justice here to these questions, but I don't think Descartes ever did abandon causal efficacy for bodies.

I think that Nadler is very much on the right track regarding the causal role of body in the production of sensation. He argues that according to Descartes the body does exercise causal efficacy in sensation (Nadler 1994).

4. Gassendi's objection concerned both the union and interaction of mind and body (AT VII 343–345/ CSM II 238–239).
5. For the view that the whole point of the union is to make interaction possible, see Radner 1971.
6. Descartes argues from the intrinsic difference between pure intellect and sensation. One might refer to this difference as a qualitative difference, but I find it hard to make sense of the idea that there is a qualitative nature to pure intellection. For this reason I will simply refer to the qualitative nature of sensation.

   Sensations are confused as a result of their qualitative nature. This is not to say that their confusion is just a matter of this qualitative nature. On Descartes's view, sensations are confused when regarded as representations of bodies. At *Principles* I.68 he says that "pain and color are clearly and distinctly perceived if they are regarded as sensations or thoughts." Whereas one might regard that position as different from the one presented in the *Meditations,* I don't think it is. When Descartes calls sensations confused and obscure in the Sixth Meditation he is assuming one takes them as representing qualities of bodies. Later in that Meditation he presents a line of thought very similar to the one in the *Principles:* He argues that our nature does not teach us to regard sensible qualities and pain as being in bodies. That claim suggests—although it does not express—the view that one can clear up the confusion we are prone to in regard to sensible qualities by seeing them as mere sensations.
7. For another interpreter who sees both aspects of sensation as showing the close union of the mind with the body, see Gilson 1976, pp. 433–434. Gueroult offers a detailed and subtle analysis of the qualitative nature of sensation and its connection with the union. See Gueroult 1953 II, pp. 123–157/ 1984 II, pp. 97–124.

   It is worth noting that there is some difference with respect to the time at which Descartes proposes the two different roles for the union. The claim that the union explains the qualitative nature of sensation is stated in the *Meditations,* and referred to in the Fourth Replies, the letter to Hyperaspistes of August 1641, and the letter to Regius of January 1642. I have not found it in later writings. Descartes focuses on the idea that the union explains interaction in the letter to Elizabeth in 1643 and in the *Principles.* This idea is not found in the *Meditations,* although Descartes refers to it in the Sixth Replies, where he writes that "the mind is so intimately joined to the brain that it is affected by the motions which occur in it" (AT VII 437/ CSM II 295). One might wonder whether this temporal order indicates some change in Descartes's thought. Steven Voss argues that in the *Meditations* Descartes espoused the position that there is "an entity composed of soul and body," but that later he adopted a more Platonistic position according to which "there is no such thing as man" (Voss 1994, p. 274).

8. Margaret Wilson remarks that the analogy with the pilot and his ship is unhelpful insofar as the pilot would notice what happens to the ship by way of sensation (Wilson 1978a, p. 210). She is right in pointing this out, but it is important in this regard that the analogy was standard among the Aristotelians. So Descartes no doubt used the analogy for the purpose of stating that he also did not accept such a Platonistic conception of the union, rather than because he thought it was a particularly apt way of explaining his own view. For Aristotle's own use of the analogy, see *De anima* 413a.8.

   The comparison with an angel being joined to a body is more apt, since presumably an angel would have no sensory states at all. It is worth noting, however, that several years later, in a letter to More of August 1649, Descartes writes that we cannot establish whether angels have sensations (AT V 402/ CSM III 380). He says there that souls that are separated from the mind have no sensation proper—*sensum proprie dictum.* But he claims that he cannot establish by natural reason alone whether angels are "created like minds distinct from bodies or like minds united to bodies."

9. Wilson is an example of an interpreter who makes this identification. See Wilson 1978a, pp. 205–220, especially pp. 211–220. She also thinks that the view that the mind is coextended with the body is expressed at *Passions* I.30, where Descartes writes that the mind is united to the whole body (Wilson 1978a, p. 211–212). But he is saying something different here. In this article Descartes gives as ground for his claim that the mind is united to the whole body that both mind and body are indivisible. The body is indivisible in the sense that its organs are such that when one is removed, the body becomes defective. But this claim does not imply that the mind is extended in any sense, and Descartes does not say it is extended. Furthermore, he says nothing in this article about the location of mind-body interaction, which, in the next article, he assigns to the pineal gland. See also Alquié's comments on this article in Alquié III, pp. 976–977.

10. The scholastics addressed this problem when discussing the question how phantasms can contribute to the production of intelligible species. Phantasms are the representations used by the imagination, and they are corporeal entities; intelligible species are spiritual entities residing in the incorporeal mind. See Aquinas, ST I.84.6; Suárez, DA IV.II; Eustachius, SP III, pp. 432–433; Coimbra Commentators, *De anima* 3.5.2.2, pp. 406–409.

11. For discussion of these models of the presence of God and mind in the physical world in various philosophers, see Grant 1981, pp. 223–228, 350 n. 127.

12. The correspondence with Elizabeth would seem to constitute an exception; there Descartes seems to treat interaction in both directions in the same way. See n. 14.

13. Grant makes clear that the model of a spiritual substance being whole in the whole and whole in the parts is different from the model of extension of

power. On the former there is a presence of the spiritual substance over and above its acting on the body. Mere extension of power was rejected by some as insufficient, as it would result in a spiritual substance acting somewhere where it is not, and thus constitute action at a distance (cf. Grant 1981, pp. 146, 157, 253–254). So we cannot assume that Descartes's talk of extension of power in the letters to More concerns the same model he proposes earlier, when he describes the union of the mind to the body as whole in the whole and whole in each of its parts. Indeed, in the Sixth Replies, for instance, he does seem to ascribe to mind an extension that goes beyond a mere extension of power (AT VII 442/ CSM II 298).

14. In the letter to Elizabeth of June 28, 1643, Descartes does write that Elizabeth may conceive of the mind as extended in order to understand interaction in both directions (AT III 694/ CSM III 228). Also, in his remarks about primitive notions in the letter of May 21, 1643, Descartes presents one primitive notion of the union as allowing a grasp of interaction in both directions. In this regard the exchange with Elizabeth is highly unusual. But it is important to note that this exchange focuses on the question how the mind acts on the body, and not on the other direction of interaction. Furthermore, Descartes never *relies on* this sense of extension for the mind to explain anything about sensation.
15. In the Sixth Replies he writes: "*mens cerebro tam intime conjuncta sit*"—The mind is so intimately joined to the brain" (AT VII 437/ CSM II 295). CSM's translation says the mind is joined to the body. Descartes uses the same phrase at *Principles* IV.189—*intime cerebro conjunctam.* On these two occasions he refers to the union to explain that motions in the brain affect the mind.
16. Although, on this interpretation it is puzzling that Descartes writes that imagination is not *required* for the essence of the mind.
17. For a defense of Descartes's account of interaction and union, see Richardson 1982. Wilson criticizes this defense in Wilson 1991, pp. 312–313. She refers to the fact that Descartes does offer an account of sensation insofar as he claims that "brain states give rise to mind states according to correlations instituted by nature." She points out that this account surely could hardly come from the senses. This is true, but in my view, after everything Descartes says about interaction, something still remains unclear about how the body can act on the mind. I think he has this in mind when he says we don't understand but only sense interaction. But I must leave this issue for another occasion.
18. *Sensus* is not the only term Descartes uses. He also uses *sensatio* and *sensuum perceptiones* (cf. *Principles* II.3, IV.197). Incidentally, Descartes uses the equivalents of 'sensation' and 'sense perception' interchangeably. I have mostly used 'sensation' (which is in accord with Descartes's frequent use of *sensus*), but sometimes 'sense perception' is more intuitive in English.
19. It is worth noting the affinity of this discussion with a certain scholastic theory of sense perception. For Descartes here describes the second grade of

sensation as a sensation of sensible qualities. He introduces perception of mechanistic qualities in the third grade, where the subject reasons on the basis of the sensation of the sensible qualities. But some scholastics held that sensible qualities produce sensations in the perceiving subject, and that mechanistic qualities were thought to be sensed indirectly by virtue of the species produced by the sensible qualities in the subject. See Maier 1968, p. 19, and Suárez, DA III.VIII.

20. Alternatively, one might think that sensation proper in the Second Meditation refers to the third grade of sensation, or to the second-order awareness that one is having a sensation. For discussion see Hoffman 1990b, p. 321. Hoffman slightly favors the view that in the Second Meditation Descartes refers to the third grade. But he brings up two considerations that support my view that sensation proper in the Second Meditation is the second grade. He notes the obvious similarity in terminology in the Second Meditation and the Sixth Replies and also points out that surely the second grade would pass the certainty test applied in the *Meditations.*
21. For an exception see Hoffman 1990b, pp. 320–321.
22. Cottingham sees this passage as a nondualistic, trialistic one, because it depicts sensation as comprising three stages (Cottingham 1985, p. 225). The second stage, he thinks, does not really fit Descartes's official dualism. But the passage does not deviate from a dualistic ontology. It analyzes the three grades of sensation as three modes, each of which belongs to either the mind or the body: the first grade belongs to body, the third clearly belongs to mind, and the second grade is also ascribed to the mind.

    Cottingham himself denies that there is an *ontological* 'trialism' in Descartes (Cottingham 1985, p. 229). But his use of the term 'ontology' and cognates differs from mine: for him ontological trialism is the view that there is a third kind of substance. I use the term 'ontology' more broadly so that it is sufficient for a third ontological category that there be a third type of mode in addition to modes of extension and modes of thought. In this sense there would be a third type of mode if sensations are not just modes of mind, nor of body, but of something else such as both mind and body, or their union. There are reasons for thinking that such trialism would imply substance trialism for Descartes, but in my use of the terms I do not wish to prejudge this question.

    One might say that the complete three-grades process constitutes a third category. Perhaps Descartes would want to call that whole process a single mode. But that does not strike me as an interesting sense in which there would be a third category. What would be interesting is if Descartes held that there are simple modes of the union or composite, not modes that can be reduced to a sequence of straightforward modes of body and mind.
23. For the view that Descartes's claim that sensations are modes of the mind is compatible with a version of trialism, see Schmaltz 1992, pp. 289–294.
24. One commentator who takes this analogy seriously is Gouhier. His interpretation of its significance is different from mine, however. He thinks the point

of the metaphor is that the mind is present to the whole body (Gouhier 1987, pp. 346–347). He refers to *Passions* I.30. But the point of that passage is quite different. See n. 9 above. And as we saw, the mixture analogy must also be distinguished from Descartes's description of the soul as whole in the whole body and whole in each of its parts.

25. The situation with respect to this analogy is similar to the one that concerns the problem of the interaction of mind and body. Descartes's critics have often claimed that his dualism founders on this problem, but they fail to explain why mind-body interaction is impossible on a dualistic view. For this point on interaction see Richardson 1982, pp. 22–26, and Wilson 1991, p. 298.
26. DA II.III.3.
27. Some twentieth-century materialists would say that such a sensation may not *consist in* a mechanistic event, or any other kind of corporeal event, but argue, for instance, that a corporeal event fulfils the functional role of such a sensation. I don't find this any easier to understand given the qualitative nature of sensation, but this point goes beyond the present concerns. My view about Descartes is that his conception of sensation as mental was motivated by his commitment to mechanistic science. Like many twentieth-century philosophers, including, in fact, many committed to materialism, he sees a problem for a materialist account of sensation. The idea that this problem meant that sensation (or a part or aspect of it) does not occur in the body was of course much more acceptable in his day. One reason is the fact that the idea that the human being includes an incorporeal component was dominant then, just as materialism is now. It addition, Descartes could not look back on the same long history of amazing scientific progress we have behind us today. The fact that in the twentieth century we can, motivates many to believe that everything about the mental will eventually also be intelligible scientifically and as corporeal.
28. The distinction between the corporeal and the incorporeal was not as absolute in scholastic thought as it is in Descartes (see chapter 4.4.2). My main point is that sensation was not regarded as occurring in the mind, which was regarded as entirely incorporeal. Although the scholastics applied the term 'immaterial' to aspects of sensation, they did regard it as occurring in the body. For discussion of this issue in Aquinas see Hoffman 1990a.
29. Gilson relates sensation to Descartes's dualism in a similar way (Gilson 1976, p. 434). See also R. Rorty 1979, pp. 59–60.
30. See *Phaedo* 65b–66c, 79c, 81b–d.
31. This point raises various interesting questions that I cannot address here. But two observations are worth making. First, when the Aristotelians ascribed to Plato the view that the soul is in its body as a pilot in his ship, they did not take the Platonic picture of the soul as mixed with the body into account. (See Aquinas, SCG II.57.) Second, Descartes's view of the relationship between mind and body does, of course, contain strong Platonic elements, as Arnauld, for instance, was quick to point out. In several respects, his dualism is closer

to Plato's views than to Aristotelian ones, even late medieval Aristotelian ones. This point should be obvious, but it is worth making, given the tendency of some recent commentators to emphasize similarities between Descartes and the Aristotelians.

32. R. C. Richardson argues that sensations are modes of the mind-body complex (Richardson 1982). According to Tad Schmaltz, sensations are modes of a third principal attribute, the union of mind and body (Schmaltz 1992). John Cottingham addresses the issue in Cottingham 1985. His position is less clear, in part because he thinks Descartes's view itself is not clear, but he regards sensations as a third category next to thought and extension (p. 229). For a subtly different view, see Hoffman 1990b. Hoffman argues that there are modes that straddle mind and body, but he leaves open the possibility that sensations are aspects or parts of these straddling modes insofar as these modes exist in the mind (p. 320).
33. Cottingham 1985, p. 218; Schmaltz 1992, pp. 286–288; Garber 1992, pp. 89–94. For a different view of the chronology of Descartes's thought on the union of mind and body, see Voss 1994.
34. Schmaltz 1992, pp. 285–289, and Laporte 1988, pp. 235–236. Laporte does not explicitly use the term 'principal attribute', but what he says comes close to describing the union as one. He does write that the union, like thought and extension, is a substance. Gouhier proposes that the union is *something like* a principal attribute: "The primitive notion of the union is then to this composite being what the principal attribute is to each substance taken separately; like each of these principal attributes it is diversified into modes [*elle se diversifie en modes*]; nevertheless since it expresses the interdependence of the two components, its modes are relations deriving from action and passion, appetites, passions, sensations, feelings connected to the effort of voluntary motion." At the same time, for Gouhier the union means interaction (Gouhier 1987, p. 335).
35. Thus Schmaltz explains that on his view "Descartes held at the time of the correspondence with Elizabeth that [sensations] are modes of a single nature with a single attribute" (Schmaltz 1992, p. 295 n).
36. For different interpretations of this letter to Elizabeth, see Garber 1983, pp. 15–32, and Mattern 1978, pp. 212–222.
37. According to Garber the differences between the Latin and French are significant. He thinks that the French is closer to the tripartition of the letter to Elizabeth than the Latin. He bases this analysis primarily on the fact that the Latin uses 'refer' where the French uses 'attribute' (Garber 1992, p. 91), but I think 'attribute' is not much clearer than 'refer'. My sense is that neither the French nor the Latin is systematically more dualistic or trialistic. Thus in the Latin Descartes says in the first part of the article that he accepts not more than two highest kinds of things—*non autem plura quam duo summa genera rerum agnosco*—intellectual and corporeal ones. The French is less clear because it merely says "And the principal distinction I notice among all created

things," *Et la principale distinction que je remarque entre toutes les chose créées* (see also Alquié's notes to this article in Alquié III, p. 119). On the other hand, the Latin says about a subspecies of the third category of items, namely, the passions of the soul, that they do not *consist in* thought alone; the French says they do not *depend on* thought alone.

38. A trialist might reply that Descartes meant to defend this view in further parts of the *Principles* that he wanted to write, but never did. Descartes mentions that he had intended to write such parts at *Principles* IV.188. (For a discussion of this plan, see Garber 1992, p. 28.) Thus one might argue that Descartes's claim that he will defend the status of sensation later dates from the time before he abandoned the plan of writing a fifth and sixth part. This could be true. But I think it is an advantage of my interpretation that it can read the remark in question in conformity with the work as it stands.
39. See Cottingham 1985, pp. 218–219.
40. It is worth pointing out that connections with behavior do not imply corporeity on all views: in Descartes's day angels were thought to be able to move spatially and act on bodies without being corporeal.
41. One might think that Descartes's claim that interaction requires the mind's union with the body does establish an essential connection between sensation and bodily stimuli. But this is not so. The need for the union arises in view of difficulties concerning mind-body interaction *on the assumption that sensations are caused by the body.* But this role for the union does not imply that sensory states are essentially connected to the bodily states that cause them. It leaves open the possibility that when a mind is separated from a body God could cause it to have sensations; and then, of course, no union with the body is needed.
42. For related observations see Shoemaker 1983, pp. 254–257.
43. See, for instance, Chappell 1994, pp. 424–426. Wilson finds evidence for the view that the union consists in interaction as well as for a different view in Descartes's writings, as I will discuss in a moment. See Wilson 1978a, pp. 205–220. Gouhier describes the union of mind and body in Descartes as a form of coexistence that consists in interaction, "*une coexistence qui consiste en une interaction*" (Gouhier 1987, p. 335).
44. I do wish to point out that one could hold yet a different view. For one could hold that for Descartes sensations are simply modes of the mind whose occurrence is caused or occasioned by motions in the brain, while, nevertheless, the union consists in more than just interaction. Daisie Radner holds that the point of the union is to *explain* interaction (Radner 1971, p. 162).
45. This chapter contains various disagreements with Wilson's interpretation of Descartes's account of sensation. But it owes much to the thought-provoking questions she raises.
46. Wilson 1978a, p. 211.
47. Descartes argues extensively that God made the best choices in establishing connections between bodily states and sensations. But it is worth noting the

limits of his explicit defense of this position in the Sixth Meditation. For he only defends the view that God made the right choices in terms of the location indicated by the sensation produced by a particular bodily motion. Thus he argues that God's decision to correlate a sensation of pain *as if in the foot* was the right one, although it can be produced by events along the entire length of the causal chain connecting the foot to the mind. But he does not attempt to explain here why God picked the sensation of pain as opposed to a ticklish sensation as a correlate for a particular state of the body. He could easily have elaborated his account, however, by arguing that God picked those sensations that produce the appropriate kind of behavior.

48. These tensions are noted in Wilson 1978a, pp. 200–220.
49. See n. 3 above.
50. On the other hand, as we saw in n. 8, in a letter to More Descartes writes: "human minds separated from body do not have sensation properly speaking" (AT V 402/ CSM III 380). This passage is hard to interpret, however. Descartes uses the phrase "properly speaking—*proprie dictum,*" which, as we saw, he uses elsewhere for the second stage of sensation (AT VII 437/ CSM II 295 and the Second Meditation, AT VII 29/ CSM II 19). But in the exchange with More, not Descartes but More had introduced the phrase. Consequently, there is a risk involved in interpreting the use of the phrase in the letter on the basis of these earlier Cartesian texts. Neither More nor Descartes explains what he means by it. So I think it would be too quick to reject the view that for Descartes sensation is possible without body on the basis of this text.
51. I interpret separability to stand for the possibility of *a* existing without *b* existing. For a very different interpretation, see Hoffman 1986, p. 343 n, and his dissertation, Hoffman 1982.
52. The distinction between different forms of dependence on body is important for understanding the implications of Descartes's argument for the existence of body from the nature of sensation in the Sixth Meditation (AT VII 79–80/ CSM II 55) and at *Principles* II.1. This argument (or at least its statement in the *Principles*) might suggest that in fact sensations cannot be clearly and distinctly understood without body. Thus one might think that they cannot be modes of just the mind—even of the mind as united to the body. The way in which Descartes infers the existence of body from sensation in this argument does not, however, imply that sensation is a mode of both mind and body, or of a third item. The argument merely implies that bodies play a causal role in the production of sensation.
53. The dependence of created substances on God is a complicated case. Descartes thinks any created substance requires God's existence. But he did not think that created substances are modes of God. They are things. If separability were all there is at stake, Descartes should have concluded that created substances are modes of God. Nevertheless, by claiming that the term 'substance' does not apply to God and creatures univocally, Descartes gives the impression that separability is the whole story (*Principles* I.51). On my view,

Descartes should not have said so, but he should have explained the difference between God and created substances in terms of the different types of dependence involved. I suspect that he saw the two types of dependence as united by the fact that either involves dependence for existence in a specific sense. A mode derives its existence from the created substance in which it inheres, a created substance derives its existence from God. And they are so dependent not just for their coming-into-being, but for their continued existence at all times. See also ch. 1 n. 10.

54. This is Richardson's position (Richardson 1982, p. 35).

Postscript

1. Rozemond 1997.
2. For this kind of criticism see recent work by Kit Fine, for instance, Fine 1994 and 1995.

References

Adams, Marilyn M. 1987. *William Ockham,* Notre Dame: University of Notre Dame Press.

Adams, Robert M. 1975. "Where Do Our Ideas Come from?—Descartes vs. Locke," in *Innate Ideas,* Stephen Stich, ed., Berkeley: University of California Press, pp. 71–87.

——— 1994. *Leibniz: Determinist, Theist, Idealist,* New York, Oxford: Oxford University Press.

Alexander, Peter. 1974. "Boyle and Locke on Primary and Secondary Qualities," *Ratio* 16, pp. 51–67.

Alquié, Fernand. 1957. "Experience ontologique et déduction systématique dans la constitution de la métaphysique de Descartes," in *Cahiers de Royaumont philosophie No. II, Descartes,* reprint, New York: Garland, 1987, pp. 10–71.

Alquié, Fernand. 1991. *La découverte métaphysique de l'homme chez Descartes,* 4th ed., Paris: Presses Universitaires de France.

Aquinas, Thomas St. 1926. *In metaphysicam Aristotelis commentaria,* M. R. Cathala, ed., Turin: Marietti.

——— 1948. *In Aristotelis librum de anima commentarium,* Angeli M. Pirotta, ed., Turin: Marietti.

——— 1951. *Aristotle's de Anima: in the Version of William of Moerbeke and the Commentary of St. Thomas Aquinas,* Kenelm Foster and Silvester Humphries, transl., London: Routledge and Kegan Paul.

——— 1954. *In octo libros physicorum Aristotelis expositio,* P. M. Maggiolo, ed., Turin: Marietti.

——— 1955. *Expositio super librum Boethii de trinitate,* Bruno Decker, ed., Leiden: E. J. Brill.

——— 1961. *Commentary on the Metaphysics of Aristotle,* John P. Rowan, transl., Chicago: Henry Regnery Company.

——— 1963. *Commentary on Aristotle's Physics by St. Thomas Aquinas,* R. J. Blackwell, R. J. Spath, and W. E. Thirlkel, transl., New Haven: Yale University Press.

——— 1964–. *Summa theologiae,* New York: Blackfriars and McGraw-Hill.

——— 1965. "On the Principles of Nature," in *Selected Writings of St. Thomas Aquinas,* Robert P. Goodwin, transl, Indianapolis: Bobbs-Merrill.

——— 1968a. *On the Unity of the Intellect against the Averroists,* Beatrice Zedler, transl., Milwaukee: Marquette University Press.

——— 1968b. *Quaestiones de anima,* James H. Robb, ed., Toronto: Pontifical Institute for Mediaeval Studies.

——— 1975. *Summa contra gentiles,* James F. Anderson, transl., Notre Dame: University of Notre Dame Press.

——— 1984. *Questions on the Soul,* James H. Robb, transl., Milwaukee: Marquette University Press.

——— 1986. *The Division and Methods of the Sciences,* Armand Maurer, transl., Toronto: Pontifical Institute of Mediaeval Studies.

Ariew, Roger. 1992. "Descartes and Scholasticism," in *The Cambridge Companion to Descartes,* John Cottingham, ed., Cambridge: Cambridge University Press, pp. 58–90.

Ariew, Roger, and Marjorie Grene, eds. 1995. *Descartes and His Contemporaries: Meditations, Objections and Replies,* Chicago and London: University of Chicago Press.

Aristotle. 1941. *The Basic Works of Aristotle,* Richard McKeon, ed., New York: Random House.

——— 1968. *De anima,* D.W. Hamlyn, ed., Oxford: Clarendon Press.

Armogathe. 1977. *Theologia cartesiana: L'explication physique de l'Eucharistie chez Descartes et Dom Desgabets,* The Hague: Nijhoff.

Ayers, M. R. 1977. "The Idea of Power and Substance in Locke's Philosophy," in *Locke on Human Understanding,* I. C. Tipton, ed., Oxford: Oxford University Press, pp. 77–104.

——— 1981. *Locke: Epistemology and Ontology,* 2 vols., London and New York: Routledge and Kegan Paul.

Beyssade, Jean-Marie. 1976. "L'analyse du morceau de cire. Contribution à l'étude des 'degrés du sens' dans la Seconde Méditation de Descartes," in *Sinnlichkeit und Verstand in der deutschen und französischen Philosophie von Descartes bis Hegel,* Hans Wagner, ed., Bonn: Bouvier Verlag Herbert Grundmann, pp. 9–25.

——— 1979. *La philosophie première de Descartes,* Paris: Flammarion.

Beyssade, Jean-Marie,and Jean-Luc Marion, eds. 1994. *Descartes: Objecter et répondre,* Paris: Presses Universitaires de France.

Broughton, Janet, and Ruth Mattern. 1971. "Reinterpreting Descartes on the Union of Mind and Body," *Journal of the History of Philosophy* 9, pp. 23–32.

Buchdahl, Gerd. 1969. *Metaphysics and the Philosophy of Science,* Oxford: Basil Blackwell.

Buroker, Jill Vance. 1991. "Descartes on Sensible Qualities," *Journal of the History of Philosophy* 29, pp. 585–611.

Burtt, E. A. 1954. *The Metaphysical Foundations of Modern Science,* Garden City, New York: Doubleday Anchor Books.

Cahiers de Royaumont, philosophie no II, Descartes. 1957. Reprint, Garland; New York, 1987.

Carraud,Vincent, and Frédéric de Buzon. 1994. *Descartes et le "Principia" II; corps et mouvement,* Paris: Presses Universitaires de France.

Carriero, John. 1986. "The Second Meditation and the Essence of the Mind," in *Essays on Descartes' Meditations,* Amélie Rorty, ed., Berkley: University of California Press.

——— 1987. "The First Meditation," *Pacific Philosophical Quarterly* 68, pp. 222–248.

Chappell, Vere. 1994. "L'homme cartésien," *in Descartes: Objecter et répondre,* Jean-Marie Beyssade and Jean-Luc Marion, eds., Paris: Presses Universitaires de France, pp. 403–426.

Coimbra Commentators. 1594. *Commentarii Conimbricenses in octo libros physicorum Aristotelis,* Lyons. Reprint, Hildesheim: Georg Olms Verlag, 1984.

——— 1604. *Commentarii Collegii Conimbricensis in tres libros de Anima Aristotelis Stagiritae,* and *Tractatus de anima separata,* Lyons.

Cottingham, John. 1985. "Cartesian Trialism," *Mind* 94, pp. 218–230.

——— 1986. *Descartes,* Oxford: Basil Blackwell.

——— ed. 1992. *The Cambridge Companion to Descartes,* Cambridge: Cambridge University Press.

Courtine, Jean-François. 1990. *Suárez et le système de la métaphysique,* Paris: Presses Universitaires de France.

Curley, E. M. 1969. *Spinoza's Metaphysics: An Essay in Interpretation,* Cambridge: Harvard University Press.

——— 1972. "Locke, Boyle and the Distinction between Primary and Secondary Qualities," *Philosophical Review* 81, pp. 438–464.

——— 1978. *Descartes against the Skeptics,* Cambridge: Harvard University Press.

Dear, Peter. 1987. "Jesuit Mathematical Science and the Reconstitution of Experience in the Early Seventeenth Century," *Studies in History and Philosophy of Science* 18, pp. 133–175.

——— 1988. *Mersenne and the Learning of the Schools,* Ithaca: Cornell University Press.

Denzinger, Heinrich. 1991. *Enchiridion symbolorum, definitionum et declarationum de rebus fidei et morum,* 37th ed., Friburgi Brisgoviae: Herder.

Descartes, René. 1963–1973. *Œuvres philosophiques de Descartes,*3 vols., Fernand Alquié, ed., Paris: Éditions Garnier.

——— 1974–1989. *Œuvres de Descartes,* 11 vols., Charles Adam and Paul Tannery, eds., Paris: Vrin.

——— 1984–1991. *The Philosophical Writings of Descartes,* 3 vols., John Cottingham, Robert Stoothoff, and Dugald Murdoch, transl., Cambridge: Cambridge University Press.

Dijksterhuis, E. J. 1961. *The Mechanization of the World Picture,* Oxford: Oxford University Press.

Doney, Willis. 1967. *Descartes: A Collection of Critical Essays,* Garden City, New York: Doubleday Anchor Books.

Eustachius of St Paul. 1609. *Summa philosophica quadripartita,* Paris: Carolus Chastellain.

Fine, Kit. 1994. "Ontological Dependence," *Aristotelian Society Proceedings* 95, pp. 268–290.

——— 1995. "Essence and Modality," *Philosophical Perspectives 8: Logic and Language,* James E. Tomberlin, ed., pp. 1–16.

Frankfurt, Harry. 1970. *Demons, Dreamers, and Madmen: The Defense of Reason in Descartes's 'Meditations',* Indianapolis: Bobbs-Merrill.

Galilei, Galileo. 1957. *Discoveries and Opinions of Galileo,* Stillman Drake, ed., Garden City, New York: Doubleday Anchor Books.

Galison, Peter. 1984. "Descartes' Comparisons: From the Invisible to the Visible," *Isis* 75, pp. 311–326.

Garber, Daniel. 1983. "Understanding Interaction: What Descartes Should Have Told Elizabeth," *Southern Journal of Philosophy* 21 (supplement), pp. 15–32.

——— 1986. "*Semel in Vita:* The Scientific Background to Descartes' *Meditations,*" in *Essays on Descartes' Meditations,* Amélie Rorty, ed., Berkeley: University of California Press, pp. 81–116.

——— 1987. "How God Causes Motion: Descartes, Divine Sustenance, and Occasionalism," *Journal of Philosophy* 84, pp. 567–580.

——— 1992. *Descartes' Metaphysical Physics,* Chicago: University of Chicago Press.

——— 1993. "Descartes and Occasionalism," in *Causation in Early Modern Philosophy,* Steven Nadler, ed., University Park: Pennsylvania State University Press, pp. 9–26.

Gassendi, Pierre. 1964. *Syntagma,* in *Opera Omnia* I, reprint, Stuttgart-Bad Cannstatt: Friedrich Frommann Verlag.

Gilson, Étienne. 1976. *René Descartes: Discours de la méthode, texte et commentaire,* 5th ed., Paris: Vrin.

——— 1979. *Index scolastico-cartésien,* 2nd ed., Paris: Vrin.

——— 1983. *Humanisme et Renaissance,* Paris: Vrin.

——— 1984. *Le rôle de la pensée médiévale dans la formation du système cartésien,* 5th ed., Paris: Vrin.

Goclenius. 1613. *Lexicon philosophicum,* Frankfurt. Reprint, Hildesheim: Georg Olms Verlag, 1964.

Gouhier. 1924. *La pensée religieuse de Descartes,* Paris: Vrin.

——— 1973. *Descartes, Essais sur le "Discours de la méthode", la métaphysique et la morale,* 3rd ed., Paris: Vrin.

——— 1987. *La pensée métaphysique de Descartes,* 4th ed., Paris: Vrin.

Gracia, Jorge J. E. 1982. *Suárez on Individuation,* Milwaukee: Marquette University Press.

Grant, Edward. 1981. *Much Ado about Nothing: Theories of Space and Vacuum from the Middle Ages to the Scientific Revolution,* Cambridge: Cambridge University Press.

Grene, Marjorie. 1986. "Die Einheit des Menschen: Descartes unter den Scholastikern," *Dialectica* 40, pp. 309–322.

——— 1991. *Descartes among the Scholastics,* Milwaukee: Marquette University Press.

Gueroult, Martial. 1953. *Descartes selon l'ordre des raisons,* 2 vols., Paris: Aubier.

——— 1984. *Descartes' Philosophy Interpreted according to the Order of Reasons,* 2 vols., Roger Ariew, transl., Minneapolis: University of Minnesota Press.

Hatfield, Gary. 1979. "Force (God) in Descartes' Physics," in *Studies in History and Philosophy of Science* 10, pp. 113–140.

——— 1985. "First Philosophy and Natural Philosophy in Descartes," in *Philosophy, Its History and Historiography,* A. J. Holland, ed., Dordrecht: Reidel, pp. 149–164.

——— 1986. "The Senses and the Fleshless Eye: The Meditations as Cognitive Exercises," in *Essays on Descartes' Meditations,* Amélie Rorty, ed., Berkeley: University of California Press, pp. 45–79.

——— 1990. "Metaphysics and the New Science," in *Reappraisals of the Scientific Revolution,* David C. Lindberg and Robert S. Westman, eds., Cambridge: Cambridge University Press, pp. 93–166.

Hoenen, P. H. J., S. J. 1967. "Descartes's Mechanicism," in *Descartes: A Collection of Critical Essays,* Willis Doney, ed., pp. 353–368.

Hoffman, Paul. 1982. *Metaphysical Foundations of Descartes' Concept of Matter,* Ann Arbor: University Microfilm International.

——— 1986. "The Unity of Descartes's Man," *Philosophical Review* 95, pp. 339–370.

——— 1990a. "St. Thomas Aquinas on the Halfway State of Sensible Being" *Philosophical Review* 99, pp. 73–92.

——— 1990b. "Cartesian Passions and Cartesian Dualism," *Pacific Philosophical Quarterly* 71, pp. 310–333.

——— 1996. "Descartes on Misrepresentation," *Journal of the History of Philosophy* pp. 357–383.

Hooker, Michael. 1978. "Descartes's Denial of Mind-Body Identity," in *Descartes: Critical and Interpretive Essays,* Michael Hooker, ed., Baltimore: Johns Hopkins University Press, pp. 171–185.

——— ed. 1978. *Descartes: Critical and Interpretive Essays,* Baltimore: Johns Hopkins University Press.

Humber, James H. 1991. "Descartes' Dream Argument and Doubt of the Material World," *The Modern Schoolman* 69, pp. 17–32.

Jolley, Nicholas. 1992. "The Reception of Descartes's Philosophy," *The Cambridge Companion to Descartes's Philosophy,* John Cottingham, ed., Cambridge: Cambridge University Press, pp. 393–423.

Kargon, Robert Hugh. 1966. *Atomism in England from Hariot to Newton,* Oxford: Clarendon Press.

Kenny, Anthony. 1968. *Descartes: A Study of His Philosophy,* New York: Random House.

Kessler, Eckhard. 1988. "The Intellective Soul," in *The Cambridge History of Renaissance Philosophy,* Charles B. Schmitt et al., ed., Cambridge: Cambridge University Press, pp. 485–534.

Kripke, Saul. 1972. "Naming and Necessity," in *Semantics of Natural Language,* Donald Davidson and Gilbert Harman, eds., Dordrecht: Reidel.

Kronen, John D. 1991. "The Importance of the Concept of Substantial Unity in Suárez's Argument for Hylomorphism," *American Catholic Philosophical Quarterly* 65, pp. 335–360.

Laporte, Jean. 1988. *Le rationalisme de Descartes,* 3rd ed., Paris: Presses Universitaires de France.

Leibniz, G. W. 1875–1890. *Philosophische Werke,* 7 vols., C. I. Gerhardt, ed., reprint, Hildesheim: Olms, 1965.

——— 1989. *Philosophical Essays,* Roger Ariew and Daniel Garber, transl., Indianapolis and Cambridge: Hackett.

Locke, John. 1975. *An Essay Concerning Human Understanding,* P. H. Nidditch, ed., Oxford: Oxford University Press.

Loeb, Louis. 1981. *From Descartes to Hume: Continental Metaphysics and the Development of Modern Philosophy,* Ithaca: Cornell University Press.

Lucretius. 1975. *De rerum natura,* Conrad Müller, ed., Zürich: Verlag Hans Rohr.

——— 1995. *On the Nature of Things,* Anthony M. Esolen, transl., Baltimore and London: Johns Hopkins University Press.

McCann, Edwin. 1986. "Cartesian Selves and Lockean Substances," *The Monist* 69, pp. 458–482.

McRae, Robert. 1972. "Descartes' Definition of Thought," in *Cartesian Studies,* R. J. Butler, ed., New York: Bobbs-Merrill.

Maier, Anneliese. 1964. "Das Problem der 'species sensibiles in medio' und die neue Naturphilosophie des 14. Jahrhunderts," in *Ausgehendes Mittelalter* II, Rome: Edizioni di Storia e Letteratura, pp. 419–451.

——— 1968. "Die Mechanisierung des Weltbilds im 17. Jahrhundert," in *Zwei Untersuchungen zur nachscholastischen Philosophie: Die Mechanisierung des Weltbilds im 17. Jahrhundert, Kant's Qualitätskategorien,* Rome: Edizioni di Storia e Letteratura, pp. 13–67.

——— 1982. "The Theory of the Elements and Their Participation in Compounds," in *On the Threshold of Exact Science,* Steven Sargent, transl., Philadelphia: University of Pennsylvania Press, pp. 124–170.

Malcolm, Norman. 1977. "Descartes' Proof that He Is Essentially a Non-Material

Thing," in *Thought and Knowledge, Essays by Norman Malcolm,* Ithaca: Cornell University Press, pp. 58–84.

Marion, Jean-Luc. 1981a. *Sur la théologie blanche de Descartes,* Paris: Quadrige/Presses Universitaires de France.

——— 1981b. *Sur l'ontologie grise de Descartes,* 2nd ed., Paris: Vrin.

——— 1986. *Sur le prisme métaphysique de Descartes,* Paris: Presses Universitaires de France.

——— 1991. *Questions cartésiennes,* Paris: Presses Universitaires de France.

Mattern, Ruth. 1978. "Descartes's Correspondence with Elizabeth: Concerning Both the Union and Distinction of Mind and Body," in *Descartes: Critical and Interpretive Essays,* Michael Hooker, ed., Baltimore: Johns Hopkins University Press, pp. 212–222.

Menn, Stephen. 1995. "The Greatest Stumbling Block: Descartes' Denial of Real Qualities," in *Descartes and His Contemporaries: Meditations, Objections and Replies,* Roger Ariew and Marjorie Grene, eds., Chicago and London: University of Chicago Press, pp. 182–207.

——— Forthcoming. "Suárez, Nominalism and Modes," in *Hispanic Philosophy in the Age of Discovery,* Washington, D.C.: Catholic University of America Press.

Mesnard, P. 1957. Discussion of "Maîtrise des passion et sagesse chez Descartes," in *Cahiers de Royaumont philosophie No. II, Descartes,* reprint, New York: Garland, 1987, pp. 228–236.

Michael, Emily, and Fred S. Michael. 1989. "Two Early Modern Concepts of Mind: Reflecting Substance vs. Thinking Substance," *Journal of the History of Philosophy* 27, pp. 29–48.

Miles, Murray Lewis. 1983. "Psycho-Physical Union: The Problem of the Person in Descartes," *Dialogue* 22, pp. 23–46.

Nadler, Steven, ed. 1993. *Causation in Early Modern Philosophy,* University Park: Pennsylvania State University Press.

——— 1994. "Descartes and Occasional Causation," *British Journal for the History of Philosophy* 2, pp. 35–54.

Nelson, Alan. 1996. "The Falsity in Sensory Ideas: Descartes and Arnauld," in *Interpreting Arnauld,* Elmar J. Kremer, ed., Toronto: University of Toronto Press, pp. 13–32.

Ockham. 1955. *Super Primum at Secundum Sententiarum,* reprint, St. Bonaventure, New York: Franciscan Institute.

——— 1980. *Quodlibeta septem,* in *Opera Theologica* IX, Joseph C. Wey, ed., St Bonaventure, New York: St. Bonaventure University.

——— 1982. *Reportatio,* in *Opera Theologica* VII, Francis E. Kelley and Girard I. Etzkorn, eds., St. Bonaventure, New York: St. Bonaventure University.

——— 1988. *Summula Philosophiae naturalis,* in *Opera philosophica* VI, Stephen F. Brown, ed., St. Bonaventure, New York: Franciscan Institute.

——— 1990. *Philosophical Writings,* Ph. Boehner, O. F. M., and S. F. Brown, transl., Indianapolis: Hackett.

Olivo, Gilles. 1993. "Descartes: l'homme en personne," in *Descartes et Regius:*

autour de l'explication de l'esprit humain, Theo Verbeek, ed., Amsterdam: Rodopi.

Olson, Mark. 1988. "Descartes' First Meditation: Mathematics and the Laws of Logic," *Journal of the History of Philosophy* 26, pp. 407–438.

Partington, J. R. 1961. *A History of Chemistry,* vol. 2, London: Macmillan.

Plato. 1980. *Phaedo,* David Gallop, transl., Oxford: Clarendon Press.

Popkin, Richard. 1979. *The History of Skepticism from Erasmus to Spinoza,* Berkeley: University of California Press.

Radner, Daisie. 1971. "Descartes's Notion of the Union of Mind and Body," *Journal of the History of Philosophy* 9, pp. 159–170.

Richardson, R. C. 1982. "The 'Scandal' of Cartesian Interactionism," *Mind* 91, pp. 20–37.

Rodis-Lewis, Geneviève. 1950. *L'individualité selon Descartes,* Paris: Vrin.

——— 1971. *L'œuvre de Descartes,* 2 vols., Paris: Vrin.

——— 1992. "Descartes' Life and the Development of His Philosophy," in *The Cambridge Companion to Descartes,* John Cottingham, ed., Cambridge: Cambridge University Press, pp. 21–57.

Rorty, Amélie, ed. 1986. *Essays on Descartes' Meditations,* Berkeley: University of California Press.

Rorty, Richard. 1979. *Philosophy and the Mirror of Nature,* Princeton: Princeton University Press.

Rozemond, Marleen. 1996. "The First Meditation and the Senses," *British Journal for the History of Philosophy* 4, pp. 21–52.

——— 1997. "Leibniz on the Union of Body and Soul," *Archiv für Geschichte der Philosophie* 79, pp. 150–178.

Russier, Jeanne. 1958. *Sagesse cartésienne et religion,* Paris: Presses Universitaires de France.

Ryle, Gilbert. 1967. "Descartes's Myth," in *Descartes: A Collection of Critical Essays,* Willis Doney, ed., Garden City, New York: Doubleday Anchor Books, pp. 338–351.

Schiffer, Stephen. 1976. "Descartes on his Essence," *Philosophical Review* 85, pp. 21–43.

Schmaltz, Tad. 1992. "Descartes and Malebranche on Mind and Mind-Body Union," *The Philosophical Review* 101, pp. 281–325.

——— 1997. "Descartes on Innate Ideas, Sensation, and Scholasticism: The Response to Regius," in *Oxford Studies in the History of Philosophy,* vol. II, M. A. Stuart, ed., Oxford: Clarendon Press.

Schmitt, Charles B., Quentin Skinner, Eckhard Kessler, and Jill Kraye, eds. 1988. *The Cambridge History of Renaissance Philosophy,* Cambridge: Cambridge University Press.

Shoemaker, Sidney. 1983. "On an Argument for Dualism," in *Knowledge and Mind,* Carl Ginet and Sydney Shoemaker, eds., Oxford: Oxford University Press, pp. 233–258.

Simmons, Alison. 1994. *Making Sense: The Problem of Phenomenal Qualities in*

Late Scholastic Aristotelianism and Descartes, Ann Arbor: University Microfilm International.

Stewart, M. A. 1997. *Oxford Studies in the History of Philosophy* vol. II, Oxford: Clarendon Press.

Suárez, Francisco. 1856. *Opera omnia,* 26 vols., Paris: Vivès.

Van Cleve, James. 1983. "Conceivability and the Cartesian Argument for Dualism," *Pacific Philosophical Quarterly* 64, pp. 35–45.

Verbeek, Theo. 1988. *René Descartes et Martin Schook: La Querelle d'Utrecht,* Paris: Les Impressions Nouvelles.

——— 1992a. "'Ens per accidens': le origini della *querelle* di Utrecht," *Giornale critico della filosofia Italiana* 71, pp. 276–288.

——— 1992b. *Descartes and the Dutch: Early Reactions to Cartesian Philosophy, 1637–1650,* Carbondale and Edwardsville: Southern Illinois University Press.

——— ed. 1993. *Descartes et Regius: autour de l'explication de l'esprit humain,* Amsterdam: Rodopi.

Voss, Stephen. 1994. "Descartes: The End of Anthropology," in *Reason, Will and Sensation: Studies in Descartes's Metaphysics,* John Cottingham, ed., Oxford: Clarendon Press, pp. 273–300.

Wagner, Steven J. 1983. "Descartes's Arguments for Mind-Body Distinctness," *Philosophy and Phenomenological Research* 43, pp. 499–517.

Walsh, W. H. 1963. *Metaphysics,* London: Hutchinson.

Weinberg, Julius. 1977. *Ockham, Descartes, and Hume: Self-Knowledge, Substance, and Causality,* Madison: University of Wisconsin Press.

Weisheipl, James A. 1985. *Nature and Motion in the Middle Ages,* Washington, D.C.: Catholic University of America Press.

Williams, Bernard. 1978. *Descartes: The Project of Pure Enquiry,* New York: Penguin.

Wilson, Margaret D. 1978a. *Descartes,* London: Henley, and Boston: Routledge and Kegan Paul.

——— 1978b. "Cartesian Dualism,"in *Descartes: Critical and Interpretative Essays,* Michael Hooker, ed., Baltimore: Johns Hopkins University Press, pp. 197–233.

——— 1979. "Superadded Properties: The Limits of Mechanism in Locke," *American Philosophical Quarterly* 16, pp. 143–150.

——— 1991. "Descartes on the Origin of Sensation," *Philosophical Topics* 19, pp. 293–323.

Wippel, John. 1977. "The Condemnations of 1270 and 1277 at Paris," *Journal of Medieval and Renaissance Studies* 7, pp. 169–201.

Zavalloni, Roberto. 1951. *Richard de Mediavilla et la controverse sur la pluralité des formes,* Louvain: Éditions de l'Institut Supérieur de Philosophie.

Index